FRENCH PIONEERS IN
THE WEST INDIES

◄■ Nellis M. Crouse ■►

FRENCH PIONEERS IN THE WEST INDIES
1624-1664

OCTAGON BOOKS

A DIVISION OF FARRAR, STRAUS AND GIROUX

New York   1977

Copyright 1940 by
Columbia University Press

Reprinted 1977
by special arrangement with Columbia University Press

OCTAGON BOOKS
A DIVISION OF FARRAR, STRAUS & GIROUX, INC.
19 Union Square West
New York, N.Y. 10003

Library of Congress Cataloging in Publication Data

Crouse, Nellis Maynard, 1884-
    French pioneers in the West Indies, 1624-1664.

    Reprint of the ed. published by Columbia University Press, New York.
    Bibliography: p.
    Includes index.
    1. West Indies, French—History. I. Title.

F2151.C84   1977   972.97'6   77-2851
ISBN 0-374-91937-2

Printed in USA by
Thomson-Shore, Inc.
Dexter, Michigan

CONTENTS

I. The Caribbee Islands	1
II. Settlement of St. Christopher	10
III. Colonization of Guadeloupe	35
IV. Arrival of De Poincy	58
V. Tortuga	80
VI. Discord in the Colonies	99
VII. Patrocles de Thoisy	125
VIII. Governor-General versus Governors	149
IX. The French Expand	175
X. Grenada and St. Lucia	193
XI. Governors Become Owners	205
XII. Trials and Tribulations of Ownership	230
XIII. End of the Pioneer Period	249
Appendix: The Islands of the French West Indies	271
Bibliography	273
Index	283

MAPS

The Caribbee Islands 4
Section of a chart entitled "The West Indies, Central America, Gulf of Mexico, and the Caribbean Sea," published by the United States Hydrographic Office of the Navy Department, 1892, with corrections up to 1916.

St. Christopher 20

Guadeloupe 48

Martinique 64
The maps of St. Christopher, Guadeloupe, and Martinique are from Du Tertre's *Histoire generale des Antilles*, edition of 1667, Vol. I.

I

THE CARIBBEE ISLANDS

EXTENDING from the eastern tip of Puerto Rico to the mouth of the Orinoco River lies a bow-shape archipelago cutting off the Atlantic Ocean from the Caribbean Sea, which in the early days was called the Caribbee Islands and to-day is known as the Lesser Antilles. This archipelago is subdivided into two major groups: the Leeward Islands and the Windward Islands—the former embracing the islands lying north of Martinique, which is situated roughly midway between Puerto Rico and the Orinoco, while the latter comprises those to the south of it. Though the Spaniards with greater meteorological accuracy spoke of the entire group as the Windward Islands and applied the term "Leeward" to the Greater Antilles or sometimes to the islands off the Spanish Main in the southern Caribbean, the British government, which now owns most of the Caribbees, has adopted the former classification in establishing the two distinct political units called the Leeward and the Windward Islands. But in the seventeenth century, the period in which our story lies, the French were the dominant nation in the Lesser Antilles. From St. Christopher (popularly known as St. Kitts), where Pierre d'Esnambuc planted his first colony, they spread out over the archipelago, seizing in the name of their king those rich islands to the south of them—Guadeloupe, Martinique, Grenada, St. Lucia, Dominica—while the English, who had likewise settled on St. Christopher, took possession of the smaller and less valuable islands, such as Nevis, Montserrat, and Antigua.

In those days the islands were prosperous, far more so than now. Their owners reaped fortunes from slave-worked plantations; buccaneers used their harbors as ports of call where they might refit their ships and spend ill-gotten gains; slave traders unloaded horrid cargoes on their shores and sold them at a handsome profit; indeed, the Caribbees offered a field of opportunity to adventurous men not overburdened with scruples, who did not hesitate to turn their hands to any profitable business without asking too many questions. During the seventeenth century, when the principle "No peace beyond the Line"[1] was tacitly recognized, these bold spirits, chiefly French and English, could here organize predatory expeditions against the Spanish possessions; for together with British Jamaica and French San Domingo[2] the Caribbees formed an outpost in that sphere of influence where Spain claimed jurisdiction, and by fortifying them they could hold the approaches to the Spanish Main. But this obvious advantage, it must be admitted, was not the motive which brought the Europeans there to appropriate and colonize. The English, for their part, were interested primarily in plantations that would enrich the mother country and serve as an outlet for a surplus population, which even at this early date roamed the countryside and collected in the towns to form a problem for the authorities. Though not so greatly troubled by a surplus population as were their British neighbors, the French, who in the seventeenth century were beginning their colonial adventures under the able leadership of Richelieu and Colbert, quickly saw the advantages of establishing colonies

[1] The "Line" was fixed by the "lines of amity" formed by the meridian of the Azores passing through the Tropic of Cancer. Beyond it the colonials could fight without endangering the peace between their respective governments in Europe.

[2] French San Domingo, known today as the Republic of Haiti, was the western portion of the island of Haiti, while the eastern part belonged to Spain. The French spoke of the island as San Domingo; the Spanish called it Hispaniola.

THE CARIBBEE ISLANDS

both in Canada and in the West Indies, which could be used to supply France with products such as furs, tobacco, and sugar and which would furnish a market for articles of French manufacture.

Impelled thus by a desire to colonize for economic reasons, the French and English pioneers had no reason to quarrel, and thanks to the large number of islands at their disposal they were able to live peacefully with each other, at least as peacefully as could be expected of two rival nations. It was not until King William III inaugurated the long series of wars that takes up so much space in the histories of the eighteenth century that the practice of capturing and recapturing each other's islands began. The period we are about to describe was, therefore, one of colonization and of wars against the native possessors of the soil.

The islands which compose the Caribbee group are of volcanic origin. They are really a mountain range rising from the ocean's bed and towering above the sea, topped by Mt. Diablotin on rugged Dominica, which raises its head to a height of more than five thousand feet. This range does not lend itself to plateau formations which would make agriculture easy; it is made up of mountain peaks whose sides, dropping away precipitately, are furrowed by deep ravines. But what nature has deprived man of in the way of accessibility, she has repaid in fertility of soil. The slopes are covered with trees and heavy vegetation, forming a veritable jungle in the more inaccessible parts, while in the cultivated portions one may see fields of sugar cane and groves of orange trees, with weed-like banana trees and stately coco palms waving in the breeze. The climate is warm and fairly uniform throughout the year, tempered by the northeasterly trade winds that blow there continually. Heavy rainfall, so necessary to tropical vegetation, occurs during the summer and early fall, and it is then that the islands are occasionally visited by that dreadful scourge, the West Indian hurricane, which sweeps the entire region, leaving havoc in its wake. The direction from which the trade winds blow causes vessels to seek shelter on the western side of the islands, and it is here that we find such harbors as the archipelago affords. Unfortunately, in some cases notably at St. Christopher, Dominica, and Montserrat there are but open roadsteads, giving only a limited protection. St. Lucia, however, has the excellent harbor of Castries, where modern steamers can tie up at the dock. Steamers can dock also at Pointe à Pitre, snugly situated between the two halves of the island of Guadeloupe, while Martinique and Antigua have a better than average shelter, and Grenada can boast of one for small craft. On the whole, harbor facilities appear to have been satisfactory for the vessels of early days, though of course they are totally inadequate for our modern leviathans.

The natives of these islands were the Caribs (whence the archipelago takes its name), a ferocious race far different from the peaceful savages of Hispaniola, whom the Spaniards so cruelly exterminated. The Caribs were the dominant stock of the West Indies, and they were to be found not only on the islands but also on the South American continent, particularly in the Guianas and in Venezuela. Shortly before the coming of the Spaniards they invaded the islands and extirpated or drove out the milder Arawaks, who when the white man made his first appearance were already confined to the island of Trinidad and the adjoining mainland. Physically the Caribs were not unattractive, though the barbarous custom of flattening the forehead by compressing the head between two boards soon after birth gave them a rather grotesque appearance. Their hair was black, worn usually in braids and heavily greased, while their complexions were hidden beneath a heavy coat of dye extracted from the juice of the annatto tree, which not only served a decorative purpose but also provided protection for the skin against the sun and the ravages of noisome insects. On important occasions they would add touches with a special coloring matter made of genip-tree sap, and thus adorned would

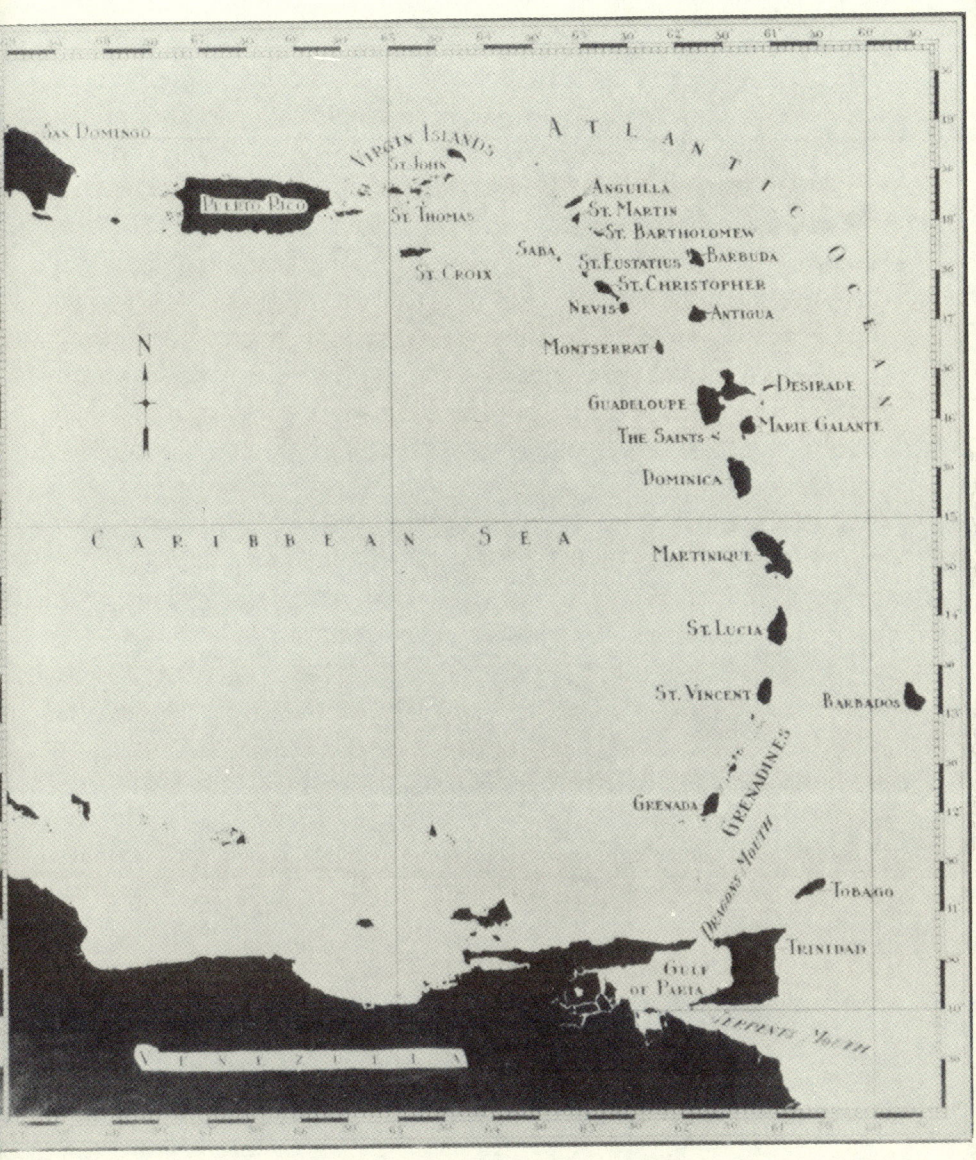

THE CARIBBEE ISLANDS

march boldly into battle or to a conference with their fellow tribesmen.

On taking the field the Carib warrior was well armed. His bow was a stout affair, fully six feet long and one and one-half inches thick in the middle, which discharged with considerable accuracy arrows about three feet long. These arrows were made of reeds tipped with barbs of hardened greenwood saturated with the juice of the manchineel tree, one of the deadliest of vegetable poisons, which because of its potency, has acquired a reputation that seems fantastic, were not the stories about it verified by actual experience. In addition to the bow and arrow the warrior carried a heavy club made of stout hardwood some three feet long, about two inches in diameter at the handle, and increasing to four or five at the business end. Thus equipped the Carib brave was a worthy antagonist for the white settler. As many of their warlike expeditions consisted of attacks on other islands, they had developed a large canoe, in some cases more than forty feet in length, capable of efficient service on the rough waters of the Caribbean, and they enjoyed the distinction of being one of the few Indian races to understand the handling of sailboats. These huge war canoes sometimes carried as many as three masts, on which small topsails were set above the courses.

Efforts to convert the Carib to Christianity met with little success, despite the earnest attempts of worthy missionaries, and the French were eventually obliged to treat him as uncivilizable. For example, Father Labat, who lived for years on the French islands, speaks of two priests who spent twenty-five years in Dominica and succeeded in baptizing only a few children and some adults *in articulo mortis*. It was not difficult, the Father admitted, to persuade them to submit to baptism, but the missionaries soon saw the folly of baptizing indiscriminately persons who had no conception of the sacrament and no intention of embracing the Christian mode of life. Taken as a whole, the Caribs were unpleasant neighbors for the European colonists, though it is difficult to say whether or not they might have proved more tractable had they met with more humane treatment. But as the French and English had little compunction in exterminating them when their destruction seemed the best policy, it is doubtful if more placid dispositions would have insured their survival. Since peace on a permanent basis was impossible with these savages, they were driven from island to island as fast as the white man advanced, until by the end of the seventeenth century they were practically confined to the two islands of Dominica and St. Vincent, where there were as yet no permanent settlements.

The first of the Caribbees to be discovered were those seen by Columbus on his second voyage. Returning to the West Indies in 1493 with a magnificent fleet and a host of adventurers eager for the riches of Cathay, the Spanish admiral's first sight of land was stately Mt. Diablotin, standing out against the horizon. It was Sunday, the eighth of November, and Columbus appropriately named the island Dominica. Yet despite the alluring appearance of the landscape, he did not land there. Lack of suitable anchorage and a desire to rejoin the little colony he had left earlier in the year at Hispaniola induced him to turn northward and to leave the beauties of Dominica behind. His course now led him through the Leeward Islands. Just north of Dominica he came to Mariegalante, which he named after his flagship. Here he landed to take possession in the name of the Spanish sovereigns; but the island was small, uninteresting, and of no particular importance, especially when he could see to the northward the lofty mountains of Guadeloupe beckoning to him. This magnificent island, largest of the Caribbees (if we except Trinidad), Columbus named after the convent of Santa Maria de Guadeloupe in Estremadura in accordance with a promise he had made the friars to call an island after their sanctuary.

Guadeloupe proved to be the headquarters of the Carib nation, whence these bold marauders set forth on their expeditions against the neighboring islands. On landing there Columbus sent his men along the shore to make a cursory investigation, with explicit orders not to venture inland. There was, however, one captain, bolder than the rest, who ventured to disobey the Admiral's orders and to lead a small number of followers on an expedition of his own, hoping to make some discovery that would redound to his glory. When night came and he did not return, Columbus sent out detachments to scour the neighboring forests in the hope of finding the lost explorers. The following day he dispatched that gallant adventurer Alonzo de Ojeda, who with a small party of men plunged into the jungle, where he wandered about for several days in a vain search for his companions. He saw much that enthralled him in this gorgeous tropical paradise: trees clothed in sparkling foliage, exotic flowers, richly colored birds, and on the macabre side of the picture he discovered gruesome evidences of the cannibalism which the savages practiced on their enemies. But he found no trace of the lost Spaniards. At last Columbus decided to leave. Believing his men irretrievably lost, he had already given orders to sail when he saw on a point of land the captain and his followers signalling desperately to the ship. By good fortune they had reached the shore in the nick of time after having wandered aimlessly about through the forests.

Columbus now sailed for Hispaniola without stopping at any other islands along his route, though the temptation to land and explore them must have been great. He contented himself with naming them as he jotted down their location in his logbook. Montserrat recalled a mountain near Barcelona; Antigua commemorated the church of Santa Maria la Antigua at Seville; the mountains of St. Christopher gave the appearance of the familiar legend of St. Christopher and the Christ child; Nevis, its peak topped by a cloud, resembled a snow-capped mountain; and lastly the multitudinous islands of the northernmost group were named the Virgin Islands after St. Ursula and the eleven thousand virgins.

Five years later, when sailing from Spain on his third voyage, Columbus made a vow to name the first land he sighted in honor of the Holy Trinity. Steering a more southerly course than on his previous voyages, his first glimpse of land was the large island that blocks off the Gulf of Paria from the Atlantic Ocean. This island he named Trinidad, and strange to say it appeared to him as he first saw it in the distance from his quarterdeck as three peaks standing out above the horizon, emblematic of the Triune God he would commemorate. Entering the Gulf of Paria by its southern approach, he sailed out through the Dragon's Mouth, as the northern entrance is called, and before he headed westward he continued far enough north to sight the islands of Grenada, which he called Conception, and Tobago, which he named Assumption. It was on his last voyage that he sighted Martinique, which for some reason always retained its Indian name—for "Martinique" is a variant of "Mantinino," by which name the Caribs knew it—and he also at this time discovered St. Lucia, situated just south of Martinique. On this voyage he may also have sighted St. Vincent and named it after the famous deacon of Saragossa, though we cannot be sure about this.[3] The island of Barbados was found somewhat later by the Spaniards, who gave it that name because its slopes reminded them of a kind of bearded fig tree called *los barbados*, at least such is the most plausible theory.

Though the Spaniards discovered the Caribbees they failed to colonize them, for these little dots of the Lesser Antilles did not offer gold and silver or vast territories as did the American continent. They were mountainous for the most part, as we have said, and covered with forests that rendered them unsuitable for cattle raising, while the fierce Caribs made colonization difficult. Furthermore, there was the question of navigation. Fleets coming from Spain picked up the trade winds off the Canaries and rode them full sail to the Caribbean Sea; but on the

---

[3] Many authorities state that St. Vincent was discovered on Jan. 22, 1498, but as the Admiral was in Spain at that time this is obviously an error.

return journey, in order to avoid the long beat to windward they sought a more northerly route through Florida Strait, where favorable winds prevailed. Thus the Caribbees could never serve as a rendezvous for the heavily laden plate fleets that sailed yearly from the Spanish Main.

And so for a hundred years these verdure-clad islands lay neglected by their discoverers, who, trusting in their title to the New World, granted to them by the Vicar of Christ, passed them by for the more imposing Cuba, Jamaica, and San Domingo. Then with the dawn of the seventeenth century, when the nations of the north began their colonial expansion, a swarm of eager, fighting colonists poured down to claim them in the names of England, France, and the United Netherlands, putting an end forever to the Spanish monopoly of the West Indies.

~ II ~

SETTLEMENT OF ST. CHRISTOPHER

TOWARD the close of the sixteenth century there lived in the parish of St. Quentin, Allouville, Normandy, a gentleman named Nicolas Belain, Sieur d'Esnambuc et de Canouville. This gentleman had married the Demoiselle Peronne, by whom he had four children: Adrienne, who married Pierre Dyel de Vaudroques (a descendant of one of the adventurers who had followed the Sieur Roberval to Canada in the days of King Francis I), François de Canouville, Pierre d'Esnambuc, and Catherine. During the wars that ravaged his neighborhood Nicolas Belain became financially hard pressed, and to relieve his necessities he borrowed from Marshal de Brissac a large sum of money, hoping to pay him back when conditions improved. But ill luck pursued him, and at last his heirs were obliged to sell their patrimony to satisfy the clamor of their creditor. In 1599 François was forced to dispose of the domain of Esnambuc, and fifteen years later Canouville met with a similar fate. There was one member of the family, however, who was determined not to be downed by such a reversal of fortune, and this was Pierre d'Esnambuc. Born in 1585, he was but a lad when his elder brother sold the fief from which he had taken his name, and at this tender age the loss of his land made an impression on him that roused in him an intense desire to win it back some day. By the time Canouville was liquidated he was nearly thirty years of age and able to translate his wishes into deeds. At his insistence there was inserted in the bill of sale a clause enabling him to buy back the family property within six years upon payment of the sale price plus a slight profit. With this as an incentive Pierre now started out in search of a fortune. Needless to say he did not intend to obtain his money by the homely process of trade or through the savings of a modest salary—the time element alone would have precluded such a method—but he proposed to make his fortune by a series of bold strokes; in short, he planned to cruise the Spanish Main in search of booty. In six years, he assured himself, he would surely meet some richly laden galleon, or he might take possession of some fertile island in the West Indies. Circumstances, moreover, were propitious for this sort of thing. The Treaty of Vervins, signed in 1598, between France and Spain had brought peace to these distracted countries; but it was a peace that applied only to Europe. Beyond "the Line," as we have pointed out, privateers could range at will on their own responsibility.

Young D'Esnambuc, for so our hero is known to history, therefore took service with a friend of his, Urbain du Roissey, Sieur de Chardonville, a native of Rouen, who was to be his companion in his coming adventures and the leader of his privateering enterprises. Years went by; not only the six, but many more, without the freebooters being able to do more than make expenses. During this time, however, they learned the art of navigation and managed to secure commissions as captains in the navy. At last, one day in the year 1625, as they were cruising off the coast of Cuba near the route taken by the plate fleet homeward bound from Cartagena, they fell in with a Spanish galleon of four hundred tons, armed with thirty-five pieces of artillery. Du Roissey's ship was but a small brigantine of four guns with a crew of forty men; but the great opportunity had arrived, and he did not hesitate. For three hours the unequal combat lasted; then Du Roissey, his ship leaking in a dozen places, his crew nearly all killed or wounded, drew off, while the Spaniard, unable to capture the plucky Frenchman, sailed away badly shaken by the punishment he had taken. It was now necessary to reach a port where the vessel could be careened and repaired, obviously a port not within the Spanish possessions; so Du Roissey steered eastward, hoping to reach one of the small uninhabited islands of the Lesser Antilles. By chance his course lay for St. Christopher, and at the end of two weeks he dropped anchor off the northern part of the island under the shadow of Mt. Misery near Pointe de Sable.

In order to understand the situation that D'Esnambuc found awaiting him at St. Christopher, it is necessary to devote a few pages to the establishment of the English colony on this island by Sir Thomas Warner, a man who played an important part in the colonization of the West Indies. Several years before, in 1620, to be exact, Thomas Warner, who since his boyhood days had dreamed of adventure, joined an expedition under Captain Roger North, sent out by a small group of wealthy men to found a settlement in that rich country between the Amazon and the Essequibo rivers, known by the name of Guiana. Upon reaching his destination North landed a number of his followers, among whom were Thomas Warner and Captain Thomas Painton, and promptly sailed home. This Captain Painton had gleaned some knowledge of the West Indies by previous voyages along the Spanish Main, and, moreover, had some theories of his own about colonization. He would form a settlement, so he explained to Warner, on one of those small, fertile islands of the Caribbee chain, where, surrounded by a sea which would keep intruders off and prevent the inhabitants from leaving, his venture would be sure to prosper. Furthermore, he knew of just such an island—the island of St. Christopher. The idea appealed to Warner, for here might be an opportunity to found a colony and to succeed where the great Raleigh had failed. At any rate, Guiana promised little, and there would be harm in glancing at St. Christopher. Warner and Painton therefore set sail in 1622 and proceeded to the Caribbees.

St. Christopher proved, indeed, a promising place for a colony.

True there was no harbor; but an open roadstead on the leeward side sheltered vessels from the prevailing winds. The soil would produce good tobacco—in fact the tobacco grown there later proved far better than that of Barbados—as well as the fruits and vegetables necessary for the support of white settlers. In the southern part lay a string of salt ponds spread out over a flat peninsula-like formation reaching almost to Nevis, which would give colonists an inexhaustible supply of this necessary condiment. Warner stepped ashore to make an inspection and managed to strike up an acquaintance with the native chief, a Carib named Tegreman, who claimed lordship over the island. Tegreman's followers, despite their reputation for ferocity, appeared friendly enough, the usual attitude of natives who have not yet been molested by the white man, and this encouraged the Englishmen to believe that they could live in peace with them.

Satisfied with what he had seen, Warner, after a sojourn of several months, during which he made a thorough survey of the island and its natural resources, returned to England and at once proceeded to look up his old friend John Jeaffreson, an experienced navigator and just the man to lead an expedition by sea, and to him he unfolded his scheme of colonization. Jeaffreson was enthusiastic, and the two at once proceeded to draw up their plans. But like most enthusiasts they lacked the necessary cash. After casting about for a financial backer they finally elected to approach one Ralph Merifield, a London merchant much interested in such enterprises. Merifield at once agreed to join them. As Captain Painton had recently died, the three adventurers determined to keep the business for themselves exclusively, and they drew up an agreement, forming a sort of partnership. Warner was to transport a small band of willing men to St. Christopher, or to some neighboring island if it should seem better to do so, and he was then to send back word of his whereabouts so that Jeaffreson could follow with a second contingent.

Warner at once went to work. He enlisted a small, adventurous group, which consisted of sixteen persons all told, including his thirteen-year-old son Edward; and having set sail for St. Christopher, he dropped anchor on January 28, 1624,[1] off the western shore of the island, in the roadstead known as Old Road Bay, about half way between its two extremities. Momentous day this, and one that should rank in the history of American colonization with those contemporary events the founding of Jamestown and the landing of the Pilgrim Fathers! For when Thomas Warner and his little band landed on the shores of St. Christopher, England began her colonial empire in the West Indies.

Once ashore, the colonists proceeded to entrench themselves. They built a rude fort, erected some houses, sowed a field of grain, and planted a crop of tobacco to be ready for Jeaffreson's arrival, living meanwhile on fish, cassava bread, potatoes, and plantains—the natural produce of the island. This done, the ship was sent back to England with the joyful news that all was ready. And now the savages, headed by Tegreman and accompanied by some French castaways (to whom we shall refer later) came to meet the newcomers. They prowled about the buildings, looking into the houses, poking fingers through the loopholes of the fort, which the English told them they had cut in the walls so that they might observe the chickens pecking about the yard, and in general making themselves a good deal of a nuisance.

Months passed. The tobacco crop ripened, the clear, warm weather of winter and spring gave way to the tempestuous rainy season; and then came that scourge of the West Indies— the hurricane. On the nineteenth of September the blow fell. Torrents of water poured down from leaden skies, while the wind blowing with terrific force tore up the tobacco plants and destroyed the flimsy dwellings, leaving wreckage in its wake. When the storm had finally spent itself, the gallant Warner, undaunted by the destruction of his settlement, drove his men to

[1] The dates will all be given in the new style according to the Gregorian calendar. Several accounts give the date of Warner's arrival as 1623, but modern scholars feel that 1624 is the correct year.

repair the damage. New houses were erected, the ground was cleared of rubbish, and soon a fresh crop of tobacco was ripening in the warm sunshine.

Meanwhile, John Jeaffreson had not been idle. With the help of Merifield he had chartered a ship, appropriately named the "Hopewell," and having loaded her with supplies, he arrived at St. Christopher on March 18, 1625. One can imagine with what joy the two leaders greeted each other on this little out-of-the-way island in the far-off West Indies, where they saw the realization of their dreams of extending the colonial empire of England in the "New World." Worthy successors of the Elizabethan heroes though they were, they did not then grasp the importance of their modest enterprise. A handful of men isolated on an insignificant island for the prosaic purpose of raising tobacco were in reality forging an important link in Britain's far-flung empire.

Early in September Warner was back in England with 9,500 pounds of tobacco to defray the costs of his expedition. During his absence important changes had taken place in the government, which were to have a significant effect on his colonial venture. King James had died and had been succeeded by his son, Charles I, whose unsuccessful matrimonial adventures with the Spanish royal family during his father's reign had crushed any affection he may have felt for Spain. In fact, when Warner landed he was already preparing an armada to attack the seaport of Cadiz. Far from sharing the fears that had held James in check when it came to a question of encroaching on the Spanish sphere of influence in America, King Charles was inclined to encourage any attempts to found colonies there. All this made matters easy for Warner, inasmuch as Merifield, well pleased with the results of his venture, determined to clinch his somewhat dubious title to St. Christopher by obtaining a charter for himself and his associates. Needless to say, he had no difficulty in securing such a document, for since the colony encroached on the Spaniard's domain, King Charles regarded it with favor and readily granted a patent on September 25, 1625, to Ralph Merifield, his partners, and his agents permitting them to traffic in the islands of St. Christopher, Nevis, Barbuda, and Montserrat. Thomas Warner and after his death John Jeaffreson were to be entrusted with their governance.[2] Thus was the possession of the settlement assured to its founders, who proceeded to develop it with renewed enthusiasm. Such, then, was the situation when D'Esnambuc and Du Roissey made their appearance off St. Christopher.

It was in the autumn season, perhaps October, when the French landed to make their first survey of the island. The possibilities of the place appealed to D'Esnambuc, who from now on assumed the leadership of the enterprise, for here was a fertile isle suitable for the production of tobacco, as he saw from the samples already planted by the English, and doubtless it would supply other valuable plants when properly cultivated. With this golden opportunity before him, D'Esnambuc now turned his attention to the question of colonists. He had with him the survivors of his crew, to whom he could add a group of stragglers who the year before had come from France to Guiana under the leadership of Captain Chantail, of Lyon, but who had been driven from that country by the Indians and had eventually found refuge in St. Christopher. These two contingents together numbered about eighty men.[3] But this was not enough; the work must be carried out on a far greater scale. For this reason he must return to France, for there only could he obtain the necessary backing and the proper number of men for the founding of a large colony.

[2]The patent is given in *Acts of the Privy Council, Colonial Series, 1613–1680*, pp. 90–91. It speaks of "Barbador" (Barbados) not "Barbuda." As there is considerable confusion in the documents of this period because of the similarity of names, one should be governed by what must be the more obvious meaning. In this case Barbuda, a near neighbor of St. Christopher, must be the island referred to, as Barbados is located far to the south and could have had no connection with the other islands mentioned in the patent.

[3]Cardinal Richelieu's patent to D'Esnambuc (which see below) mentions eighty Frenchmen on St. Christopher.

While waiting for his brigantine to be repaired he made overtures to Thomas Warner's men for a protective alliance against the savages. It was a wise move and one which the English fortunately accepted, for in November and again in December a band of Caribs, five hundred strong, came from a neighboring island to raid the little colony; but the combined efforts of the French and English, now united under one command, succeeded in driving them back. With the Indians of St. Christopher, however, the white men appear to have lived in amity for the time being.

At the end of six months the brigantine was again seaworthy, and D'Esnambuc felt that he had the situation well enough in hand to warrant his returning home. Having placed the colony in charge of a subordinate he embarked with Du Roissey; and with a cargo of tobacco as evidence of his success he set sail for France, arriving there in the summer of 1626. By good fortune the tobacco brought a fancy price, and our two adventurers, now flush with money, set themselves up in style. They purchased a supply of clothing suitable to men of their station, and procuring a carriage with a team of horses set out for Paris to sell their project to the public. By dint of liberal spending, pardonable under the circumstances, they soon persuaded a number of French capitalists to take a share in their enterprise.

The moment for such an undertaking was propitious. Cardinal Richelieu had recently inaugurated a plan to raise the French navy to the position he felt it should occupy among the sea powers of the world. With the reorganization of the navy there went hand in hand the policy of colonial expansion, which was now beginning to occupy the Cardinal's attention. Inspired by the examples of England and the Netherlands, he determined to follow in their steps by organizing huge trading companies in which merchants were to be encouraged to invest their capital by offering them special privileges, such as freedom of customs duties for a period of years or exclusive trading rights in specified localities. This system, he believed, would be far more efficient than the old arrangements, according to which private individuals sent out small vessels which easily became the prey of freebooters. Thus it was that when D'Esnambuc and Du Roissey arrived in Paris the Company of the Hundred Associates was already in process of formation—nearly ready to take over the colonies, then little more than trading stations, which Samuel de Champlain had established in Canada. This company, according to the original plan, was to control all colonial activities in lands bordering on the Atlantic Ocean and its tributaries; but as such a vast monopoly raised too much opposition, it became necessary to restrict its activities to Canada, where it continued to play a dominant role in the affairs of that colony for many years, leaving other fields open to other organizations.

Such being the situation, when the two pioneers presented themselves before the distinguished minister, they succeeded in convincing him that St. Christopher and its surrounding archipelago offered the opportunity for the founding of a colonial empire in the West Indies and that they were the very men to head such an undertaking. Thus it was that when in the month of October Richelieu finally had himself appointed Grand Master of Navigation and Commerce, a position which gave him supreme authority in maritime affairs, his first act in this capacity was to close a deal with D'Esnambuc. A corporation with a capital of 45,000 francs known as the Company of St. Christopher, in which Richelieu was the largest shareholder, was formed for the purpose of colonizing the islands of St. Christopher, Barbuda, and, as the charter quaintly puts it, "other [islands] at the entrance to Peru, between the eleventh and eighteenth parallels, not possessed [it does not say "claimed"] by any Christian prince."

The purpose of this venture, so the patent tells us, was to instruct the natives in the Catholic faith and to cultivate the resources of the land for a period of twenty years. Three ships were to be purchased and immediately fitted out for the coming expedition. The members of the corporation were to bear all the expenses necessary to finance the enterprise, in return for which they were to receive half the crops raised and half the goods manufactured on the island, while D'Esnambuc and Du Roissey were to have 10 percent of the profits on all business transactions. They were also to turn over to the company the fort they had recently built at Pointe de Sable in return for 3,000 francs. Prospective settlers who wished to join the expedition were to be accepted, upon condition that they would agree to remain in the colony for three years. At the same time Richelieu issued a commission to D'Esnambuc and Du Roissey which recited with great redundancy the terms upon which they were engaged as commanders and which emphasized particularly that one-tenth of the revenue should be reserved for the King.[4] Armed with this authority, D'Esnambuc went at once to Havre, where he raised 322 men for his ship, "La Catholique"; while in Brittany Du Roissey secured 210 for "La Victoire" and "La Cardinale." They sailed on February 24, 1627, and they landed at Pointe de Sable on the eighth of May. Unfortunately the expedition was badly managed from the start. Provisions ran low, disease broke out, and by the time St. Christopher was sighted the few who managed to survive had to be rescued by those they had come to save. About half the original number of those who had left France died either during the crossing or shortly after landing.

While D'Esnambuc was absent in France, Indian troubles again broke out this time among the natives of the island. Alarmed at the rapidly increasing number of white men, the savages determined to strike a blow before it was too late. These foreigners, so the Indians reasoned, and with considerable logic, had come from afar only to massacre them as the Spaniards had massacred their ancestors on the larger islands. To make sure of success in the coming uprising they sent envoys to the neighboring islands to obtain assistance, and assistance was eagerly furnished. Fortunately for the white men, an Indian woman whom

[4]These documents, both dated Oct. 31, 1626, are to be found in Du Tertre, *Histoire generale des Antilles*, I, 8–15.

the English had always treated kindly disclosed the plot. Warner's position was too precarious for him to trouble about the means he used to protect his colony. His handful of followers, even when reinforced by the French, would be no match for a concerted attack by the savages. "Like a wise man and a good soldier" he seized his advantage, and gathering all his men together he fell upon the Indians while they were engaged in a drinking bout, killing a large portion of them, including Chief Tegreman, and putting the rest to flight.

But this was not the end of the affair, for there were still reinforcements to come to the Indians from the other islands. Rushing his men down to the shore, Warner hastily threw up barricades behind which they kept watch night and day for the coming of the savages. At last they saw a vast fleet of war canoes, containing some three or four thousand braves armed with spears and clubs, swarming toward them. The vanguard of this force was permitted to land and approach within range. Then the colonists opened fire. At the first volley the front ranks fell, and the rest, seeing for the first time the deadly effects of the white man's weapons, turned and fled ignominiously to their canoes. They were pursued by the victorious pioneers, who quickly launched their boats and gave chase. As a result of this battle the Caribs, or a least the greater part of them, were driven from St. Christopher. Thus began the expulsion of the Indians from their native islands, a sanguinary page of West Indian history that reflects little glory on the European conquerors, but which may, in the eternal scheme of things, have been inevitable.

The presence of two separate colonies, belonging to different nations and located within such a limited territory, might have led to difficulties, especially as the population began to increase rapidly, had not the leaders solved the problem by the sensible expedient of dividing the island between them. A treaty of partition was drawn up on May 13, 1627, an epoch-making date, indeed, whereby the English reserved the middle section of the

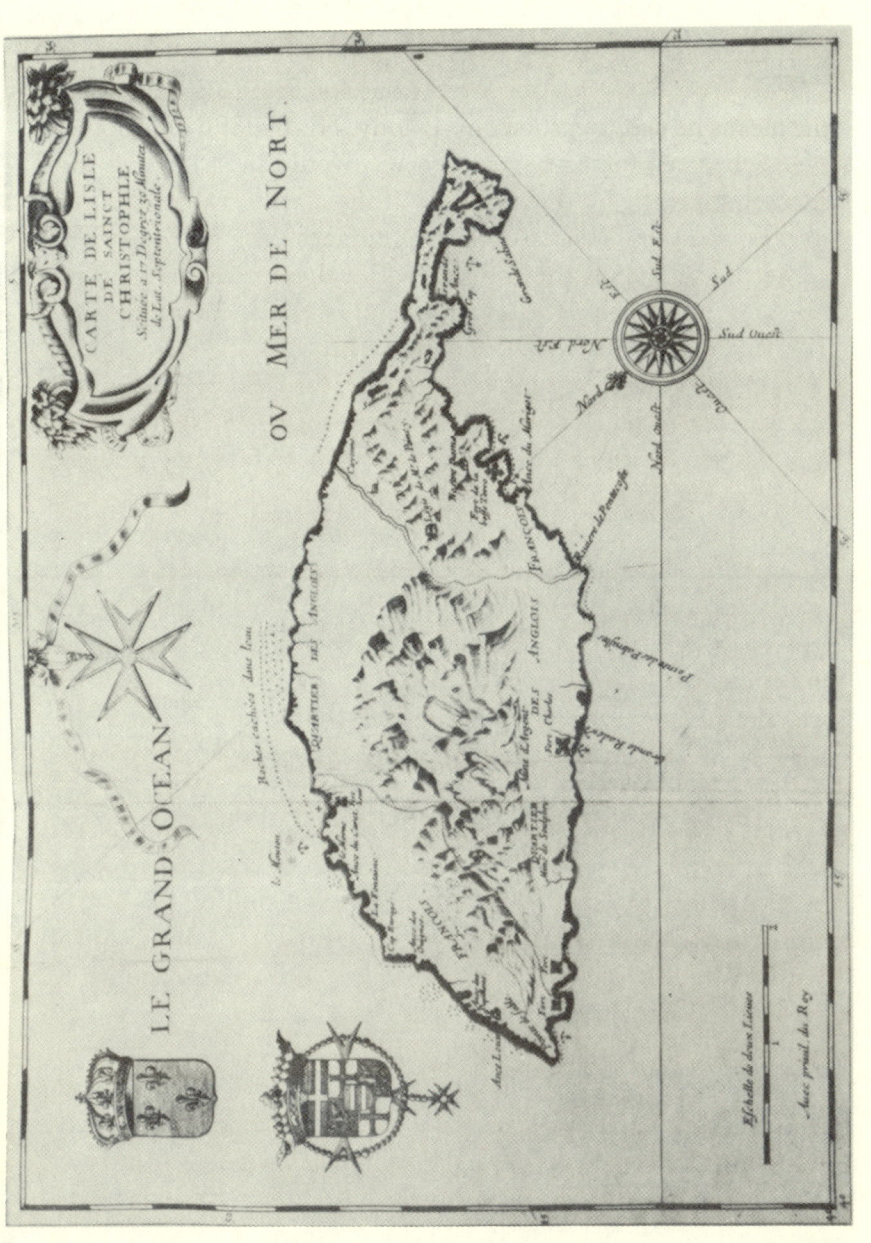

ST. CHRISTOPHER

island, and the French the two extremities. Furthermore, D'Esnambuc took the northern or *capesterre* portion, with headquarters at Pointe de Sable, while Du Roissey selected the southern part called *basseterre*, where he settled on the site of modern Basseterre and built a fort.[5] A glance at the map will show the division lines. This partition was bolstered by numerous clauses in the treaty calculated to maintain peace and insure mutual coöperation between the contracting parties. They agreed to aid each other in case of an attack by the Spaniards and to unite in wars against the natives when occasion required. Each nation was to regulate trade with its own nationals: no English ship could land its cargo without consent of the English governor, nor could a French vessel trade without permission of the French commander. Dutch merchantmen, which were even now beginning to put in an appearance, must obtain the approval of both. Quarrels between men of the two different nations were to be judged by both governors—the culprit to be sent back to his own people for punishment. But most important of all the clauses in the treaty, and the one that stands out unique in colonial history, was the one by which each agreed to refrain from hostilities against the other in case war broke out between France and England unless specifically ordered to fight by their respective governments, and even in this case the aggressor must give due notice to the other of his intention to attack. As war had already broken out between the two parent countries, the colonists had this clause inserted, since they saw the folly of ruining their embryo settlements by becoming involved in a quarrel in which they had no direct interest.[6]

The wretched condition of the D'Esnambuc-Du Roissey relief expedition had such a bad effect on the colony that the leaders

---

[5]"Capesterre" (possibly from *caput terrae*) was the name generally applied to the eastern or northern part of a Caribbee island, *basseterre* to the southern or western part. Since the prevailing winds were the northeast trades, the windward side was considered the higher side, the leeward the lower.

[6]For the text of the treaty see Du Tertre, I, 17–20. The treaty was renewed in 1638, 1644, 1649, 1655, and 1662.

decided to apply again to France in order to save the venture from utter ruin. The ships were therefore loaded with tobacco and whatever commodities could be obtained on the island and dispatched to France in charge of Du Roissey. No sooner, however, had he reached his destination than he was importuned by Commander Isaac de Razilly, an officer greatly interested in promoting French colonization, to sell his tobacco, guns, and merchandise and undertake a secret expedition to Ireland. With the greatest indifference to the fate of his fellow colonists he left France for several months on this strange business. It would have gone badly with the wretched people at St. Christopher had not a Dutch merchant chanced to arrive with a cargo of supplies which he was willing to unload on credit against a future crop of tobacco. When Du Roissey returned to France the Company of St. Christopher managed to secure his services again—after all there was no one else they could send—and dispatched him with "La Cardinale" and 150 men. He reached St. Christopher in May, 1628, in no better condition than on the first expedition; nearly all his men were sick or thoroughly exhausted.

Meanwhile, Warner appears to have been more successful than his French allies in his efforts to bring in new colonists. This was due to some extent to the greater experience the Englishmen had had in transporting and settling large bodies of people, for they had been experimenting with the problem for twenty years in Virginia, where they had learned something from their misfortunes. But more to the point was the apparent inexhaustibility of the surplus population of England, which furnished a reservoir of man power from which Warner could draw at will with the blessing and good wishes of the government officials. Thus, with the exception of the setback in 1629, which will be described presently, the colony grew apace, until in 1637 the English population was estimated at twelve to thirteen thousand souls, though these figures seem somewhat high. The popular method of securing plantation workers for the colonists was to transport men as indentured servants under a contract to serve their masters for a given number of years before they could become free citizens. This method was used by both the French and the English. The persons thus obtained were not particularly desirable from what contemporary records tell us. General Venables, who captured Jamaica in 1655, recruited a number of these men in Barbados and St. Christopher, and he describes them as "being bold only in mischief, not to be commanded as soldiers nor to be kept in any civil order: being the most profane debauched persons that we ever saw, scorners of religion, and indeed men kept so loose as not to be kept under discipline, and so cowardly as not to be made to fight." The French servants, since no one seems to have denounced them so scathingly, may have been a little better. At least we should give them the benefit of the doubt. They consisted of younger sons in search of adventure; debtors fleeing from their creditors; persons with an unsavory past; quarrelsome youths who wished to escape Richelieu's edicts against dueling; peasants tired of the *corvées* and low pay; and poor artisans out of work.

Traffic in these people was an important industry in Dieppe, Havre, and St. Malo, where agents lured their prospects to sign up by painting the West Indies as a land of milk and honey where one could live well with little effort. To make matters worse unscrupulous shipmasters were not above enticing them on board and boldly kidnapping them. When such unpromising material was dumped on their shores the planters were not likely to exert themselves to bring out whatever latent good qualities they might have had. The treatment of these unfortunate beings, from what we can learn, was harsh in the extreme, and some authorities assert that they were treated with less consideration than were negro slaves, who, after all, cost money.

The pressure of population soon made itself felt in St. Christopher, and it was not long before the inhabitants sought relief by founding settlements on neighboring islands. The first of these was the English colony on Nevis, founded under the following circumstances.

At this time there came to St. Christopher a young man named Anthony Hilton, who had been sent to Virginia by some English adventurers, but had happened to stop off on the island. During his brief stay there he became so impressed with its fertility that he determined to obtain the necessary backing to establish a plantation. On returning home he landed in Ireland, where by virtue of the glowing description he gave of the West Indies he succeeded in interesting some merchants in the possibilities of a colony. They provided him with a ship, sufficient funds, and a small following of settlers to carry out his project. When he landed at Old Road Bay he had no difficulty in obtaining Warner's permission to settle on the windward side of the island, and here he proceeded to erect dwellings and clear the land. But his good fortune did not last long. A tribe of Caribs, remnants of King Tegreman's band, lived in the vicinity, and the memory of the recent massacre was fresh in their minds. They had had enough of the white man and would not tolerate his intrusion on the eastern side of the island. Rising against Hilton's colony, they destroyed his houses, tore up his plantation, killed several of his men. Wise enough to see the folly of trying to maintain himself in this locality, Hilton retreated to the neighborhood of Warner's settlement, where he managed to raise a crop of tobacco which he carried back to Ireland as evidence of his industry.

As it happened, he had among his followers some English planters, and they now persuaded him to abandon his Irish connections and to come with them to London, where a certain merchant was planning to found a colony on some island near St. Christopher. Thomas Littleton, for such was the merchant's name, had obtained a patent from the Earl of Carlisle (who himself had just received a royal charter for the entire Caribbee group) granting him the island of Barbuda or any other island in the Earl's domain which he might care to select. The virtues of this island had been greatly exaggerated to Littleton and his associates, and they called it Dulcina. The scheme of settling

SETTLEMENT OF ST. CHRISTOPHER

here appealed to Hilton, for by founding a colony on an unclaimed island he could eventually become its governor—a position he could never hope to attain at St. Christopher. He therefore accepted Littleton's offer to assume the leadership of an expedition, in the hope that Dulcina would live up to its poetic name.

On reaching this none-too-attractive spot, however, he gave it but a brief inspection, then turned his attention elsewhere. Antigua and Montserrat, the latter a really beautiful island, were also considered, but quickly discarded, and at last after cruising for many days through the Leeward group his choice fell on Nevis, an adjunct of St. Christopher, separated from it by a narrow strait about a mile in width. Here Anthony Hilton landed on July 22, 1628, with a band of one hundred men, and he founded a settlement that grew and prospered until it eventually made that rugged isle one of the social centers of the British West Indies.

The English colony at St. Christopher, as we have said, also increased and prospered; but the French population remained static. As might be expected, such a condition gave rise to disturbances. Why, the English asked, should a small munber of men occupy nearly two-thirds of the island? And to this question the French could find no better answer than to point to the treaty. But treaties of this kind do not always stand up in the face of economic changes, and soon the English began to encroach on French territory—even going so far as to forbid their neighbors to fortify Pointe de Sable in their own domain. Fearing he might eventually lose his foothold on the island, D'Esnambuc decided to return to France and to lay his problem at the feet of the Cardinal, hoping to obtain assistance in the shape of reinforcements for the sadly dwindling colony.

The Cardinal proved sympathetic, much more so than D'Esnambuc had dared to hope. Moreover, he acted promptly. A fleet of ten vessels was collected and placed under the command of the Sieur de Cahuzac, and orders were issued in February,

1629, to assist the colonists in getting complete control of the island or, if this could not be done, to bring about an alliance with the English against the Spaniards.[7] The cessation of hostilities between France and England, which took place in April, caused, it is true, the bellicose portion of these instructions to be modified; but the orders to form an alliance against the Spaniards held good.

There were strong reasons for this alliance, for the Cardinal had just learned through one of his many sources of information that King Philip IV of Spain had no intention of permitting foreigners—particularly heretics, as the English were—to settle in his cherished West Indies without making a strenuous effort to drive them out. The clauses in the charters of Warner and of D'Esnambuc authorizing them to settle in lands not *possessed* by any Christian prince did not, in the eyes of his Catholic Majesty, apply to St. Christopher. All the West Indies were his by right of prior discovery whether or not they were actually settled by Spaniards. Moreover, Philip had at this time a splendid instrument for enforcing his claims. The recent capture of the plate fleet by the Dutchman, Peter Hein, had caused the Spanish government to organize a powerful squadron under Admiral Don Fadrique de Toledo to serve as escort for merchantmen going to Cartagena. With this armada at his command the King could kill two birds with one stone: after convoying the merchantmen the fleet could drive the intruders from St. Christopher. It was to save the island from this threat that Richelieu collected and dispatched the ships under Cahuzac.

Cahuzac was late in starting, and he did not reach his destination until July. He anchored off Basseterre in the southern part of the island, where D'Esnambuc landed for a conference with Du Roissey, having taken with him some three hundred colonists supplied him by the company. He found the situation much better than it had been when he left, for the Dutch had again been there with a cargo of supplies, while during his absence the

[7]Margry, *Belain d'Esnambuc*, p. 32.

company had sent over a shipload of settlers. It was but natural that the arrival of Cahuzac's fleet should increase the confidence of the Frenchmen. Brushing aside the English superiority of numbers as inconsequential, since in French opinion the British colonists consisted chiefly of wretched indentured servants fit only to till the soil, Cahuzac and D'Ensambuc sent an ultimatum to Edward Warner, who governed during his father's absence in England, ordering him to withdraw at once from French territory and to retire within the limits prescribed by the treaty. Warner stalled for time, hoping to get word to a small English fleet in the offing; but Cahuzac would not be put off. Weighing anchor with his six ships—the rest had wandered off during the crossing—he sailed to the English roadstead and opened fire on the vessels lying off shore. The reply was brisk and spirited. For three hours the battle raged, the guns from the British redoubt, Fort Charles, joining in the fracas, until the French had captured three vessels, driven three ashore, and scattered the rest.

The victory was complete. The following day Warner arrived under a flag of truce to make a formal protest against the actions of the French. Cahuzac received him on board his flagship, the "Trois Rois," and again insisted that the English evacuate French territory, adding this time that they must abandon their efforts to prevent D'Esnambuc from fortifying Pointe de Sable. Warner tried to avoid the issue by saying he must first communicate with his Sovereign to learn his pleasure in the matter, but Cahuzac would not be delayed, and he answered bluntly: "Make up your mind quickly to give me the satisfaction I demand or I shall begin hostilities again." To Warner's further request for a delay of five days the French commander offered to wait only until the morrow. The following day Warner again boarded the flagship where the officers had gathered. A friendly spirit pervaded the group. Cahuzac entertained them all at luncheon, and the customary toasts to the reigning monarchs were given amid salvos of artillery. A new treaty, embodying the demands of the French, was signed, and as a mark of courtesy Cahuzac presented the English with the ships he had captured from them in the battle.

Cahuzac now considered his duty done. After dispatching his lieutenant, Captain Giron, on a tour of reconnaissance (which failed to reveal any trace of the Spanish fleet) he sailed to the little island of St. Eustatius, just north of St. Christopher, thinking that Don Fadrique had gone elsewhere. Here he broke up his command. "La Cardinale" was sent back to France; two vessels set sail on a cruise of their own; Captain Giron, his ship dismasted in a storm, sought refuge in the nearby island of St. Martin. Thus the French commander had only two vessels left when the Spanish armada finally hove in sight, and he was unable to be of any assistance to D'Esnambuc and Du Roissey. Through an error of judgment he had failed in the principal objective of his expedition.

Let us now return to Nevis, where we left Governor Hilton and his promising little colony. At this time the Earl of Carlisle, somewhat disturbed by reports he had received concerning Barbados and Nevis, had sent out as his representative a man named Henry Hawley with orders to investigate the situation. Hawley proceeded first to Barbados, where he distinguished himself by the brutal and high-handed manner with which he treated the local governor. This done he set sail for Nevis. Governor Hilton, however, had been forewarned of what he might expect from Hawley, and had sailed for England to appeal to Carlisle, leaving the colony in the hands of a deputy. He left in the nick of time, for his ship was stopped by Hawley as it left the roadstead, and he managed to escape only by stating that he was a peaceful trader bound for the Windward Islands.

When Hawley landed he was welcomed by the planters, who escorted him to the Governor's residence. There they entertained him "with wine and good victuals"; but after this civility had been complied with, they refused to acknowledge his authority until Hilton returned with instructions from Carlisle. Thus checkmated Hawley could do nothing. He realized instinctively that the ruthless methods he had used at Barbados would not be appropriate here, so he invited the deputy on board his ship, hoping to accomplish something by means of kindness and persuasion. As the two leaders sat down to dinner, the air was split by a detonation; it was the long gun at Pelican Point welcoming the Spanish fleet. Rushing up on deck Hawley saw through the haze of the early September evening the mighty armada of Don Fadrique, consisting of sixteen galleons, twenty-nine ships, and eight galiots, advancing to the roadstead. The Englishman did not hesitate. He cut his cable, set his sails, and ran for St. Christopher; nor did he stop until he had piled his vessel up on the shore of Basseterre.

The planters, meanwhile, took a more dignified course of action. The gun on Pelican Point was served adroitly, battering a Spanish vessel so hard as to put it out of commission. But the indentured servants, representatives of that surplus population which England was trying to dispose of in the New World, feeling that any fate would be better than their present bondage, swam out to the ships and revealed to the attackers the true condition of the island. The soldiers proved no better—most of them were servants—and deserting their leaders ran to the shore crying: "Liberty, joyful liberty!"

Resistance under these conditions was obviously impossible. Governor Hilton's brother, John, took charge of the situation and rowed out to the flagship with an interpreter. He found Don Fadrique well disposed. The Admiral received him with true Spanish courtesy, informing him that all would go smoothly if the English would only yield to his master that which they had so wrongfully usurped. He even went so far as to offer ships for transporting the colonists back to England—that is, if they would give hostages for the return of the vessels, for after all one must be businesslike. When John Hilton went ashore to report the result of his interview to the assembled planters, they demurred a trifle; then, there being no alternative, they accepted the Admiral's offer with thanks. Don Fadrique was as good as his word. He came ashore and complimented the Englishmen on their good sense, even offering favorable terms of employment to any wishing to join the Spanish forces. The conference ended in a feast at the Governor's house with the copious eating and drinking appropriate to such an occasion. It was a happy ending to what might have been an unpleasant affair. In the afternoon Don Fadrique set sail for St. Christopher.

On the evening of the sixth of September the Spanish fleet appeared off Basseterre and saluted the fort with a salvo of guns, sending ashore at the same time an envoy with a flag of truce; for Don Fadrique hoped to capture the place in the same peaceful way in which he had taken Nevis. Du Roissey, for his part, appears to have misjudged the Spaniard's intentions, for he replied to the friendly salute with shotted guns and immediately sent messengers to Edward Warner and D'Esnambuc apprising them of the arrival of the enemy's fleet. The French commander, unwilling to leave his settlement undefended, could spare but one hundred men; but Warner, thanks to a large supply of servants recently arrived from England, replied generously with a contingent of eight times that number. With these reinforcements Du Roissey was ready to put up a stout defense, and he spent the night erecting a barricade along the shore. Next morning the Spanish admiral, seeing that the islanders were determined to fight, sent ashore a detachment of sappers to build a line of trenches paralleling the French fortifications. When this work was completed, a large body of men was disembarked to begin the attack.

There was among the French forces a young officer named Simon Dyel du Parquet, eldest son of D'Esnambuc's sister, Adrienne, who stood apart watching with considerable disgust Du Roissey's arrangements for fighting a defensive battle. Fearing that this lack of initiative might discourage his men, he begged the commander's permission to attack, asking that worthy officer somewhat sarcastically if he intended to remain behind his barricade all day without striking a blow. Stung by the

SETTLEMENT OF ST. CHRISTOPHER 31

taunt Du Roissey at once gave his consent, hoping that the outcome would teach the young man a lesson. Du Parquet needed no further encouragement, and having collected a handful of eager volunteers he hurled himself at the enemy's outpost. The Spaniards, taken by surprise, gave way as the Frenchman rushed at them sword in hand. But his followers had none of his spirit, and soon he was left alone with only three men to support him. The young man, however, proved equal to the emergency. He sought out and killed the Spanish leader, but only to be borne to the ground by superior numbers. From this predicament he was rescued, not by his own men, who long ago had turned tail or been killed, but by a Spanish officer, who in admiration for the lad's bravery caused him to be carried aboard the flagship. There he was given every care by the generous Don Fadrique. He lived only a month, vainly struggling to regain his strength, and at his death was buried with all honors by his enemies, who appreciated his valor more than did his own countrymen.

When Du Parquet fell, the Anglo-French resistance collapsed, and, if we can believe the historian Du Tertre, a panic seized the little army. Du Roissey in person led the retreat. Throwing himself into a boat with his officers, he hurried to Pointe de Sable, leaving his men to make their way overland to safety as best they could. The soldiers, if we can call the plantation hands that made up the army by such a name, were now leaderless, and they broke into a run, throwing away guns and ammunition in their haste to escape from the Spaniards. On landing at Pointe de Sable Du Roissey called the demoralized settlers together and ordered them to hurry on board two vessels which were anchored off the shore and to abandon the island. D'Esnambuc did his best to quiet the panicky commander, pointing to the military advantages of the place and to the difficulty Don Fadrique would have in attacking it. But neither reason nor an appeal to his sense of honor had any effect on the terrified Du Roissey. He called together a council of war, dominated it by appealing to the fears of the colonists, and insisted on an immediate evacuation of the island, at the same time threatening his colleague with death if he should dare to interfere. There was nothing D'Esnambuc could do; all save a handful of colonists were swayed by Du Roissey's arguments, and in a few days the entire colony of about four hundred persons had clambered aboard the ships and sailed for Antigua. Such is the account of the fall of St. Christopher as given by Father du Tertre—an account which we have no means of checking, but which seems almost unbelievable, inasmuch as the picture it gives of Du Roissey is so at variance with the story of his gallant attack on the Spanish galleon in the face of overwhelming odds. Were it not for his subsequent conduct, we should be inclined to dismiss it as a slander spread by his enemies.

The English thus deserted by their allies felt unable to continue the unequal contest by themselves. When the Spaniards landed and seized the French fort at Basseterre, they offered to surrender if ships were provided to take them back to England. Apparently Don Fadrique acted humanely in his treatment of the fallen enemy. Seven hundred men and boys were transported first to Cartagena, then to Havana, where they were dispersed among several Spanish vessels. Their fate was probably no worse, and it may have been better, than their position as indentured servants at St. Christopher, if we may judge by the way their fellow-sufferers welcomed the Spaniards as deliverers when the fleet put in at Nevis. An effort was made later to return some to their native land when three hundred were put on board the "David of Lubeck" and sent to Plymouth.[8] Yet despite all the efforts of Don Fadrique's men, a few remnants of the English settlement remained in the mountain fastnesses of St. Christopher to form the germ of a new colony.

So hasty had been the departure of the French that they failed to take on board sufficient supplies, and the pangs of hunger soon made themselves felt. For three weeks the refugees were buffetted by storms and contrary winds until at last, only too glad

[8]*Calendar of State Papers, Colonial, 1574–1660*, p. 118.

SETTLEMENT OF ST. CHRISTOPHER

to set foot again on dry land, they disembarked at St. Martin. This island proved barren, its water brackish, and here Du Roissey for a second time played the craven. Despairing of ever maintaining a colony in such an unfavorable locality, he suborned the captain of one of the ships and despite the entreaties of D'Esnambuc persuaded that officer to sail him back to France, leaving his erstwhile comrade-in-arms to manage the colony as best he could. We are pleased to record, however, that when Du Roissey made his report to Cardinal Richelieu, he was promptly thrown into the Bastille, where he remained, presumably, for a long time. At any rate, he disappeared forever from West Indian history.

Next day D'Esnambuc called his followers together, cheered them by promising not to desert them, and announced his intention of continuing his voyage to Antigua. The number left after Du Roissey's defection was rather large for one ship, so a few remained on St. Martin, while small detachments were placed on the neighboring islands of Anguilla and St. Bartholomew. Then the main party sailed for Antigua. After three or four days they reached the island, only to find it, or rather that portion of it upon which they chanced to land, swampy and ill-suited for colonization. But by good fortune D'Esnambuc here met Captain Giron, Cahuzac's lieutenant, who professed himself eager to aid the refugees in any way he could. With his assistance the French governor was able to get his people to Montserrat, where they remained while Giron went to St. Christopher to reconnoiter.

At St. Christopher Giron found the English remnant of the colony in virtual possession of the entire island. After the departure of the Spanish fleet those who had fled inland determined to come forth from their retreat and to face the situation rather than to remain forever in hiding, gambling on the probability that the Spaniards would never return after so signal a victory. There were a few Frenchmen among them, but the English predominated, and they refused to allow Giron to land, hoping to secure the island exclusively for themselves. Giron, however, had no intention of seeing France lose her rightful possessions, so without further ado he attacked two English vessels riding peacefully at anchor and carried them off. With the aid of these ships he now gathered the scattered colonists at Montserrat, St. Martin, and the other islands, and advancing on St. Christopher 350 strong he succeeded in re-establishing the French colony without striking a blow.

With the return of the French the dual settlement of St. Christopher takes on an aspect of permanence. The colonists lived for many years, not altogether in harmony, it must be admitted, for where French and English dwell together there must always be a certain amount of bickering, but at least without serious open rupture. Sir Thomas Warner threw himself into the various problems of government, providing for the defense of the island, training men, stationing guards, and going the rounds day and night. John Jeaffreson, appointed colonel of militia, also contributed to the general welfare by drilling soldiers and constructing fortifications, besides attending to his duties as a prominent planter. The English colony grew by leaps and bounds. D'Esnambuc, on the other hand, ruled a settlement that did not enjoy, for a while, at least, the prosperity of its English neighbor. When he returned from Montserrat it numbered all told only some four hundred souls. But after the formation of a new company in France to take over the business of the old one, it began to show signs of increase, until it, too, found need of expansion in other islands of the Caribbee group.

~ III ~

COLONIZATION OF GUADELOUPE

WHEN Belain d'Esnambuc returned to St. Christopher with his followers, after his ignominious expulsion by the Spaniards, he found it necessary to start again from the very beginning. His men, it is true, were eager and energetic; but he himself had lost faith in the willingness of the company to support him in his struggles against the raids of Spanish squadrons and the attacks of his English neighbors, who now far outnumbered the French. For once the brave pioneer despaired. In his agony of doubt and uncertainty he lost the confidence that had sustained him throughout all the vicissitudes of the past four years and gave orders to return to France. Acting on this decision the settlers stopped planting vegetables for the coming season and concentrated on the production of as large a crop of tobacco as possible, as it was the one commodity that could be taken back to France and sold at a profit.

Then came a change. The tobacco proved exceptionally abundant, and the Dutch merchant, who had visited them so opportunely the year before, now arrived with an ample supply of flour, wine, meat, and clothing material to be exchanged for all the available tobacco as a down payment, with a six-month credit for the balance. Perhaps, then, if the Dutch were eager enough for tobacco to send ships across the Atlantic with goods to be exchanged for it on such favorable terms, the colony could prosper on Dutch trade despite the apathy of the company at home. Providence, indeed, had rebuked D'Esnambuc for his lack of faith.

The immediate needs of his colonists thus provided for, D'Esnambuc attacked with renewed vigor the problem of establishing his settlement on a permanent basis. He divided his men into separate companies, each of which, in addition to doing its share of work on the fortifications, was to busy itself in the district allotted to it with the cultivation of tobacco, cotton, and pimento, that is, crops which could be readily exchanged for merchandise. Since the English neighbors, who now numbered about six thousand, were constantly encroaching on French territory despite the terms of the treaty, D'Esnambuc to meet their threat secured the close co-operation of the two halves of his colony so that reinforcements could be rushed from one to the other through the intervening English territory whenever hostilities became imminent. At this time, too, D'Esnambuc was called upon to settle a problem that threatened to disrupt his economic system. The master planters were attempting to hold their indentured servants to a five-year term of service in violation of the company's charter, which limited it to three. The servants, of course, far outnumbered their masters, and being well armed they threatened to turn the plantations upside down unless their wrongs were righted. According to simple justice they were obviously in the right, and D'Esnambuc by virtue of his authority as governor canceled the contracts of those who had already served three years and established them in the colony as free citizens.

These domestic problems had hardly been solved, when there arose difficulties with the company at home. The profitable stroke of business which the Dutch merchantman had been able to do in the time of D'Esnambuc's need had encouraged others of his nationality to build up a trade with St. Christopher, with the result that the French capitalists who had financed the enterprise were left with little return on their investment.

To their loud complaints the colonists replied in a spirited manner, pointing out that the company had failed to keep its part of the bargain, thus leaving them so poorly supplied that they could not subsist if cut off from the Dutch traders. Struck by the truth of this observation, the company made a half-hearted attempt to set matters right. The good ship "La Cardinale" was again sent out (in 1631), this time with a small delegation consisting chiefly of military men who were empowered to enter into negotiations with the colonists with a view to reducing the dues they were paying the company. They brought with them little in the way of merchandise. Thus treated, the settlers had no choice, if they would survive, but to send the greater part of their tobacco to Holland and England, where they could get excellent prices, reserving only a small portion of their trade for certain French merchants not affiliated with the company. They then took the money received from these transactions to France, where they secured additional servants to take back to St. Christopher. By this procedure the English and Dutch merchants were the real beneficiaries of the business, while the French capitalists who had financed the undertaking received no returns; for they were powerless to stop the natural flow of business. At last, when the directors attempted to rectify the trouble, they applied the very worst remedy possible. Instead of sending well-laden ships to their colony, they begged the King for an edict forbidding all vessels to trade at St. Christopher without their permission. This edict, signed November 25, 1634, did more harm than good to every one concerned. The colonists, disgusted with the company, turned over all their business to the English and Dutch, thus cutting off the independent French traders. While the company, seeing its trade vanish entirely, prepared to give up the venture as unprofitable.

Yet there were among the merchant adventurers some who did not despair. If the English and Dutch could make money from the tobacco crop at St. Christopher, there was evidently ample opportunity for French traders to do likewise, if only the situation could be properly adjusted. A conference was accordingly held with Cardinal Richelieu, at which it was decided to dissolve the Company of St. Christopher and to organize in its place a new one with broader powers.

As a result of this meeting and of several subsequent meetings a charter was issued by the Cardinal on February 12, 1635, incorporating the Company of the Isles of America, which was to take over the property, privileges, and authority of the Company of St. Christopher. In brief, the new associates bound themselves to continue the establishment at St. Christopher and to bend every effort to plant new colonies on neighboring islands not already occupied by any Christian prince. The associates also pledged themselves to transport to the Caribbees during the next twenty years at least four thousand persons of both sexes, all of whom were to be Roman Catholics in good standing, for neither King nor Cardinal had any intention of permitting the religious dissensions which had caused such turmoil in France to be re-enacted in the newly established colonies. There would be trouble enough as it was. The King, moreover, was graciously pleased to bestow these islands on the new corporation without the payment of dues, a mere formal act of homage paid to him and his successors being deemed a sufficient obligation. He reserved, of course, the power of appointing civil and military officials. During the twenty-year period of the grant all persons save members of the company were forbidden to trespass on the islands under its jurisdiction or even to trade with them without the express permission of the directors, and all who ventured to disregard this ordinance were subject to the confiscation of their ships and merchandise. Furthermore, the King would permit all descendants of French settlers and Indians who made profession of the Faith to be reckoned as French subjects with all the privileges appertaining thereto.

Armed with this liberal document, the associates immediately started to infuse new life into their moribund venture. As soon as the King ratified the Cardinal's arrangement by formal letters patent, which he did the following month, the merchants began to enlist prospective colonists. So rapidly was this work pushed that they were soon able to send out an imposing number of people, properly equipped for the business at hand. An innovation in the selection of clergymen to accompany the expedition, and one that was destined to have a great influence on the colony, was also made at this time. Hitherto the priests had been chosen on the hit or miss plan, with the result that on reaching St. Christopher they generally confined their duties to the celebration of mass and routine visits to the sick. The establishment of missions among the savages was neglected. To please the King, who was sincerely interested in the conversion of his Carib subjects, the directors asked the Provincial of the Capuchins in Normandy to select priests whom he considered specially fitted for such work. This he did, assigning Fathers Jerome, Marc (no family names are given), and Pacifique de Provins to the colony. These worthy men came to St. Christopher and established convents—one in the northern section, at the foot of Mt. Misery, the other, which became the headquarters of their evangelical labors, near D'Esnambuc's home. (M. d'Esnambuc had shifted his residence to Basseterre after the departure of Du Roissey and had erected a dwelling in the foothills back of the town. From that time Basseterre may be regarded as the capital of the French West Indies.)

A piece of good fortune awaited the newcomers at St. Christopher. A privateersman named Pitrecotté had arrived with a cargo of negroes, recently captured from a Spanish trader, which he sold at a handsome profit. Whatever one may say of the ethical aspects of slavery, it is certain that the colonies could never have attained a high degree of agricultural development without a plentiful supply of cheap labor. The need for slaves was even greater in the French than in the English colonies, for France did not have a large surplus population. While the English settlers could and did import thousands of their fellow countrymen as indentured servants, the French were obliged to get along as best they could with comparatively few. Thus the importation of negroes was a necessity if they were to develop and hold the larger islands of the archipelago. Moreover, it is extremely doubtful if the savage blacks who were brought from their native wilds in Africa could ever have been made to labor on the plantations under any other system than chattel slavery.

The slave system in the French islands, however, came very near being wrecked at the outset by a peculiar law of great antiquity, which held that all those who reached the domains of the King of France became free. It was only with difficulty that his councillors could prevail on Louis XIII to abrogate this law in favor of the Caribbee Islands, and then they succeeded only by an appeal to his piety, pointing out that it was the one method by which these savages could be brought under Christian influence and saved from idolatry. Once the institution of slavery had received official sanction, French companies were organized to carry on the traffic, though the settlers also secured their human chattels from English, Dutch, and Danish interlopers. The French Guinea Company obtained its blacks from the coast of Benin, where men suited for the arduous labors of the fields could be procured, while those imported by the Senegal Company were better for household duties. Upon arriving at his destination the slave trader displayed his wares and sold them. The slaves were then taken by their masters to the plantations and subjected for a week to special treatment calculated to limber them up after the long sea voyage, to acclimatize them, and to strengthen them for work. Father Labat, who devoted some time to studying the subject at first hand, describes at length the method of treating the newly arrived slaves. He deplored the harsher system used by owners who put their people to work before they had time to recover their strength. When the slaves arrived at the plantation they were quartered among the older hands, from whom they soon learned the ropes and a smattering of the language. No time was lost in giving them the necessary religious instruction to prepare them for baptism, and in this the negroes already baptized were of great help in dealing with the new ones, for they carefully explained that they did not regard them as equals until they had become professed Christians. Slavery, then, became the basis of the economic system in the Caribbee Islands, for the English also bought slaves to supplement their free labor. It was not abolished until the nineteenth century.

Reinforced in this fortunate manner, D'Esnambuc determined to resist the encroachments of the English colonists, who, far outnumbering his people, had established themselves on French territory. There was at this time a huge banyan tree near the seashore at Pointe de Sable, which was used as a marker for the line of demarcation separating the northern French territory from that of the English. For some time Warner's men had been extending their boundary by taking their bearings from a different part of the tree which, like all its species, dropped aerial roots from its branches to the ground, thus extending itself over a considerable area. By taking a bearing from the point of the tree extending farthest into French territory to Mt. Misery, the English had been able to get an angle that threw the boundary line well over on the French side.

D'Esnambuc at first tried peaceful means to bring about a reasonable adjustment of the dispute. But when negotiations proved inadequate, he prepared for war, choosing to fight rather than yield an inch of territory. Word was sent to the planters, who rose in a body and armed their slaves, promising them freedom if they would fight. From the salt ponds of Basseterre to the slopes of Mt. Misery the clans gathered in a common cause that almost took on the nature of a crusade. Parish priests accompanied their flocks, carrying a huge cross and exhorting them to stand fast against the heretics. Slaves to the number of five or six hundred made their appearance under the command of French officers at the edge of the forests, gazing down on the English houses, ready to kill and burn. Alarmed by the terrifying sight of these black savages, Sir Thomas Warner hastened to a rendezvous with D'Esnambuc under the banyan tree, where he met the French commander surrounded by his staff. D'Esnambuc had arranged his negro hordes behind him with the dark forest as background—a dramatic setting calculated to put fear into the hearts of his enemies. For these negroes were, not the semicivilized colored hands of a modern plantation, but the savages of the African jungle, armed with knives and clubs, their half-naked bodies glistening in the sunlight, ready to kill when their leader raised his hand. D'Esnambuc at once saw his advantage and promptly seized it. Driving his sword into the ground on the far side of the banyan tree he pointed to the summit of Mt. Misery and swore that the line between the two would hereafter serve as the boundary line separating the two nations. It was a highhanded manner of beginning a conference, and Warner was disposed for a moment to resist; but a glance about him at the savage countenances of the French slaves, who were only too willing to fall upon his people, decided the issue, and he capitulated.

The tension broken, an agreement was drawn up confirming the new frontier, and the two leaders drank the healths of their sovereigns, vowing to respect each other's rights. Peace thus restored, a friendly intercourse of trade soon arose between the two colonies. French and Dutch vessels touched at the island, bringing besides the usual cargoes of merchandise an occasional shipload of blacks gathered on the Guinea coast or filched from a Spanish slave trader off Brazil. With the return of prosperity came the time for the French to think about colonizing other islands.

There happened to be in St. Christopher at this time a wealthy planter named Charles Liénard, Sieur de l'Olive, whom Richelieu had appointed lieutenant-governor of the island. He was a bold, ambitious man, ruthless in his methods, impulsive, and not likely to be held back by overconscientiousness. When he arrived, in the latter part of 1631, D'Esnambuc, out of respect for his position, gave him Du Roissey's former home for his residence and appointed as his assistant a young man named Guillaume d'Orange, whose experience made him just the person to advise his superior in matters concerning the development of his property and his dealings with the inhabitants. L'Olive's affairs prospered, yet mindful of Richelieu's desire to expand the colony he presently purchased a flyboat and sent D'Orange with a small party to make a thorough survey of the three large islands to the south of St. Christopher: Guadeloupe, Dominica, and Martinique. D'Orange did an excellent job of the business entrusted to him, for thanks to his familiarity with Indian ways he was able to penetrate into the interior of these islands despite the general hostility of the natives. On his return he reported to L'Olive that Guadeloupe was the most promising of the three islands, a conclusion D'Esnambuc had already reached through independent investigation.

After receiving this report L'Olive promptly set sail for France with D'Orange, and he arrived at Dieppe toward the end of 1634. Here he had the good fortune to meet Jean Duplessis, Sieur d'Ossonville, a former member of Cahuzac's famous expedition, who was busily engaged in fitting out a ship for a trading voyage to the West Indies. Duplessis was a quiet, likable man, not given to bluster, a man easy to get on with, just the man for the domineering Sieur de l'Olive to have as partner. The two of them, L'Olive quickly saw, would work well together. L'Olive accordingly laid his plans before Duplessis, spread D'Orange's report on the table, and painted in glowing colors the wealth and beauty of Guadeloupe, tickling his auditor's ambition by pointing out the possibilities of building there a colony that might in time overshadow St. Christopher and make its founders the leaders of the French West Indies. Duplessis allowed himself to be convinced, and in truth one cannot blame him, for here was the opportunity of a lifetime to become a real figure in the new scheme of colonial expansion.

The two partners hastened to Paris, arriving in time to witness the dissolution of the old Company of St. Christopher and the birth of the new Company of the Isles. It was, indeed, a propitious time for them, as the new organization was eager to develop its possessions and to begin the work of sending out the four thousand colonists it had obligated itself to furnish under the terms of its charter. Within two days after Cardinal Richelieu had signed the patent the directors under the presidency of M. Fouquet had closed a deal with L'Olive and Duplessis granting them the privilege of colonizing in either Guadeloupe, Martinique, or Dominica.

The terms granted the two adventurers were indeed favorable. They were appointed governors of their colony for a period of ten years, and sums of two thousand francs in cash and three thousand in munitions were placed at their disposal—the latter to remain the property of the company. Furthermore, the company agreed to claim only sixty pounds of tobacco or forty of cotton for each man sent out during the first six years. In return for these privileges the two adventurers bound themselves to send overseas two hundred men within two months and to erect a fort the first year and a storehouse the second. For the next five years one hundred men a year were to be sent out, and fifty a year for the following four years, so that at the end of the term mentioned in the charter they would have transported nine hundred men, not counting women and children. The company reserved the right to transport as many settlers as it pleased, who were to be supported for a year by L'Olive and Duplessis. Of course, all were to be Frenchmen and Catholics. Their term of service was to be limited to three years. The island was to be governed by a council, at which the *commis*, or factor—to borrow a title from the Hudson's Bay Company—who represented the financial interests of the company was to have a seat. At the same time the Cardinal made arrangements to strengthen the royal authority in the West Indies by a slight though important innovation. The company, as we have pointed out, had the power to select the governors and, if it deemed it necessary, the lieutenant-governors of their island possessions. Over these officials the Cardinal now arranged to superimpose a governor-general appointed by the King. There could, of course, be but one person entitled to such a post, and on March 7, 1635, His Majesty signed a commission designating the Sieur d'Esnambuc to this high office.

When the Cardinal had established the new company, he saw fit to give the religious situation in the colony his serious consideration. Before this, as we have seen, little had been done for St. Christopher save to send the three Capuchins. But now His Eminence proposed to see that Guadeloupe had a suitable mission. With this object in view he decided to act along the lines recently set by the company in dealing with the situation at St. Christopher, and he suggested to the directors that they ask Father Carré, Superior of the Dominican convent in Paris, to designate members of his order who would be qualified for this work. Father Carré was pleased at this mark of the Cardinal's esteem and promptly selected four priests to accompany the expedition. They were: Pierre Pelican, who was to act as superior, Raymond Breton, who devoted much time to studying the Carib language, Nicolas Bréchet, and Pierre Gryphon. These men were to be the founders of the first mission to the Caribs outside St. Christopher, the forerunners of many others who attempted, though with little success, to convert the Indians to the Faith. Their appointment was ratified by the Pope himself, who sent a brief blessing their mission.

With their charter signed, sealed, and delivered, MM. de l'Olive and Duplessis returned to Dieppe and sat down to think the matter over. It was a big assignment, bigger than they had expected, and common sense showed them that it was necessary to obtain help if they would carry out so vast a project. To secure the much-needed assistance they signed an agreement with four merchants of the city, who promised to send the proposed colony 2,500 able-bodied men, besides women and children, within the next six years. In return for this the company agreed to give these merchants exclusive rights to trade and the privilege of importing into France twenty pounds of cotton or tobacco for every man they sent over.

Three months after Richelieu had set his hand to the charter the necessary complement of colonists had been raised—there were more than five hundred of them—and the two pioneers set sail from Dieppe on May 25, 1635, with their followers safely ensconsed in two stout ships. The transatlantic voyage was quickly made; just one month after leaving Dieppe the expedition sighted Martinique. Attracted by its beauty, the leaders determined to land and explore it, for the place might after all be more favorable than Guadeloupe. Having anchored off the western side, L'Olive and Duplessis accordingly went ashore near the Rivière du Carbet, which flows from a triple-peaked mountain to the sea about half way between the two extremities of the island. Here was performed the ceremony of the annexation of the island to the Crown of France. A rudely fashioned cross was planted on a prominent spot close by the shore, and to it was fastened the coat of arms of His Majesty. Then, intoning the *Vexilla regis*, which was so often sung on such occasions, the kneeling crowd bowed their heads while the Sieur de l'Olive pronounced the words that proclaimed King Louis XIII the lawful ruler of this little domain. But on further inspection the island appeared inhospitable, as indeed it is in the neighborhood of their landing place. The terrain there is rugged—hardly suitable for cultivation. Perhaps, too, they may have had an encounter with the fer-de-lance, the deadly reptile of the island, that discouraged them from further exploration. Without attempting a more thorough investigation of the lovely island, which today is one of the most thickly populated spots in the world, they set sail, and, passing by beautiful Dominica, they dropped anchor three days later off the northern shore of Guadeloupe near the modern village of Ste. Rose.

The island of Guadeloupe, as we have said, is the largest of

COLONIZATION OF GUADELOUPE

the Caribbees. In reality it consists of two distinct islands separated by a narrow salt-water stream, barely navigable for small boats, a stream so narrow that unless one looks closely at the map one would never suspect that the island was actually divided into two halves. The western half is mountainous, furrowed by deep ravines and innumerable rivers. A mountain range runs north and south, rising through the clouds to its crowning height in La Soufrière, which is more than five thousand feet above the sea. Indeed, Guadeloupe and Dominica share the distinction of being the most imposing islands of this beautiful archipelago. Although the western half is mountainous, the eastern half is flat by contrast and offers little to dazzle the eye. Even its plains are unattractive, for due to a lack of rivers to supply the necessary irrigation they have few agricultural advantages to offer. At the southern extremity of the isthmus which joins the two halves an excellent harbor is located, where the modern city of Pointe à Pitre is situated.

L'Olive and Duplessis naturally knew nothing of this shelter, so they anchored at Ste. Rose, where a certain amount of protection is afforded, thanks to a string of small islands lying a short distance off the shore. Here they landed and took possession of the island with ceremonies similar to those at Martinique. This done, the two leaders took up separate stations not far from each other—L'Olive to build a fort, which he called St. Pierre, on the Vieux Fort River, while Duplessis settled to the east of him on the Petit Fort River. The choice of this site for the location of a permanent colony was not a fortunate one. The soil was scarcely suitable for cultivation. It was red and of a quality, so Father du Tertre tells us, more adapted to the making of bricks than to any other use. Thus the little colony was handicapped at the outset by a lack of proper nourishment.

The two leaders now divided the men between them—each one also taking his share of the tools and supplies. The colonists who had paid their own way and brought indentured servants with them were given concessions of land in return for certain obligations they were expected to fulfill, such as the payment of specified dues, guard duty, and the construction of fortifications and public works. Like their Canadian prototypes, these men were called habitans. They were to become the backbone of the colony.

Now that they were settled on this wonderful island their troubles began in earnest. The expedition had, in fact, been poorly supplied from the start. Actuated by greed, the merchants who provisioned the ships had furnished a poor quality of meat and other food; and so small had been the quantity of cider supplied for the passengers that it was found necessary to dilute it with salt water, a process that caused a violent outbreak of dysentery. Thus, despite the rapidity of the voyage disease was rampant, and many died as soon as they reached land. To add to these misfortunes the settlers had brought from France provisions for only two months; then the ship had failed to touch at Barbados where the directors of the company had arranged for a fresh food supply, so that after landing they soon found starvation staring them in the face.

Nor was lack of food the sole cause of all their ills. These Frenchmen, who had never before experienced a tropical climate, failed to take even the elementary precautions necessary for a European who would survive in the Torrid Zone. They worked for long hours unprotected from the glaring sun, then burning with thirst they drank copiously of cold water and threw themselves down to rest in the insufficient shade of the nearest tree. Unlike the Caribs, who wisely left shady groves standing in the midst of their fields, the French cut and slashed right and left, intent only on clearing the ground as rapidly as possible and without a thought of future protection from the sun. They tore up the earth, which, loosened for the first time, gave forth an unhealthy exhalation which was often fatal to the laborers in their weakened condition. Thus, caught between malnutrition and insanitary surroundings, the wretched pioneers quickly succumbed to disease. To make matters worse

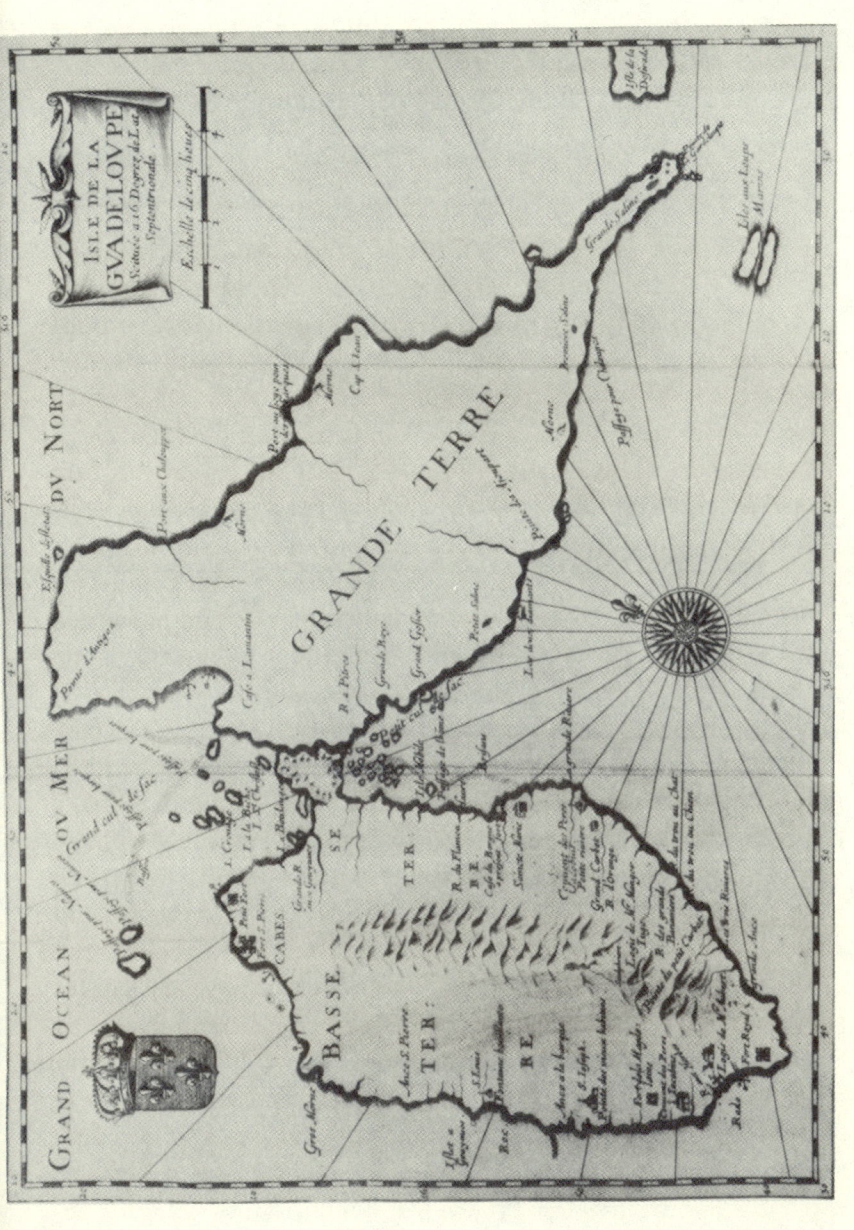

GUADELOUPE

the habitans treated their servants with great severity. These wretched men, enfeebled by sickness and privation, were driven to work by overseers armed with clubs and forced to labor in the burning sun, so that, as Du Tertre tells us, "some who had been captives in Barbary cursed the hour they had left there, publicly invoking the devil and giving themselves to him if only he would take them back to France, and what is more horrible, some died with these frightful blasphemies on their lips." To remedy this desperate situation L'Olive and Duplessis attempted to obtain supplies at St. Christopher, only to return in a few days with very little in the way of food.

It was now merely a matter of surviving by any means possible. Some prowled along the shore to catch turtles, whose flesh, though it relieved hunger temporarily, caused them to fall ill and die. Some escaped to the savages, who, be it said to their credit, treated them humanely. Others ate what they could find—dogs, rats, and boiled leather, even ointment stolen from the surgeon's stores was devoured to relieve the frightful hunger. A few frantic men dug up the dead to satisfy their cravings. The entire population was reduced to a desperation that verged on insanity. In the midst of all this suffering the four Dominicans labored zealously to prevent the members of their flock from taking their own lives. They dragged back some who had thrown themselves into the sea and cut down others who had tried to hang themselves. The leaders did what they could to prevent the theft of the fast-dwindling provisions, throwing thieves in jail or flogging them. One fellow, who had already been branded twice and saved from the gallows by the intercession of Father Breton, vowed he would steal again and be hanged rather than endure the pangs of a slow death by starvation.

At last, on the sixteenth of September, there appeared the ship which the merchants of Dieppe had promised to send over with a supply of provisions. The miserable colonists swarmed out of their huts to welcome the new arrivals; but their cries of welcome met with no enthusiastic response, and as the ship's boats slid up on the beach there tumbled from them 140 half-starved creatures no better off than the men they had come to relieve. Again the merchants had proved themselves niggardly, drivers of a hard bargain, whose only wish was to send over enough men to form the quota required by the company. But perhaps we are likely to judge them too harshly; their shortcomings may have been due more to ignorance of the true conditions in Guadeloupe than to inhuman indifference to the sufferings of their people. Doubtless, in order to secure the necessary backing for their enterprise L'Olive and Duplessis had painted a lovely picture of West Indian abundance and of Guadeloupe as a land where men could live with very little effort. Thus the gullible merchants thought of the island as overrun with fruit trees, game, and vegetables which could all be had for the asking; while the two adventurers who had spread these reports were made the victims of their own exaggerations.

Be this as it may, the settlers now saw that drastic measures must be taken if they were to survive. The relief ship—if it can be called such—at once sailed for home, the captain stoutly protesting that he had barely enough food to get him back to France without leaving any at Guadeloupe. It was then that L'Olive proved himself the evil genius of the colony by advocating a measure contrary to the policy of the company and the dictates of conscience: he would attack the Caribs and rob them of their provisions. Duplessis, to his credit be it said, opposed the plan, vowing he would rather starve with his men than be a party to such an outrage. But L'Olive was a persistent man, strong in his opinions; and, moreover, there were many rendered desperate by their privations who were ready to join in any plan that promised immediate relief. Unable to move his companion, L'Olive hurried to St. Christopher, where he hoped to enlist the aid of D'Esnambuc. The latter, however, he found as stubbornly opposed to him as Duplessis, for the experienced

Governor saw the dangers that would result from an unprovoked attack on the natives. At first he tried persuasion; then, when this failed to move the pig-headed commander, he threatened to report the matter to the King, since His Majesty had insisted on a humane policy toward the natives. Faced with such strong opposition L'Olive might have yielded had not an untoward event thrown the entire situation into his hands. During his absence from Guadeloupe Duplessis fell gravely ill. Already weakened by privations, the condition of his wife who was also stricken had so preyed upon him that he became despondent. His health grew rapidly worse, and on the fourth of December he died, leaving M. de l'Olive the sole commander of the expedition.

Upon receiving the news of his partner's death L'Olive immediately hastened back to Guadeloupe. He was now master of the situation; and, deaf to all entreaties and even to the pleasure of his Sovereign, he determined to put his plan into execution. To do this he had no difficulty in gathering about him a group of men whose sufferings had blunted their senses and who were in no mood to weigh the ethics of the situation when it was a question of obtaining food. On January 26, 1636, he decided definitely to declare war on the savages. Yet, trained in the European school of warfare, he felt it necessary to have a *casus belli*. Fortunately for him an incident soon presented itself which by dint of sophistry he managed to regard as an excuse for an unprovoked attack upon a friendly people. Some Caribs had taken a roll of cotton cloth without permission, though in exchange for it they had left a pig and some fruit, thinking, no doubt, that their action was a legitimate business transaction. This was all L'Olive needed; here was a robbery to be punished, and on this flimsy pretext he declared war on a race which had succored many of his people in their time of need.

L'Olive began his campaign by dispatching his lieutenant, La Fontaine, in a boat with fifteen soldiers to make a complete reconnaissance of the western shore and pick up quietly any

Frenchmen he might find among savages. La Fontaine was well received by the friendly Caribs, who gladly surrendered their French guests, little dreaming that they would soon need them as hostages, and even pointed out in evidence of their friendship that they had refused to trade with a boatload of Englishmen who had recently come there anxious to do business with them. Three days after La Fontaine's return L'Olive began his preparations. Under pretense of looking for a better location he embarked in one of his boats and made his way to the Carib encampment, located near the southern tip of the island in the vicinity of modern Basseterre. Apparently the savages had got wind of the expedition. Perhaps a member of La Fontaine's detachment—more conscientious or more loose-tongued than his companions—had tipped them off; for when L'Olive landed he found that they had fled with their squaws after having burned their huts to the ground. They had, however, left behind an aged chief, 120 years old according to tradition, with two or three young men who had remained to care for him. His name was Captain Yance, at least that is what the French called him. When L'Olive landed, the old man was preparing to embark in a canoe; but he promptly gave himself up when assured that no harm would be done him. Once he had the Carib chief in his power, the French commander quickly changed his manner and accused him of conspiring to destroy the white men, heaping threats and reproaches on his devoted head. All this the unfortunate Indian vehemently denied, protesting that there was not one of his men who would not do anything to please the French. He defended himself, says Du Tertre, with all the strength and positiveness of one entirely innocent. Then L'Olive drew his watch and showed it to the chief, saying that it was a French devil who had told of the treachery he had planned against the white men. Captain Yance, astonished at the strange mechanism, believed the commander, but protested loudly against this lying devil, swearing that neither he nor his fellow savages had ever plotted to harm the French.

L'Olive now ordered the Carib to send one of his men to bring back the squaws, who had halted a short distance from the smoldering village. The chief complied at once; but the youth dispatched on this errand gave the alarm instead of obeying and led the frightened women to the eastern part of the island toward the place where the settlement of Ste. Marie was later built. Enraged at this, L'Olive caused Captain Yance to be bound and thrown into a canoe with one of his grandsons, who was speedily stabbed to death before the eyes of his distracted grandfather. Then the soldiers hurled themselves upon the aged chief, slashed him with their swords, and finally threw him overboard, bearing him down beneath the waves with their oars.

This done, they seized two other savages and compelled them to lead the way to the place where the squaws had taken refuge. One of these guides, the son of a Carib called Captain Baron, a chief of considerable influence, who had always been known for his friendliness to the French, broke away from his tormentors and threw himself over a steep precipice, landing in some bushes that checked his fall. Uninjured, he managed to make his way to the eastern part of the island, where he found the squaws and warned them of the coming attack. L'Olive now forced his other captive to act as guide. This youth led the white men all day through the jungle, then at night when all were asleep, exhausted by the long march, he cut his bonds and disappeared into the forest. Foiled in their attempt to reach the camp of the squaws, the French made their way with considerable difficulty back to Basseterre, collected all the provisions they could find, and, leaving a few men to guard what they could not remove, sailed to Fort St. Pierre, where they proceeded to encourage their fellow colonists to complete the work they had begun.

But now a reaction set in. Father Breton, who had been absent from the fort when the expedition started, had returned by this time. Shocked at the treatment of the Caribs, he violently denounced the brutality of the undertaking and personally berated L'Olive, boldly pointing out to him that his action was in direct disobedience to the orders of the King and of the directors, who wished for peace with the savages at any cost in the hope that the Dominican Fathers would succeed in converting them to the Faith. The clique surrounding L'Olive were enraged at the father's presumption and endeavored to persuade the commander that the priest was a Spaniard in disguise who should be driven from Guadeloupe. But the popularity which Breton and his fellow religious enjoyed amongst the rank and file was too great for the war party, and the Dominicans were left in peace.

If L'Olive and his precious gang of scoundrels expected to improve their position by this unprovoked assault on the Caribs, they were quickly undeceived. The Indians had been in the habit of aiding the French in a small way by bringing them an occasional canoe load of potatoes, bananas, and figs; but now all such attentions ceased. They withdrew from Guadeloupe to Dominica, where, in conjunction with the natives they established a headquarters for spasmodic raids on the French, which they managed so well as to capture or kill from sixty to eighty of their enemies. For three years, so Father du Tertre tells us, the raids continued. The Caribs succeeded in enlisting not only their fellow savages in Dominica but those in St. Vincent as well. Their method of attack was to hurl themselves upon isolated groups which had wandered from the protection of the fort—an excellent bit of strategy, to be sure, yet one that did not always meet with success, since the French were continually on the watch for these raids.

On one occasion the Caribs learned of a detachment at work some distance from the fort. Having collected two or three hundred men, they bore down in their canoes on the unsuspecting colonists. As the Caribs advanced under cover of a shower of arrows, the French seized the muskets which they always kept near at hand when working in the fields and replied with a spirited volley. The Caribs fought well, but they could not hold their own against the galling fire of the enemy, who enjoyed some protection from a hastily constructed barricade, and after a stubborn fight they were forced to retreat, carrying their wounded with them.

Nevertheless, successful repulses of Indian raids did not relieve the colonists of the fear of attack under which they constantly lived. Like their contemporaries in Canada who went to work gun in hand, ever on the alert for the Iroquois war whoop, the French in Guadeloupe quickly learned that eternal vigilance was the price of safety. Hard pressed for food the Governor was now obliged to send his men along the shore to gather turtles, whose flesh could in a pinch stave off hunger. To insure the safety of these hunters he divided them into two companies, each in turn to go out fully armed. But the savages kept up a continual guerrilla warfare, picking off stragglers with such success that sorties of this kind became less and less frequent and famine gradually gained the upper hand.

M. de l'Olive now put forth his best efforts to save the colony. From his plantation in St. Christopher he drew enough to relieve the immediate wants of his men, but, even so, ill luck appeared to pursue him. A ship which he loaded and sent to Guadeloupe was driven back by the sudden appearance of a Spanish squadron; and another boat, dispatched from Guadeloupe to St. Christopher for supplies, disappeared forever, her crew evidently more interested in escaping from the famine-stricken island than in rescuing their dying comrades. It was every man for himself. As always happens in such a crisis the rank and file turned against the leader, blaming him for all their misfortunes. L'Olive's assault on the Caribs now rose up to haunt him, for this treacherous action was popularly regarded as the cause of all the trouble. When the true state of affairs became known in France, the criticism was much the same. It was suggested that he be given a colleague to replace Duplessis, that his commission be revoked, that he be deprived of his office, in short that as the one responsible for the misery of the colony he should in some manner be called to account. For once the home critics appeared to be in the right. In desperation L'Olive appealed to Father Pelican to undertake a mission to France in order to place what he considered to be the true state of affairs before the directors and to request immediate help and a renewal of his commission as Governor of Guadeloupe.

Father Pelican left the island in the year 1636 to carry out the wishes of his commander and also, while he was about it, to obtain for himself and his colleagues the grant of a small tract of land where they could erect a dwelling and live in an atmosphere suitable to their calling. After his arrival in France he presented himself promptly before the directors of the company, who immediately granted his request for the ecclesiastical establishment; indeed, the directors went a bit further in their willingness to please him by ordering L'Olive to build a residence for the clergy. But when it came to the question of renewing the commission of a man who had nearly wrecked the enterprise by his unprovoked assault on the Caribs, they demurred.

On receiving the directors' order to erect a dwelling for the fathers L'Olive saw fit to disregard it, for the continual attacks of the Indians made it dangerous for anyone even to venture from the fort, to say nothing of setting up a separate establishment. Angered at the Governor's refusal to obey instructions, Father Gryphon proceeded to France to add his entreaties to those of Father Pelican. The two placed the matter before their superior, Father Carré, who after listening patiently to the tales of suffering poured into his ear, went in person before the directors to request immediate aid. To his amazement he was informed that the company no longer felt itself responsible for the actions of the Governor, since it was he, according to their contract, who had undertaken to transport the colonists, which, of course, included the clergy, and it was now for him to decide what was best for them. Disgusted at this attitude—

although it was doubtless strictly correct from the purely legal point of view—Father Carré ordered his clergy to leave the island.

Father Breton, however, had no desire to abandon his flock, since he was the only priest in Guadeloupe (Father Bréchet had just gone to St. Christopher), but, unwilling to be guilty of direct disobedience, he prepared to leave. Hearing this the colonists swarmed about him, begging him with tears in their eyes not to desert them, and when this proved ineffectual, they restrained him by main force. The good father, nothing loath to surrender to *force majeure*, agreed to stay; and to settle the difficulty he wrote to the directors of the company, suggesting that they issue an order to Governor l'Olive definitely instructing him to provide the clergy with a suitable tract of land. The directors at once complied, and on January 26, 1637, M. de l'Olive signed a grant giving the Dominicans a tract at the mouth of the Rivière des Galions, near the modern town of Basseterre. Thither the Governor presently moved his own colony, as the location at Fort St. Pierre had been made untenable by the Caribs, and, moreover, the southern portion of the island was the one best suited for settlement and cultivation.

In consideration of the land granted to his mission, Father Carré appealed to the Cardinal on behalf of M. de l'Olive and urged him to bring his influence to bear on the directors in order to secure his reappointment. This the Cardinal was pleased to do; and the directors, bowing to the wishes of their eminent patron, wrote to L'Olive on December 12, 1637, apprising him of their decision to continue him at his post. M. de l'Olive was in St. Christopher when he received the joyful news of his reappointment together with letters from the company promising a generous supply of men and provisions. He returned at once to Guadeloupe, sent for Father Breton, and read him the letters from France, assuring him he would never forget the services of the fathers in his behalf.

IV

ARRIVAL OF DE POINCY

WHEN NEWS of L'Olive's seizure of Guadeloupe reached D'Esnambuc, he was immediately goaded into action. The settlement of this great island had long been a pet project of his, and he resented its pre-emption by another. But unable to do anything about it, since L'Olive had a patent from the company, he wisely put resentment aside and proceeded with his own preparations for annexing Martinique. During the latter part of August, 1635, he collected a band of 150 picked men, all experienced colonists, thoroughly acclimatized, and well versed in the art of earning a living in the West Indies. This gave him at the outset a decided advantage over his neighbors in Guadeloupe, who had been recruited from the streets of Dieppe and the fields of Normandy, and who were totally unfamiliar, as we have seen, with the conditions they were called upon to face. To made sure of proper nourishment for his men D'Esnambuc took with him a plentiful supply of peas, beans, and sweet potatoes, for he did not propose to have his people live for any length of time entirely on native fruits; experience had shown him the dangers of such a diet. Each man took with him also his musket and an assortment of garden tools, so that all were prepared for war or for the peaceful pursuits of agriculture.

The expedition set out late in August, and after a brief voyage it reached Martinique on the first of September.[1] D'Esnambuc

[1]This is the date given in D'Esnambuc's letter to Cardinal Richelieu of Nov.

ARRIVAL OF DE POINCY

did not land at the same spot where L'Olive had set up the cross two months before. Sailing past threatening Mt. Pelee, he came to anchor at the mouth of Rivière du Fort, somewhat north of L'Olive's landing place. The shelter offered here for vessels is not particularly good. It is merely an open roadstead or bight, giving protection of a sort from the easterly trade winds, but useless in a storm. Had D'Esnambuc continued southward he would have come to the excellent harbor of Cul de Sac Royal where modern Fort de France, chief town of the island, now stands. At Rivière du Fort he constructed on the northern bank of the stream a substantial fort, which he named St. Pierre, probably to commemorate his own Christian name, and armed it with the guns he had brought from St. Christopher. Like L'Olive and Duplessis, he took formal possession of the island, not knowing they had already done so. In a ceremony held on the fifteenth of the month a cross was erected, the flag unfurled, and a proclamation read declaring Martinique to be a French colony in the name of the King, the Cardinal, and the company, all for the "augmentation of the Faith, Catholic, Apostolic, and Roman, and to derive a profit from the island for the King and our masters."

D'Esnambuc did not remain long in Martinique—only long enough to complete the fort and get his people settled—for the more pressing duties of his large colony in St. Christopher needed his immediate attention. Fortunately, he had with him an able lieutenant in the person of Jean du Pont to whom he could entrust the governance of the place during his absence. This done, he left the island about the middle of November. As he skirted the western shore line of Dominica, the thought occurred to him that now was the opportunity to take possession

---

12, 1635. Margry, *Belain d'Esnambuc*, p. 55. Du Tertre tells us he landed early in July on the octave of the feast of Sts. Peter and Paul. But it is hardly probable that D'Esnambuc was mistaken as to the date, and, moreover, he could not have heard of L'Olive's arrival in Guadeloupe in time to get his expedition ready by early July.

of this beautiful island, so that France would have clear title to the three major islands of the Leeward group. He therefore cast anchor off the shore—we do not know at what spot—and landed on the seventeenth of the month to take formal possession and to draw up a report of his action to send to the authorities at home. A small detachment was left there in command of Philippe Levayer de la Vallée, who may be regarded as the island's first governor. His administration did not last long, and the island was soon abandoned by all save the clergy who maintained a mission there. At this time D'Esnambuc also took possession of the little volcanic cone known as Saba, a short distance north of St. Christopher.

Meanwhile, Governor du Pont was having troubles in Martinique. The Caribs of this island, unlike those of Guadeloupe, viewed the arrival of strangers with suspicion and determined to drive them out before they themselves were attacked. They carried on a sort of guerrilla warfare, though with small results, as the French were too strongly entrenched in their fort to be assaulted successfully, and they never ventured forth unless heavily armed. At last, despairing of ever being able to do the job themselves, the savages sent out a call for assistance. From Dominica, Guadeloupe, and even from St. Vincent reinforcements soon poured in, until a respectable army of no less than 1,500 men was assembled for the attack. Du Pont, who had got wind of the affair, was ready to receive them. He withdrew his men into the fort, placed his three cannons in position, and loaded them to the muzzle with musket balls, nails, and assorted bits of hardware. Seeing the French retreat within their walls, the Caribs took heart. They gathered together in a body and rushed the fortifications. Du Pont allowed them to approach the walls until they were within range, then he gave the signal to open fire. The effect was terrific. The Caribs fled, and "thinking that all the devils of France had burst from the muzzles of the guns to destroy them, they ran with incredible speed to their canoes and put out to sea, so terrified by the effect of the cannon that, contrary to custom, they did not stop to pick up either the dead or the wounded."

The effect of this blast was lasting. The Caribs had learned their lesson, and Du Pont was now able to send his men abroad to clear the land and plant vegetables for their own needs and tobacco for the export trade. The colony prospered and carried on a lively business with ships which were attracted there by the excellent quality of the tobacco the planters had to offer. At last the Indians, seeing the futility of trying to dislodge these newcomers, sued for peace. Governor du Pont received them affably, for he was not a man to harbor a grudge, and before long a truce was concluded which enabled the French to devote their entire time to peaceful pursuits. Now that everything was in good order, the Governor decided to pay a visit to St. Christopher to give an account of his stewardship to M. d'Esnambuc. He set sail; but unfortunately he was picked up by a Spanish vessel and taken to San Domingo, where he was kept prisoner for three years.

When news of this loss reached D'Esnambuc, he was already stricken with the malady that was destined to carry him off. It was therefore necessary for him to appoint at once a successor to Du Pont, and it was but natural that he should turn in such an emergency to a member of his own family. D'Esnambuc himself was a bachelor. For some unknown reason he had never married, despite what must have been a yearning to transmit the fruits of his great achievement to a son and heir. Lacking children of his own, he took a keen interest in his nephews. His sister, Adrienne Dyel de Vaudroques, had welcomed him to her home when his fief was sold to satisfy his father's creditors, and to repay her for her kindness he had invited her sons to the West Indies to share in the great colonial empire he was building. Adrienne had five sons: Simon, who had died fighting the soldiers of Don Fadrique; Pierre, who remained in Normandy, but became, thanks to his descendants who migrated to the West Indies, an ancestor of the Empress Josephine; a third, whose first name is unknown;

Adrien, who was made a captain by his uncle on the death of Simon, but soon returned to France; and Jacques, Sieur du Parquet.

Jacques was a new arrival at St. Christopher. He had served as captain in a regiment of Picardy and was holding an important post in Calais when, sensing intuitively that greater fortune awaited him beyond the seas, he decided to sail for St. Christopher in 1634. He arrived in time to be selected as the new Governor of Martinique. The choice made by D'Esnambuc was an excellent one, for Du Parquet was destined to become one of the leading figures in the early history of the French West Indies, a worthy successor to his distinguished uncle. Du Parquet left at once to assume his new duties, and taking with him some fifteen men he proceeded to Martinique where he was received with open arms.

D'Esnambuc's condition was now rapidly becoming worse. For ten years he had devoted his life to the founding and building up of his colony—protecting it against foreign enemies, superintending the cultivation of its fields, dispensing justice to its people, ironing out its problems at home—until now the settlement numbered some four or five thousand souls. In addition he had just laid the foundations of colonies at Martinique and Dominica, while an erstwhile lieutenant had established a colony at Guadeloupe. It was but natural, then, that he should seek to gain a moment's respite from his arduous labors in order to visit again, perhaps for the last time, his beloved Normandy. But the company needed his presence in the West Indies, where three colonies, especially Guadeloupe, were still in inexperienced hands. To his request for a leave of absence the directors answered in the negative. "It shall be written to the Sieur d'Esnambuc," so ran the minutes of their meeting, "that the company consider him too useful to the service of His Majesty and the well-being of the company to consent that he leave the islands to make a voyage to France, and that his absence might cause harm to the establishment at Martinique, to the preservation of St. Christopher and to the help he can give to those at Guadeloupe and Dominica." It was a sincere compliment, not merely a politely worded refusal, but it brought little comfort to the failing man. As the year 1636 drew to its close, the Governor grew worse and sometime in the month of December he passed away in the settlement to which he had devoted the best years of his life.

Pierre Belain d'Esnambuc may be truly regarded as the founder of the French colonial empire in the West Indies. With the exception of San Domingo and that little island home of the buccaneers off its northern coast, known as Tortuga, the Caribbean colonies of France all sprang directly or indirectly from the seed he planted at St. Christopher. As the French possessions grew, the greater settlements at Martinique and Guadeloupe gradually overshadowed the mother colony and became the chief care and pride of France. In time the clashing interests of France and England drew them into that long series of duels known sometimes as the Second Hundred Years' War, a conflict which, of course, had its repercussions in the Caribbean. The various islands of the Lesser Antilles were captured and recaptured, only to be traded back and forth by the various treaties of peace. It was during this time that St. Christopher was lost to France and became entirely English. On this island his name is now almost forgotten, but his glory has been transferred to Martinique, where a statue has been erected to him in the public square of its capital, Fort de France.

The death of Belain d'Esnambuc hastened the confirmation of Du Parquet's position. The company, anxious to do something in recognition of the services so well performed by its late Governor, issued on December 2, 1637, a commission to his nephew appointing him lieutenant-governor of Martinique for a period of three years. In doing so the company promised to place no one above him, so that during his entire incumbency he retained this title instead of that of governor, though he was in supreme command. The commission signed, it was at once sent to the appointee. When it was received, the militia companies, such as they were, were drawn up on the parade ground before the fort, and it was read to the assembled colonists. By this ceremony the lieutenant-governor was formally inducted into office.

Now that he was master *de jure* as well as *de facto* Du Parquet proceeded to his duties with fresh enthusiasm. Fortunately for him Martinique had certain advantages. Owing to its situation as the most southerly of the French islands it was the one first visited by vessels from France, which always headed southward after leaving port in order to pick up the trade winds. Thanks to the cordial reception Du Parquet extended to strangers, many who had stopped there on their way to Guadeloupe decided to remain despite the evil reports they had heard of the fer-de-lance. On one occasion a ship came to anchor in the harbor, and a few passengers ventured ashore. Du Parquet took them to his own house and gave them a sample of French colonial hospitality. The following day no less than sixty people left the vessel to become permanent settlers in Martinique, and from that time on the French commander experienced little difficulty in obtaining colonists.

Since the population was increasing rapidly, Du Parquet applied himself to the problems of organization, security, and the betterment of living conditions. To encourage agriculture he generously surrendered his revenue from the tobacco crop and introduced methods for improving the quality of the plant. There was also the question of a harbor. Fort St. Pierre was located on an open roadstead and was scarcely suitable; but there was, however, the Cul de Sac Royal, where large ships could ride an anchor protected from all winds save those blowing directly from the south. Smaller boats could find complete shelter in its inner bays. On the northern shore of this harbor a tongue of land reached out to form an excellent basin, called the Carénage, where ships could be careened, and on this little peninsula Du Parquet built the fort he named Fort Royal. Here, also, a second colony was started, which became in time the

MARTINIQUE

chief town of the island and took the name of Fort de France. For the time being, however, St. Pierre remained the capital. Du Parquet made a bid for foreign trade by throwing open the Carénage to all comers during July, August, and September, a time when storms were to be expected, and even furnished a pilot to guide them through the channel. Within two years the colony had increased to seven hundred inhabitants.

As the colony grew under Du Parquet's wise leadership, it was presently divided into four settlements, or *quartiers*, as the French called them, the principal one of which was the Quartier du Fort St. Pierre, for many years the capital of the island. Here Du Parquet erected a good-size fort, strongly built of masonry and mounting some nine or ten cannons that protected the roadstead. The Dominican fathers resided near by in a substantial house which Du Tertre mentions with pride. Next door to them was the estate of M. d'Orange, where he took up his residence in 1649, after he had been driven from Guadeloupe. On his grounds was located a fountain of fresh water, evidently the only one in the district, which he generously threw open to the public. There were also in this settlement the Church of St. Peter and St. Paul, a government building where Du Parquet met his council once a month, and several stores—the entire group of buildings forming a sort of hamlet.

North of St. Pierre was the Quartier du Prêcheur, so called because a rock projecting into the sea bore some rough resemblance to a preacher in his pulpit. It was not an important settlement, though one dear to Father du Tertre, who once acted as rector of the local parish of St. Joseph. South of St. Pierre lay the Quartier du Carbet, where lived the Governor. Here a river of that name falls into the sea, and on an island which divides its mouth into two branches M. du Parquet erected a brick dwelling, where he lived until he moved to Fort St. Pierre. The building was then given to the Jesuit Fathers. Farther south, along the coast, was the Quartier de la Case Pilote, so called because it was the residence of the pilot mentioned above. It boasted of a church dedicated to the Virgin, a government weighing scale for the benefit of local planters, and several stores. M. de la Vallée, after leaving Dominica, became one of its leading citizens.

After the death of Pierre d'Esnambuc the company cast about for his successor as governor-general of the archipelago. Fortunately for the immediate needs of St. Christopher, they had appointed a short while before the Sieur du Halde, a worthy native of Gascony, as lieutenant-governor of the island, and after the demise of his chief he was appointed governor. He appears to have been a good, if not particularly distinguished, official, but one who had little enthusiasm for his position, for as soon as he received a formal commission designating him governor he petitioned to be allowed to return to France. At that time such a desertion would have been a serious blow to the colony and the directors lost no time in begging the King to use the weight of his authority to keep the newly appointed governor at his post. Louis acquiesced without hesitation; on September 9, 1637, he issued a royal order forbidding the recalcitrant Du Halde from leaving his command without the express permission of the company.

While this temporarily settled the vexed question of St. Christopher, it did not solve the greater problem of the governor-generalship of the Caribbee Islands. Du Parquet, though in good odor with everybody, was too young and inexperienced; Du Halde had already shown his true colors; L'Olive could scarcely be regarded as a successful commander; there remained, then, but one course open—to select someone in France. Despite its obvious objections the company had no choice but to proceed with this plan, and having glanced about for a suitable candidate they presently chose René de Beculat, Sieur de la Grange Fromenteau, a gentleman whom Du Tertre describes as a man of exemplary piety and affable personality, richly endowed with all the qualities necessary for a successful governor. Such is Du Tertre's opinion; we shall see how La Grange lived up to it.

ARRIVAL OF DE POINCY

M. de la Grange accepted with alacrity, but on second thought he decided that the expense incident to his establishing himself at St. Christopher was greater than he could conveniently afford, so he suggested a substitute in the person of Philippe de Lonvilliers de Poincy, Knight of Malta, commander of Oyzemont, sometime vice-admiral in the French navy—a dashing blade who at this time was idling away his days in Paris, thanks to a misunderstanding with the Archbishop of Bordeaux which had deprived him of his former occupation. La Grange made his offer with the proviso that he would reserve for himself the position of lieutenant under De Poincy and that the latter should lend him four thousand francs with which to defray the expenses of his voyage to St. Christopher. The proposition appealed to De Poincy. Here, indeed, might be an opportunity to carve out a name for himself and perhaps add a tidy bit to his fortune. He closed the deal at once, even lending La Grange five hundred francs more than the sum at first requested. As for the directors, they quickly voiced their approval of M. de Poincy. They placed his name before the Cardinal who presented the candidate to the King, suggesting that he be appointed governor-general of all the islands for a period of three years. Louis, relying on his minister's judgment, issued a commission to this effect on February 15, 1638, as a matter of course. The company also made him Governor of St. Christopher. Thus for the first time a man of distinguished position was to be lieutenant of the King of France in the West Indies. The colonies founded by Pierre d'Esnambuc were indeed growing in importance.

As soon as he received his commission, De Poincy dispatched La Grange, now his subordinate, to prepare a residence for him at St. Christopher. La Grange set forth in April with his wife, his son, and several gentlemen, and on reaching his destination was welcomed by the inhabitants in a manner that may have caused him to regret the minor part he had chosen. To make up for this he at once set out to provide for himself in the grand manner, forgetting completely the arrangements he was to make for his superior. He purchased some excellent property and added to it by taking over some vacant land adjoining it. To his credit be it said, however, that he took a keen interest in public welfare. He built Fort St. Pierre, at Basseterre; he encouraged foreign trade to the great benefit of the colony; and he gained the good will of the people and the clergy by his friendly disposition.

That the colonists appreciated keenly the honor done them by the appointment of such a prominent member of the French aristocracy as M. de Poincy is shown by the enthusiastic reception they accorded him when he arrived in the West Indies the following year. De Poincy sailed from France on January 12, 1639, accompanied by a retinue of gentlemen, soldiers, and artisans, in the dual capacity of governor of St. Christopher for the company and governor-general of the islands for the King. He arrived in due course at Martinique, where he anchored off Fort Royal. He was received on land by Du Parquet, whose militiamen were drawn up along the shore, while the guns barked out a salute from the fort. All stood uncovered while the King's commission was read, then Du Parquet and his men took the oath of fidelity to the new incumbent. In Guadeloupe, however, the Governor-General met with quite a different reception. There was no one to receive him at the landing, for the unfortunate colonists were too much occupied with their Carib enemies and chronic famine to take much interest in visiting dignitaries. De Poincy made his way as best he could to the fort, where he found the wretched L'Olive ill and half blind, voicing profane objections to what he considered a usurpation of his authority. The Governor-General had the good taste not to argue with the sick man, who, moreover, did not recognize him. On the contrary he spent some time beside him trying to calm his anger, and only when he had brought the patient to a more reasonable frame of mind did he disclose his identity. When he learned who his visitor was, L'Olive expressed regret at the violence of his language, and the two men parted in a friendly spirit.

ARRIVAL OF DE POINCY

The Governor-General arrived at St. Christopher on the twentieth of February, where, at the settlement of Basseterre, he made a formal entry into his capital. Never before in the history of the West Indies had a French governor made his appearance with such éclat. Arrayed in the full dress uniform of a Knight of Malta, he stepped ashore accompanied by his gentlemen and guards clad in rich scarlet cloaks embroidered with the white cross of the order and advanced between two rows of awe-struck colonists, drawn up on each side of the roadway to welcome him. With this retinue he proceeded to the church, where he was received by M. de la Grange. A *Te Deum* was sung in his honor, the leading planters pressed forward to assure him of their fidelity, and even Sir Thomas Warner was so impressed by the importance of the new incumbent that he sent his aide to welcome him in behalf of the English colony and came to Basseterre four days later to pay his respects in person. De Poincy was equal to the occasion. He promptly returned the visit, accompanied by an impressive escort, and addressed to his host, through an interpreter, the usual remarks appropriate to such an occasion.

Governor De Poincy landed, as we have said, on the twentieth of February, and the rest of the year, that is until La Grange's return to France in November, was taken up by an *opéra bouffe* exhibition of domestic difficulties. The trouble began when De Poincy failed to find a suitable residence prepared for his reception, which it had been La Grange's business to provide. The unfortunate lieutenant was soundly berated for his negligence—in truth the stricture was well merited—and threatened with the seizure of his property and expulsion from the colony. In vain he offered De Poincy his own house; the choleric Governor spurned the offer and purchased instead the former plantation of M. D'Esnambuc, situated among the foothills at some distance from Basseterre. Eventually the ill feeling engendered by this contretemps died down, thanks largely to the efforts of the Capuchin fathers, who were extremely partial to La Grange, until, in appearance at least, the two men were quite friendly.

But there were not lacking those who thought that they could profit by any trouble that might arise between the commanders. Rumors were spread abroad that revived the old feeling of distrust, and La Grange was summarily ordered to the northern part of the island. For this harsh procedure De Poincy gave certain reasons in presenting his account of the affair to the president of the company: first, before his arrival Mme de la Grange used his name to force several planters to sell their property to her at a price determined by herself, a proceeding which embittered many toward the Governor; secondly, the lieutenant had seized seventy-eight negroes of a consignment brought in by a Dutch trader and had sent to his superior an assorted group of eighteen slaves, mostly sick and useless and including a couple of corpses, as his share of the cargo. But the third reason injected a humorous element into the situation. It arose from the arrival of a consignment of young women sent over by the paternally inclined directors as wives for the colonists. La Grange, for no particular reason so far as we know, immediately branded most of these ladies with his disapproval. He vowed they had been imported to form the nucleus of a harem for M. de Poincy and cast aspersions on their virtue, refusing to allow his officers to marry any save a select few. Matters came to a head when the Governor-General seized a girl who was described as "perfectly beautiful and capable of inspiring love." She was, not one of the new arrivals, but the daughter of a wealthy planter named Bellestre, and she was taken from him on the ground that he was a hopeless drunkard and totally unfit to care for such a lovely creature. She was placed in the house of Mme de la Grange, where De Poincy paid her frequent visits. Such an opportunity was not to be lost by the wife of the irate lieutenant, who, in order to shield the young lady's reputation, talked loudly about the matter to the neighbors.

To make matters worse a relative of Mme de la Grange, the Sieur Quérolon, composed a pasquinade about De Poincy's

ARRIVAL OF DE POINCY

amours entitled *Prosopopée de la nymphe Christophorine*, a bit of witticism that received the warm approval of La Grange himself. It contained principally a collection of poems, doubtless rather mediocre verse, concerning the reputation of several girls, especially the young woman who had elicited the Governor-General's admiration. Mme de la Grange circulated this bit of literature throughout the community, even going so far as to furnish Sir Thomas Warner with a copy, amplifying it with comments of her own. This was the last straw. The hue and cry was now raised after Quérolon, who fled St. Christopher and took refuge in the Dutch colony at St. Eustatius. De Poincy wrote the Governor of this island requesting him to surrender the fellow and received an answer promising full co-operation; but Mme de la Grange used her influence with Sir Thomas and induced him to bring pressure on the Dutch commander in behalf of the fugitive poet. Quérolon was therefore placed on an English vessel that chanced to be in the harbor and permitted to make his escape. De Poincy thus unable to secure his man caused him to be tried *in absentia* and condemned to death. His property was confiscated and the capital sentence was carried out on his effigy by the local headsman.

The badgered Governor-General now felt that he could stand no more from the ill-disposed La Granges. Fortunately for him he held the whip hand, thanks to the loan he had made to his subordinate, and he now took action against him, charging him with lese majesty for the affronts offered him as representative of the King. In vain did La Grange offer to pay all he owed and ship his loose-tongued wife back to France by the first vessel if only the matter were dropped. De Poincy was inexorable. He felt, as he later wrote to M. Fouquet, that La Grange's ambition had been fired by the possibilities of the West Indies, that he had repented of his bargain, and that he was using every means, fair or foul, to procure his (De Poincy's) recall. For this reason the Governor-General started a civil and criminal action against La Grange in the court presided over by M. Renou, an action which La Grange sought to nullify on the ground that since the judge was beneath him in rank he was not obliged to bow to his authority. M. Renou, however, thought otherwise and presently rendered a decision depriving the defendant of more than 2,500 francs and all his slaves, some twenty-odd negroes and negresses, and sentenced him and his wife to prison for lese majesty despite the protests of the Capuchin fathers, who stood stoutly by them.

M. and Mme de la Grange were at once incarcerated in the Basseterre prison with their eight-year-old son. Apparently they were not kept in strict confinement, and the way of escape was easy, as numerous friends pointed out to them. But they preferred to take no chances of running into an ambush and being shot as fugitives. Mme de la Grange relieved her feelings by writing to the directors a hysterical letter accusing De Poincy of all manner of atrocities inflicted on the helpless colonists to accomplish his selfish aims, actions she asserted, which would assuredly have brought on a revolt had it not been for the influence of her husband. La Grange also wrote the directors asking for a review of the sentence passed on him by M. Renou. While awaiting the results of this appeal an incident occurred which nearly cost them their lives. Two of their servants were found one night prowling about the powder magazine near De Poincy's residence. Their actions roused suspicion. The Governor-General had them questioned, using, no doubt, some rough-and-ready methods to make them talk; but they held firm to their story, saying that they had merely wandered there by chance during an evening walk and had not been sent there by La Grange to blow up the place. Shortly after this, and largely because of the suspicions that this incident engendered, the La Granges were sent back to France, accompanied by a letter in which De Poincy assured the directors that he would have had his prisoners beheaded if he had found them guilty of attempting his life. Thus peace, at least domestic peace, was restored to the unhappy island.

While this serio-comic business was taking up so much of his

ARRIVAL OF DE POINCY

time De Poincy was able to inaugurate several drastic changes in the colony. To weaken La Grange's influence he replaced several La Grange men by creatures of his own. An ex-brewer of Dieppe was named judge; a former surgeon who had served under Duplessis was appointed the Governor-General's assistant in civil matters; and the unfortunate La Grange found himself cut off from all his friends save the Capuchin fathers.

De Poincy's most notable achievement, however, was the founding of an excellent hospital for those who could not receive proper treatment at home, as well as for strangers who fell ill during their stay on the island. Arrangements were also made by him for placing orphans in suitable houses and caring for them at his expense. He also caused Fort Pierre, recently erected by La Grange, to be demolished and ordered a new fort of more substantial construction, called by him Fort Basseterre, to be built in its place. It was second in point of strength to the one known as "the Citadel" at Pointe de Sable near the line of demarcation separating the French and the English colonies. There was also another fort in the northern part of Capesterre, called St. Louis, and one at Anse à Louve; while the English boasted of two: Fort Charles, at Old Road Town, and one opposite the Citadel.

Though busily engaged with his plan of public works, De Poincy did not lose sight of the fact that he owed himself a residence in keeping with his position as representative of the King. He had already purchased the estate formerly belonging to Governor d'Esnambuc, a beautiful piece of property connected with Basseterre by a road lined with lemon and orange trees, and it was here that he now erected his dwelling. This house, sometimes referred to in contemporary documents as "the Château," was without exception the most pretentious dwelling on the island, or, for that matter, in the archipelago. Designed in the style of an Italian villa, it rose four stories to a height of thirty-six feet and was topped by a flat roof that served as an observation platform from which one could obtain a magnificent panorama of the southern portion of the island. Its shape was nearly square, about fifty feet on each side. Its walls were built of cut stone and brick. The front faced the east and overlooked the fertile valleys covered with sugar cane and ginger plants, while in the rear was a large vegetable garden, behind which arose the mountains, cutting off further view. A stream of clear water, skillfully brought down from its source in the hills, poured into a basin in the garden and furnished refreshment for the cattle of the neighborhood, which would otherwise have died during the dry season. In front lay a broad terrace surrounded by a low wall, behind which were mounted several guns; for De Poincy regarded his house as a place of refuge in case of trouble. On one side of the Château was D'Esnambuc's former home, now converted into a chapel, while two brick buildings served as quarters for the servants. On the other side, at some distance from the mansion, was a settlement inhabited by the slaves of De Poincy, who numbered about three hundred. Altogether the establishment was intended to be a self-sufficient one, capable of supporting itself in case of an uprising. The representative of His Christian Majesty was, indeed, well established.

The settlement at Basseterre could scarcely be called a town at this time, though it was the capital of St. Christopher and also in a sense the capital of the archipelago, since De Poincy, like D'Esnambuc before him, had taken up his residence there. Grouped about the fort was a small cluster of stores, some built of brick, some of wood, roofed over with tile or covered with sugar-cane stalks or palm leaves. The more prominent merchants, Dutch as well as French, had their stores there. A large building, called the "Magazin de Monsieur," served as a council hall for the Governor and his advisers. In their storehouses the traders kept on hand a plentiful supply of wine and beer, wool and silk, or whatever goods had to be imported. The Church of Notre Dame served the religious needs of the people at the settlement. It was a substantial structure built on a solid

ARRIVAL OF DE POINCY

foundation of cut stone and covered by a roof of red tile. The priests in charge of this establishment, as well as of the church at Cayonne on the northern side of the island and the two churches in Capesterre, were the Capuchin fathers. These clergymen held their posts until they were driven from the island by De Poincy in 1646. They were then replaced by Jesuits and Carmelites, whom the Governor-General at once provided with suitable houses and a sufficient number of slaves to keep them in comfort.

During this time certain difficulties arose with the English settlers which well-nigh led to armed conflict. The principal cause of this trouble was a shortage of salt from the ponds in the southern part of the island. These ponds were free to the inhabitants of both nations, according to the terms of the original treaty of partition, and usually they yielded enough and to spare for everyone; but in the year 1639 they failed to produce a sufficient amount. The result was a scramble for the precious condiment which resulted in the death of a number of persons on both sides. On the advice of a council of war, called to consider the situation, De Poincy ordered his officers to arm their men against a possible attack by the English.

M. de la Grange was at this time commanding the northern part of the island, and orders were sent him by De Poincy to put his frontier in a proper condition to resist invasion. As might be expected, La Grange did no such thing; but, calling his officers together, he indulged in a diatribe against the Governor-General, accusing him of wishing to launch a wanton attack on the English for his own private reasons and announcing that he (La Grange) washed his hands of the entire business.

De Poincy, however, decided to face the situation without the help of his rebellious subordinate. He began by making overtures of peace, sending Jean Soulon, Sieur de Sabouïlly, major-general of the archipelago, then commanding at Pointe de Sable, with full powers to negotiate a treaty. The effort failed, and the Governor-General prepared for an attack, despite the presence of two English ships of forty guns each which lay at anchor near enough the shore to support the troops with their fire. When all hope of a peaceful settlement had been abandoned, De Poincy was surprised to receive a communication from John Jeaffreson, now in command of the British forces, asking for a conference in the hope that the differences could be settled by arbitration. Anxious to avoid bloodshed, De Poincy at once agreed, and an honest attempt was made to draw up a satisfactory treaty for adjustment of the salt-pond question and various other differences that had arisen. It was decided that the right to hunt and the right to gather wood, held in common by both nations in all parts of the island, were now to be restricted for each nation to its own territory, but as it proved impossible to reach a satisfactory agreement regarding the salt ponds, the parties decided to suspend hostilities—the ponds to be used in common temporarily by both nations—while the matter was referred to their French and English Majesties for a final pronouncement.

Scarcely had this difference been amicably adjusted, when a problem which had been hanging fire for some time came to a head. For several years the British government had viewed with apprehension the large volume of tobacco that was flooding the market and playing havoc with the price. Within the two years before De Poincy's arrival at St. Christopher the English West Indian colonists had shipped to London a little more than one million pounds to be added to nearly 3,500,000 sent home from Virginia. To ease the situation a law had been passed forbidding the cultivation of the plant in England, but its attempted enforcement had produced riots. King Charles now made preparations for sending out an officer to his Caribbean colonies to look into the situation and to take steps to curb the excessive volume which was being produced. In France, too, the question was causing grave concern. The company had made a ruling limiting its production to 900 pounds, annually, for each planter and prohibiting its cultivation every second year. Thus it happened that a few weeks after the conference about the salt ponds De Poincy and Warner agreed on a suppression of the tobacco industry for eighteen months. Notices to this effect were placed on church doors, and the colonists were instructed to uproot their tobacco without sparing a single plant, beginning on the last day of October, and to plant no more for a year and a half thereafter under penalty of losing their property.

This decree marks the beginning of the decline of tobacco as the staple product of the Caribbee Islands. Not that it ended abruptly, for we find the planters exporting it for several years to come; but owing to the decrease in its value they were obliged to replace it with something else. Orders were given by the company to its agent in St. Christopher to compel the colonists there and in Martinique to plant cotton as a substitute. Other staples were suggested, such as roucou and indigo; but it was soon discovered that sugar cane was the plant best suited to replace tobacco, for cane was indigenous to the Western Hemisphere—the earliest settlers had found it growing wild in the Lesser Antilles, though they did not understand the process by which the sap is extracted and refined. As early as 1638 the directors had discussed the possibilities of sugar cane as the staple product of their colonies, and the following year they had reached an agreement with a Dutch merchant, the Sieur Trezel, a man who understood its cultivation, to develop the art in Martinique.

Trezel proceeded at once to Martinique with a contract in his pocket granting him 2,400 arpents of land, a monopoly of the business for six years, and the privilege of establishing plantations in Guadeloupe, in return for which he would pay the company one-tenth of all the sugar raised, confine his trading to France, and refrain from raising tobacco. Trezel found the difficulties of establishing himself greater than he had expected. He demanded and obtained further concessions from the company in the shape of exemption from payment of the tenth, permission to employ fifteen men to grow tobacco, and the privilege of trading with foreigners for foodstuffs if necessary. He seems, furthermore, to have met with many obstacles. His manufacturing apparatus, he says, was scattered and probably lost, while his plantation was sold for debt.

On the whole the arrangement proved a failure, and the company felt obliged to undertake the work itself. Slaves were accordingly purchased to till the fields, workmen were employed to erect factories, and the entire business was placed under the direction of Charles Houël, Sieur de Petit-Pré, one of the directors who had just returned from a survey of the islands. He was made Governor of Guadeloupe, with complete authority over all slaves and employees of the company, and given a bonus of one-tenth of all the sugar produced there. We shall have occasion later to speak at great length of M. Houël, for he became one of the most distinguished commanders in the French West Indies.

Gradually the sugar cane industry replaced the cultivation of tobacco throughout the islands, until it became the principal source of wealth. De Poincy was anxious to introduce it into St. Christopher as early as 1639. At first it seemed as though his efforts might be checkmated because of an insufficient water supply, but this difficulty was gradually overcome, and within a few years six mills were operating full blast in the island—three on his estate and three in Cayonne. Trezel, too, was soon back on his feet, and we presently find him the chief producer of the commodity in Martinique. In Guadeloupe Houël for several years raised all the sugar cane, while his planters still cultivated tobacco.

When De Poincy first published his edict against tobacco raising in St. Christopher, he sought to carry out the same measure in the other islands under his jurisdiction. In Guadeloupe, however, he struck a snag. M. de l'Olive refused to be bound by the Governor-General's order, claiming that the agreement he had made with the merchants of Dieppe, whereby they would take all the tobacco at ten *sols* the pound which he could grow in six years, absolved him from compliance with his superior's orders. To obey would cause him too much loss. Unable to reach an agreement on this point the two men referred their differences to the company at home.

It was while waiting for an answer to this appeal that L'Olive, who had been ailing for some time, grew suddenly worse. The anxieties of his position as head of a none-too-successful colony began to prey on him. The merchants of Dieppe had refused to send over the men they had promised, with the result that there were not enough hands to gather the ripening crops. Seized with an attack of melancholy that amounted to a frenzy and now totally blind, the unfortunate man was carried to Nevis, where he tried to regain his strength by taking the sulphur baths for which the island was famous. The cure proved of little value, and at last, as the hopelessness of his condition dawned upon him, he proceeded to St. Christopher to beg assistance from De Poincy for the protection of his wretched colonists, who were suffering from the continual attacks of the Caribs. De Poincy, now that he had the recalcitrant Governor in his power, placed him under nominal arrest (though out of consideration for his helpless condition he ordered that he should be treated with kindness) and proceeded to carry out a plan which had been maturing in his mind for some time. But before discussing this we shall devote a few pages to the events that were taking place in the island of Tortuga.

V

TORTUGA

Off the northwestern coast of San Domingo, a few miles west of Cape Hatien, lies the little island of Tortuga, separated from the mainland by a channel only two miles wide. During the seventeenth century, this island rose to a position of importance far out of proportion to its size, for it became one of the strongholds of the buccaneers who preyed on the Spanish Main. San Domingo, or rather the northern part of it, was the original home of the buccaneers, for here they lived by hunting the wild cattle that roamed about the island.

They were a precious crew, these freebooters, chiefly natives of France and England who had been thrown by a turn of the wheel of fortune onto the desert shores of this savage island. Whence they came or why they came no one knows, but they were probably deserters and castaways who had despaired of ever returning home and had determined to make the best of their new mode of life. It was from their means of livelihood that they obtained the name "buccaneers," for they were accustomed to cure the meat they obtained by drying it slowly over a fire of coals, Indian fashion; and as the place where this process was carried on was called a *boucan*, they became known as *boucaniers*, or buccaneers. They had no government, being guided in their dealings with each other by laws and customs of their own, which formed a code known as the *coutume de la côte*, that proved sufficient for their needs. It was from this outlaw settlement on San Domingo that there gradually developed that freemasonry of freebooters, men of all nations, though chiefly French and English, who for nearly a century hunted the fleets of His Catholic Majesty.

The first definite system of government among the buccaneers was set up in Tortuga when a group of Englishmen arrived from Nevis under the leadership of Anthony Hilton, whom the reader will recall as the founder of the colony on that island. Governor Hilton, as we pointed out in a previous chapter, left Nevis for London just before the unexpected arrival of Don Fadrique in order to discuss his difficulties with the Earl of Carlisle. During his stay he had many interviews with his backer, Thomas Littleton, and there developed during these conversations certain misunderstandings over the finances of the settlement. Consequently, when Hilton at last returned to Nevis he did so solely for the purpose of securing recruits to found a colony of his own. Thanks to a wide acquaintance among sea captains of questionable antecedents, he had gained considerable knowledge of various places where he could settle without molestation, and he selected the island of Tortuga as the one best suited to his purpose.

Thither he moved with his followers in the year 1630, and he took up his residence on the southern side of the island, where he found a fairly good harbor. The island proved satisfactory to the pioneers, but being poor men themselves they felt the need of proper financial backing if they were to make a success of their undertaking. After duly considering the matter they decided to make overtures to the Providence Company, which at this time was carrying on its colonizing activities in the Bahama Islands. The company responded quickly. A select group, consisting of Anthony Hilton, Christopher Wormeley, and three or four others, were invited to associate themselves with the Providence organization under an arrangement by which each man was to contribute forty pounds for every seventy subscribed by a member of the company. An enlargement of the company's original grant to include Tortuga was obtained from the King; and the company was given title to the island in return for a 20 percent cut of the profits on all commodities raised by the new settlers. The directors also agreed to send out six cannon and a supply of ammunition for the protection of the little harbor. Government of the settlement was to be vested in Anthony Hilton, with Wormeley as his assistant and successor. Officially Tortuga was to be known as the Island of Association, and it is so referred to in contemporary English documents, though elsewhere it is always called by its proper name. The chief product of the island, the one on which the merchant adventurers relied almost entirely for a return on their investment, was dye wood, of which there was a large quantity ready to be cut down and shipped.

For a few years the island experienced a fair degree of quiet and prosperity. The buccaneers from nearby San Domingo proved friendly, and brought their cured meat to exchange for gunpowder and other supplies necessary to their mode of life. Two or three vessels manned by colonists and loaded with provisions were sent out from England. Negro slaves were introduced for the planters, who were thus able to obtain the dye wood in localities where the white man would not venture. Governor Hilton died in 1634, and he was succeeded by Christopher Wormeley.

At this time, however, it happened that an Irish renegade named John Murphy had made his way to the Spanish colony on the southern coast of San Domingo and had persuaded the Governor that the capture of Tortuga would be a simple matter, as the settlement then consisted of only six hundred men capable of bearing arms. The Spaniard needed no urging. As commander of Spain's oldest colony in the New World he resented the presence of the English on Tortuga as an encroachment on his own domain, especially as they were in cahoots with the buccaneers, who had long been a thorn in his flesh. In accepting Murphy's suggestion, which he did with alacrity, the Governor evidently had a poor opinion of the English and French (a number of

Frenchmen had joined the colony) as fighters, or else he could not spare a large detachment, for he entrusted the business to a force of only 250 soldiers, under the command of Rui Fernandez de Fuermayor.

Thus it happened that shortly after sunrise on a January morning in the year 1635 the little armada of ships bearing these men presented itself at the mouth of the harbor of Tortuga, where they spoiled what would otherwise have been an imposing entrance by running aground on a reef not far from the shore. Here they remained stranded, while Don Rui sought to capture his objective by means of a small landing party. He managed to get some thirty men ashore in canoes and at once seized the fort, driving off a body of colonists who advanced to retake it, killing their leader, and breaking down whatever resistance they could offer.

Governor Wormeley, it appears, thought of nothing but saving his own skin and as much of his property as he could. At the head of a large number of his followers he quickly transferred his stores to some vessels in the harbor and promptly sailed away, leaving Fuermayor to enjoy the fruits of an empty victory and to wreak his displeasure on the inhabitants left behind. With true Spanish thoroughness Fuermayor landed his soldiers and spread them over the island to exterminate the fleeing settlers. Many were hunted down; some surrendered, only to be promptly hanged; while a handful managed to conceal themselves in out-of-the-way recesses until the Spaniards, carrying with them four banners and a supply of muskets as trophies of victory, sailed back to San Domingo. As for Governor Wormeley, he was tried for cowardice and deprived of his office—a blow which does not seem to have harmed him greatly, for he eventually settled in Virginia and played an important part in the life of that colony.

For several years Tortuga remained deserted, save for a few French stragglers. The Providence Company, it is true, made a desultory effort to resettle the place; but their colonists became more interested in cattle hunting than in cruising the forests for dye wood, and they soon moved over to San Domingo to the great annoyance of the Spaniards, who organized squads of militia to destroy them. Gradually, however, pioneers again made their appearance, and by the end of 1639 the population had risen to three hundred persons, most of them Englishmen who had migrated there from St. Christopher. As leader they now selected one of their own countrymen, a man referred to in various documents as Captain James, who took the title "president" of the colony. He appears to have been a person of some ability, but he soon antagonized the few Frenchmen on the island by the favoritism he showed his fellow-countrymen. There was, however, in the colony a certain French adventurer who became tired of this tyranny and determined to obtain assistance for a plan he had evolved to seize the island. He embarked secretly in a vessel bound for St. Christopher and managed to reach Basseterre and place the situation before Governor de Poincy, pointing out to him the possibilities of capturing the island for France.

To Governor de Poincy this was indeed a welcome opportunity, for he had a domestic problem on his hands that might be solved by the acquisition of Tortuga. The charter of the company, it so happened, stressed the necessity of spreading the Faith among the savages and specified that only Roman Catholics were to be transported to any of its colonies. Yet there had crept in among the faithful a number of Huguenots, refugees from the disastrous siege of La Rochelle, whose presence was in violation of the implied promise the company had made the King and the Cardinal. As these people were good citizens and added much by their industry to the wealth of the colony, they were not molested, though they were strictly forbidden to have any ministers or to practice their faith openly.

Efforts were, of course, made to convert them, and these efforts appear on the whole to have met with some measure of success—if not at this time, at least later on. Father Pelleprat, who visited the islands about 1555, tells us that often as many as thirty or forty were converted in a month, and we know from other sources that many renounced their heretical beliefs and returned to the religion of their forefathers. Nor is this to be wondered at, for the Huguenot colonist transplanted to a far-off settlement where his religion was proscribed, himself now a member of a small minority in the midst of a large Catholic population, felt, no doubt, few qualms when he re-entered the established church of his fellow countrymen. After all he was merely accepting the faith which had sustained his ancestors for generations. When a Huguenot was admitted to the Church an elaborate certificate was made out, duly signed by him, showing that he had abjured his errors and embraced the true Faith.

There was among these heretics a M. le Vasseur, one of D'Esnambuc's original companions, a man of considerable ability upon whom De Poincy continually relied for advice, particularly in military affairs, for he was well versed in the construction of fortifications, having served his apprenticeship at La Rochelle. No fort was built without his being consulted as to its location and general plan. Needless to say the presence of this man constantly at his elbow gave De Poincy's numerous enemies just grounds for lodging a complaint against him before the directors, who did not fail to notify him of their displeasure. Here, then, was an opportunity of getting rid of many of these troublesome Huguenots by founding a colony at Tortuga and of "kicking his friend upstairs" by appointing him its governor.

To make the scheme more palatable De Poincy offered Le Vasseur a charter which contained under Article One a clause quite unusual in those days and likely to cause trouble with the government if it became known. It guaranteed liberty of conscience to both Protestants and Catholics. The rest of the document contained provisions regarding the political and economic set-up of the new colony—the principal item dealing with the question of a division of profits. It was decided that after one-tenth had been set aside for the Crown half should go to the company and half to Le Vasseur and his officers. Provisions were also made for the erection of the necessary buildings for trade and fortifications for protection. The Governor-General signed the document in the presence of Le Vasseur on November 2, 1641.

M. Le Vasseur was pleased with the scheme. He immediately gathered together some forty or fifty of his Huguenot co-religionists and set sail in May, 1642,[1] in a vessel which he and De Poincy had bought for the purpose. Stopping at Port à Margot in San Domingo he persuaded about fifty buccaneers, most of them Protestants, to join his expedition. After lingering in San Domingo for three months he reached Tortuga late in August.

At Tortuga, Le Vasseur posed as an avenger of wrongs. He sent word to Captain James that it was his intention to exact vengeance for the death of several Frenchmen who had been recently killed there by expelling the English from the island and that if they did not leave within twenty-four hours he would give quarter to none. Captain James did not make even a show of resistance, for not only did he have Le Vasseur's men to face but he also had many Frenchmen in his own ranks who were ready to join the men from St. Christopher at the first sign of trouble. Within a few hours James and his men had piled pell mell into one of their ships and departed for New Providence, in the Bahamas, leaving Le Vasseur master of the situation.

Mindful of the former invasion of the Spaniards, the French

---

[1]The date given by Du Tertre for this expedition is 1640. But there are objections to this. The charter was signed on Nov. 2, 1641, and we know that Le Vasseur did not undertake his expedition before he received it. Moreover, a document in *Calendar of State Papers, Col. 1574-1660*, p. 316, date, Dec. 26, 1640, shows that James was still in command at Tortuga on that date. Since, as we shall see, Le Vasseur drove James from the island in August it could not have been the August of 1640. The expedition in all probability took place in 1642.

commander determined to put his newly acquired prize in an adequate state of defense. Since he himself was a skilled engineer, he had no difficulty in selecting the correct spot for building his fort. There happened to be some five or six hundred paces from the harbor's edge a hill topped by a flat summit, in the middle of which stood a rock about thirty feet in height. At the base of this rock was a spring of fresh water. It was an ideal natural formation for his purpose. On the platform of the summit he constructed terraces capable of sheltering four hundred men, while for his personal use he chose the top of the rock which could be reached by a series of steps surmounted by an iron ladder. Here he erected his dwelling and the storehouse for his ammunition. Several guns were mounted on this rock, and several more on the platform below—the entire battery being so placed as to command the harbor. The citadel was named Fort de la Roche.

Once firmly entrenched in Tortuga, Le Vasseur's colony began to attract the buccaneers and rovers who infested northern San Domingo. They brought their hides and cured meat to the settlement, exchanged them for ammunition, and returned to the island ready for further depredations. Needless to say this did not escape the watchful eye of the Governor of San Domingo, who became alarmed at the close proximity of this French outpost and determined to destroy it before it became too powerful. For this purpose he organized in 1643 a fleet of six vessels, manned by a force of five hundred men, and sent it forth against the heretic stronghold, thinking that he would have no more trouble than he had had before. But the situation, thanks to the fort, was now quite different. From his eyrie on the rock Le Vasseur saw the fleet coming in the distance, and he made ready to receive it. As the ships came within range, the battery opened fire with such telling effect that one vessel was quickly sunk and the others scurried away to safety, coming to anchor about two leagues from the fort at a place called Cayonne. Here the army made a landing. Le Vasseur did not oppose them, but threw his men into an ambuscade as they approached and attacked them valiantly, driving them back to their ships with a loss of two hundred men.

While Le Vasseur was meeting with such success in Tortuga, De Poincy, who kept a watchful eye on the situation, began to experience certain qualms. Perhaps this plan of his would lead to the establishment of a powerful Huguenot colony in the West Indies, and the government would hold him responsible. It might be well, then, to lure the Governor of Tortuga away from his jurisdiction before he became too powerful. In order to set the trap he now dispatched his nephew, Robert de Lonvilliers, and Roi de Courpon, Sieur de la Vernade, to Tortuga. These gentlemen opened their mission with the proper diplomatic approach. They complimented M. Le Vasseur roundly on the condition of his colony, his various achievements, and especially on his recent victory over the Spaniards, which had so impressed M. de Poincy, they said, that he wished to see him in order to discuss plans for establishing a settlement on San Domingo itself. Le Vasseur saw through the plot, but he kept his own counsel and answered politely that there was grave danger of an early return of the Spaniards with additional forces and that much as he would like to see M. de Poincy, he felt it would be a grave dereliction of duty for him to leave the island at this critical time. It was apparent that each party saw through the other; and such being the case MM. de Lonvilliers and La Vernade could do nothing but bid their host farewell and return to St. Christopher to report the failure of their mission.

The character of Le Vasseur now appears to have undergone a change. The once moderate, wise, and generous man became a tyrant, cruel, arrogant, and violent. Doubtless the memory of the injustices his coreligionists had suffered at the hands of Catholics in France now awoke the Huguenot within him and started him on a program of vengeance, for he suspended the exercise of the Catholic religion, and to show that he meant business he burned the chapel and drove away the priest who served it, a worthy Capuchin named Father Marc. Nor did he, strange to say, spare the Huguenots, whom he persecuted with the same bitterness he had visited on the Catholic population, and he expelled M. de Rochefort, the Protestant minister, from the colony. To enrich himself he levied a special tax on the hides brought in from San Domingo, and he squeezed every possible cent from the revenues to which he was entitled. But despite all this Le Vasseur was careful not to come out in open rebellion against his superior at St. Christopher. M. de Poincy, for his part, continued his policy of trying to draw his subordinate away from Tortuga by means of flattery, to which Le Vasseur replied in terms of mock humility.

At last, feeling himself secure, the Governor decided to defy his superior. An opportunity to do this occurred when some buccaneers who had seized a Spanish ship brought home a valuable statue of the Madonna wrought in solid silver and turned it over to Le Vasseur. On hearing this De Poincy sent him a request for the statue, pointing out that it was an object more precious to him than to a heretic. Le Vasseur, however, decided to amuse himself at the Governor-General's expense and sent him a replica carved out of wood, pointing out at the same time that Catholics were doubtless too spiritual to notice the difference, while as for him he preferred the metal one because of its intrinsic value. After this piece of insolence De Poincy could no longer contain himself. He cast about for some means to punish his subordinate, but before he could work out a plan he found himself drawn into a long struggle with Patrocles de Thoisy (which will be described later) who had been sent out by the King to replace the Governor-General.

Years passed, and Le Vasseur's power and arrogance waxed strong. He made his colony the headquarters for buccaneers and sea rovers, a haven for all who might have business that would be frowned upon by the more regular authorities of the French, English, and Spanish colonies. He made a special effort to attract Protestant settlers from the various islands, for he aimed at founding a sort of semi-independent Huguenot settlement, and to this end he persuaded his people to accept him as their ruler. But such a situation could not last forever. Governor de Poincy became more and more alarmed as time went on, for he had not reported to the King the clause in the charter which guaranteed religious liberty, and should Le Vasseur succeed in maintaining his independence from the seat of government at St. Christopher, De Poincy might well be accused at Court of having been instrumental in turning over an important post to a group of heretics.

While the Governor-General was casting about for a way out of this impasse there anchored off Basseterre a handsome frigate of the Royal Navy, commanded by the Chevalier de Fontenay, who had stopped there to seek replacements for the losses he had sustained in battle. De Poincy at once saw his opportunity. He approached the Chevalier and offered him the governorship of Tortuga if he would undertake its subjugation. The terms he suggested were liberal in the extreme. The Chevalier was to become ruler of the island (under the Governor-General, of course) and was to receive for his services one-half the land, which was to be his as long as he remained in office. He was also to share equally with his superior the tax of one hundred pounds of tobacco levied yearly on each inhabitant. The two contracting parties were to divide equally between them all Le Vasseur's property, his silver, jewels, lands, furniture, and agricultural machinery, for he had become enormously wealthy by his dealings with the rovers who brought their prizes to his port, while Fontenay was to make a complete report of all the derelictions of the rebellious governor in order to give De Poincy just cause for removing him from his post. This agreement was signed by De Poincy on May 12, 1652, and two months later the Governor-General appointed his nephew, M. de Treval, to accompany the coming expedition as his representative and to make a careful inventory of the confiscated property. The adventurous Fontenay accepted this proposal with alacrity and at once began his preparations for taking over his new duties.

The attack on Tortuga was to be in the nature of a surprise, for Le Vasseur was too strongly entrenched on his rock to be dislodged by any force De Poincy could spare unless he were taken unaware. The greatest secrecy was therefore used in getting ready the expedition. Fontenay was urged to get his recruits together as quickly as possible under pretext of undertaking a series of raids on the Spanish Main and then to sail to Port à l'Écu on the northern coast of San Domingo, where he would meet M. de Treval, who would join him in the attack on Tortuga. After Fontenay's departure De Poincy scurried about to raise his nephew's contingent. With considerable effort he succeeded in enlisting a force equal to that of the Chevalier, which he placed in a frigate and sent to Port à l'Écu. Here the two leaders met to make their final arrangements. But while they were busy with their preparations an astounding bit of news arrived from Tortuga, which changed the situation entirely.

When M. Le Vasseur had succeeded in consolidating his power, he had selected two men from among his followers to act as his confidants. According to some authorities these men, Tibaut and Martin, were his nephews; but, be this as it may, he adopted them and made them heirs to his power and fortune, for he had no children of his own. This arrangement might have turned out well if the Governor had not seen fit to impose upon Tibaut's good nature by taking from him a handsome girl he was keeping as his mistress. Enraged at this desecration of what he considered his home, the jealous Tibaut persuaded Martin to aid him in seeking revenge. It was no difficult task to persuade Martin, for he as well as Tibaut fell heir to the government of Tortuga in the event of the Governor's demise. Knowing Le Vasseur to be in bad odor with the authorities above him, they also hoped to secure the good will of the King and De Poincy by ridding the island of the rebellious commander and returning it to its rightful rulers.

The plot was not difficult to carry out. Waiting one day until Le Vasseur came down from his residence on the rock to inspect the storehouse on the esplanade, they rushed in upon him. Tibaut discharged his musket, inflicting a slight wound. The Governor snatched his sword from a slave and started to defend himself, but as Martin rushed in to grapple with him, he turned his head and saw Tibaut standing with the smoking weapon in his hand. The sight of this treacherous rascal on whom he had showered favors paralyzed him for a moment, and before he had time to recover Tibaut stretched him dead with a blow of his dagger.

Upon hearing this news Fontenay and Treval determined to strike at once, for they feared that this desperate pair might put up a stout resistance. Anchors were accordingly raised, and the two ships proceeded to the attack. As was the case of the Spanish fleet a few years before, they were met by a brisk fire from the redoubt as they sailed into the harbor, and similarly they retreated to Cayonne, where they landed a force of five hundred men. The settlers, however, had no stomach for a fight, and they failed to rally to the support of their new chiefs. Trusting that the murder of Le Vasseur would be condoned by the authorities at St. Christopher, Tibaut and Martin sent an emissary to offer the surrender of the place on condition that no punishment would be visited on them for the death of their benefactor. In this they were not mistaken, for Fontenay was naturally pleased to take the place without bloodshed, and, after all, Le Vasseur was a rebellious heretic. A brief parley was held, and the island was quietly surrendered into his hands. After the fall of the Huguenot colony the Catholic refugees in San Domingo quickly returned, the chapel was rebuilt, a priest was secured to serve as pastor, and the colony again resumed the more-or-less even tenor of its way.

But peace was not to endure for long. The Chevalier de Fontenay was an active man, accustomed from his youth to warfare, and once the colony's affairs had been put in order he began to send out ships for piratical raids on San Domingo and Cartagena —a form of activity in which he was so successful that he finally disrupted the commerce of these two places. To aid him in this work he sent for his younger brother, M. Hotman, a kindred spirit, who quickly joined him, bringing a shipload of things most needed by the colonists. To express his joy at the young man's arrival Fontenay gathered his men on the esplanade of the fort to introduce him, knocked in a few bungholes, and served wine to the assembled colonists. As they were thus engaged in drinking the health of the newcomer, a buccaneer appeared in the harbor with news that a huge Spanish flotilla was heading for the island.

The raids of the Chevalier on Spanish shipping had had their effect. Merchants had complained to governors, governors to officials at home, and officials had sent orders to San Domingo to destroy this nest of pirates. Calling together his council in November, 1653, the Governor of San Domingo placed the situation before them, and as a result of their deliberations Don Gabriel de Valle Figueroa was put in charge of a select detachment of 180 well-seasoned soldiers, who were embarked in an imposing fleet of five large ships and several small ones. On the way to Tortuga they fell in with three buccaneers, captured two, but let the third escape. He it was who now entered the harbor with news of the impending attack.

On the tenth of January, the Spanish fleet appeared at the entrance of the harbor, and like its predecessor it anchored off Cayonne once it had tasted the reception given it by Fort de la Roche. Here the leaders prepared to make a landing. Seeing this, Hotman placed himself at the head of a detachment and proceeded overland to oppose them, but they kept their men so well covered by artillery that he could make no impression and was obliged to content himself with spreading his men over the neighboring hills as sharpshooters to harass the enemy. It was, however, but a vain gesture, and he was soon back in the fort, having left the Spaniards safely encamped along the shore.

For three days both forces remained inactive—the Spaniards reconnoitering the ground, the French strengthening their defenses and preparing the garrison to meet the coming attack, confident that the fort was impregnable. But, as often happens in such cases, there was a weak spot in their armor. The two large bastions of the fort were located against the side of a hill which dominated it—a hill which was considered inaccessible, since its sides were so steep and broken that two men could scarcely climb them abreast. Finding this place unguarded, Don Gabriel decided to attempt the impossible and transport his artillery to the summit, where he would be able to command the French stronghold. The guns were therefore dismounted and strapped to beams supported by crosspieces in such a way that they could be carried on the shoulders of men. In the night a large number of slaves were requisitioned and forced to carry the artillery up the mountainside, so that by morning a battery of eight or ten pieces was ready for business. The first intimation the French had concerning this maneuver was a cannon ball that came crashing through the Governor's house, which stood on the top of the thirty-foot rock silhouetted against the sky. This was followed by another and still another, until the place became untenable. Fontenay, however, showed great resourcefulness. When night fell he set his men to work to build a breastwork on the esplanade, which was to consist of two rows of beams, six feet apart, the space between filled in with earth well tamped down to resist gunfire. Next morning the French, crouching behind this defense, were able to withstand the fire of the Spaniards; but they, seeing how they were checked, promptly moved their battery to a neighboring hill where they were able to sweep the breastwork.

Fontenay now determined on a sortie. To lead it he selected his brother, whom he placed in command of a detachment of sixty men with orders to attack the Spanish battery and destroy it. Hotman started out at nine in the evening, expecting to make a surprise attack in the dark; but unfortunately his plan was betrayed by a slave, who hoped by this treacherous action to obtain his liberty from the Spaniards when they became masters of the island. Thus, on reaching the enemy's camp Hotman found all were under arms ready to receive him, with reinforcements hurrying to their support. There was no time to work out a careful plan of action. Hotman gave the signal, and his men rushed in, fought their way to the powder magazine (which they managed to blow up), then fought their way back to safety, leaving sixteen Spaniards dead on the field. Next day the Spaniards brought up a fresh supply of powder, and the bombardment began again in earnest.

It was not long, however, before the enemy began to lose heart. Heavy rains made their maneuvers increasingly difficult, and sickness broke out among the officers and men. The leaders were already seriously considering raising the siege, when they were heartened by the appearance of a traitor from the French camp, who told them that all was not well within the fort and that Fontenay would soon be obliged to surrender. He spoke the truth, for there was loud murmuring among the French forces. After a second attempt to destroy the Spanish battery had failed, the colonists gave voice to their complaints against Fontenay, who stubbornly refused to surrender. Sadly battered by the cannonading of the last few days, they were ready to quit. The Spaniards, they felt, would be reasonable in their demands on the vanquished, so having collected all the weapons in the fort they sent a delegation to Fontenay, headed by one Noël Bedel, to insist that he surrender the place on the best terms obtainable. Livid with rage at this cowardly spirit, the Governor drew his pistol and shot Bedel; then he rebuked the others of the delegation with such severity that they promised shamefacedly to return to their posts. But it was only a flash in the pan; on the following day they were as mutinous as ever. When evening came on, some traitor fired on Hotman as he was making his rounds and dashed off to the Spanish camp with the story that he had slain the Governor's brother. Don Gabriel disgusted with the contemptible fellow, sent over a flag of truce to learn if the report was really true, for he was determined, if it were so, to hang the murderer in sight of the entire French army.

The Spaniards, now advised by so many deserters of the dissatisfaction among the French colonists, could not but feel that something was wrong. They redoubled their efforts, and soon Fontenay sent word that he was ready to yield, for after all he could not hold the fort by himself. An armistice was requested and as readily granted, for the attackers were as weary as the beseiged. As to terms, the French asked to be given the honors of war when they surrendered—for even in this buccaneer stronghold the niceties of military etiquette must be observed—and these being conceded by the chivalrous Spaniard, they left the fort with drums beating, flags flying, and muskets loaded. They were also given permission to repair two ships that lay damaged in the harbor—in fact the Spaniards urged them at the point of the sword to do so—since they had no other means of transportation to France.

Don Gabriel appears to have acted fairly enough, though he did use threats to speed the colonists in their work on the ships; but when he saw the French ready to put to sea in the only full-sized vessels at Tortuga and remembered the smallness of his own craft, it suddenly occurred to him that Fontenay might lie in wait for him when he returned to San Domingo. He therefore requested that the Sieur Hotman be placed in his hands as a hostage, agreeing in exchange for him to furnish the French with provisions and to refrain from all acts of hostility until he was released. This done, Don Gabriel returned to San Domingo, taking Hotman with him.

The young Frenchman was well received by the elderly Spanish Governor, who took a great liking to him and kept him at his residence for five or six months, more as a guest than as a hostage. When the time came for him to return to his brother, he was sent back by the solicitous Governor with a retinue of fifty men to ensure his safe arrival. When he landed in Tortuga he found that preparations had already been made by the Chevalier to evacuate the island. The colonists had been divided into two groups: one had embarked in the ship to which MM. Tibaut and Martin had been assigned as commanders, the other in Fontenay's vessel. Hotman, of course, joined the latter. The fate of the first shipload was tragic. Tibaut and Martin appear to have set sail without any definite idea of where they were going. For some time they beat back and forth, then they decided to make for the Spanish Main to see what they could pick up in the way of plunder. Handicapped by a number of women, children, and other noncombatants, they decided to rid themselves of these superfluous passengers by putting them ashore, and being near the little Cayman group, north of Jamaica, they placed them on these barren islets and left them there to shift for themselves. Fortunately they were presently rescued by a Dutch vessel, which happened by just in the nick of time. What eventually became of Tibaut and Martin is not known—and no one cares.

Fontenay and Hotman now found themselves in possession of a ship, but they were without the necessary equipment or provisions to enable them to reach France. Before they could undertake such a lengthy voyage it was necessary to secure fresh canvas, rope, and the hundred and one things needed to handle a ship at sea. Therefore they put into Port à Margot to see if something could be procured there, and by good fortune they met a Dutch trader who generously supplied them with the required tackle and even sent over his own men to assist in making the necessary repairs.

When his vessel was again in seaworthy condition, Fontenay decided to return to Tortuga and wipe out the disgrace of his surrender. His decision did not, however, meet with an enthusiastic reception, for of his three hundred men only one-third volunteered to accompany him. Anxious to attack before their ardor had cooled off, Fontenay and Hotman divided the command of these men equally between them and set out at once for Tortuga, where they landed at Cayonne. The Spanish force which awaited them offered no resistance and hastily retreated to a spot near the fort, where they lay in ambush. Warned of the trap by the barking of a dog, the French attacked the ambush vigorously and drove the enemy back into the fort. Fortunately the two leaders had not forgotten the battery which the Spaniards had erected overlooking Fort de la Roche. Rushing up the mountainside, they assaulted the place with such vigor that they slew all the garrison save one, who was spared to carry the news to his comrades. The French now turned the guns on the esplanade, sweeping it from end to end, and doubtless they would have destroyed the entire garrison if the Spaniards had not rushed a company of two hundred men to its support. When these reinforcements arrived, Fontenay saw that the game was up, and he gave the order to retreat. By skillful maneuvering he managed to get his men back to the shore, where he embarked for Port à Margot. Here he disbanded his crew, took on board those who were tired of the adventure, and sailed back to France—never to return to the West Indies.

Thus ended, for a while at least, French jurisdiction in Tortuga; and for a few years the little island was left to shift for itself. Then came Governor d'Ogeron who re-established the claims of his King over the former colony, spread his authority over western San Domingo, and founded the French colony that was to endure until the time of Napoleon.

~ VI ~

DISCORD IN THE COLONIES

GOVERNOR DE POINCY, as we have said in a preceding chapter, was preparing in the year 1640 to carry out a plan which he had been considering for some time—the sale of St. Christopher to the English and the removal of the French colonists with their slaves, livestock, and portable property to Guadeloupe, which would then become the capital of the archipelago. The idea was by no means an unreasonable one, for the advantages of this large island from the point of view of location, resources, and harbor facilities were too obvious to need discussion. The benefits that would accrue to the proprietors if the colonists could get away from their none-too-friendly English neighbors and settle on an island where they could be supreme were many. Moreover, such a settlement would in time become the nucleus of an expanding colony that would spread out over the adjacent islands and be ruled from a capital of such magnitude that it could be made almost impregnable—a citadel no enemy could capture. It was De Poincy's intention, of course, to remain Governor-General of the French West Indies, but in order to lessen the burden of his duties in the new and larger colony he planned to have the company appoint his protégé, M. de Sabouïlly, Governor of the island.

For placing the details of his scheme before the directors and the government authorities De Poincy selected as his emissary the Sieur Jean Aubert. This man, who was destined to play an important and somewhat tragic part in Guadeloupe, had come to St. Christopher as a surgeon—a useful calling, to be sure, but one which carried with it no social prestige, surgery in those days being regarded more as a trade than as a profession. Yet despite this, by sheer native ability backed by unusual courage Aubert had been able to carve out a respectable position for himself. His skill in commanding men, his knowledge of colonial affairs and the needs of colonists, his intelligent management of business—all these qualities had recommended him to Governor d'Esnambuc, who had appointed him lieutenant in the militia. In addition to this he married the widow of Jean Duplessis, former governor of Guadeloupe, which made him one of the wealthiest colonists, for the lady on the death of her husband had acquired his extensive property. De Poincy, who was as much impressed with the man's engaging qualities as his predecessor had been, sent him as his agent to France.

While awaiting the return of M. Aubert, Governor de Poincy found plenty to occupy him in the island of St. Christopher. Toward the close of 1639 a slave insurrection broke out in the Capesterre section. Negroes, angered by the brutal treatment meted out to them by their masters, fled to the woods on the slopes of Mt. Misery with their women and children, where they established a sort of headquarters for raids on the planters. To put an end to these disorders De Poincy raised a body of five hundred armed men and sent them out to suppress the uprising. It proved to be a not very difficult task, for the negroes were poorly armed, and though they built a formidable camp high up on the mountainside their numbers were not sufficiently large to permit them to offer serious resistance. It was not long before most of them were killed in skirmishes, while the rest were captured and hanged, drawn, and quartered to serve as a warning to those who might be tempted to rebel.

There was, however, one negro, a gigantic fellow, who for three years had eluded capture, carrying on a one-man reign of terror by his murders and serving as a rallying point for the disaffected slaves. He played a lone hand in the forests of Mt. Misery, living apart from his fellow rebels through fear of betrayal by some fugitive who might wish to curry favor with the authorities. Like most leaders of his kind he was well served by the men of his race who regarded him as the personification of freedom from slavery, and a living threat against their masters. Thus he was kept well informed of what was going on in the settlements. His success in evading all attempts to take him was so amazing that the rumor soon spread abroad that he was aided by supernatural powers.

Governor de Poincy, realizing the disturbing influence wielded by such a man, determined to kill him or capture him at any cost. For this purpose he detailed some half dozen soldiers and sent them out heavily armed to scour the slopes of Mt. Misery. They were not long in finding their quarry, for the plan of action had been worked out in secrecy to prevent the blacks from getting an inkling of what was going on, and therefore they had no opportunity to send word to the rebel. When the negro came in sight, the soldiers blazed away at him, but strange to say every musket missed fire, and the infuriated African charged on them with his sword, putting the entire band to flight. This amazing incident, as might be supposed, quickly gave rise to the rumor that he possessed certain magic charms against firearms—a superstition that gained popular credence, as this was not the first time he had escaped the bullets of his pursuers. It was necessary, therefore, to strike quickly. The following day De Poincy sent forth another squad, which soon surrounded the man and fired at point blank range without even wounding him. No doubt the marksmanship was deplorable, but the soldiers felt that they had to deal with diabolical powers, and this may have unnerved them when they took aim. At last they closed in on him, and by good fortune the sergeant managed to dispatch him with a bullet through the head—a lucky shot, for, as De Poincy said, it is doubtful if a dozen men could have captured him.

Scarcely had this trouble been settled when word came from M. de Sabouïlly, who had picked up the news while on a short visit to Martinique, that England and Spain had signed an agreement by which the former was to furnish eighteen ships manned by Irishmen to be added to twenty-five supplied by the latter to form a fleet to drive the Dutch from Guiana. Afterward they would proceed to attack the French at St. Christopher in the hope of expelling them from the island and replacing them with Irish settlers. On receiving this disturbing news De Poincy wrote frantically to the company urging them to send out at the first possible moment 10,000 pounds of powder, 1,000 muskets, 1,000 pikes, and 200 halberds. Turning then to the business at hand, he began to strengthen his own fortifications at Basseterre and in the Capesterre section. Fortunately the attack never materialized, for the Dutch annihilated the Spaniards when they descended on Pernambuco.

While Aubert was still in France carrying out the orders of his superior an opportunity to gain control of Guadeloupe presented itself to M. de Poincy. Shortly after L'Olive left the island a series of attacks was launched by the savages which bade fair to destroy the colony. In desperation the company's factor, M. Voléry, then acting as governor, sent a messenger post haste to St. Christopher requesting immediate assistance if the colony was to be saved. Here, then, was De Poincy's opportunity to make an armed invasion of the island, drive off the Caribs, and establish himself as protector. Once this was done the company would doubtless be glad to confer the title of governor on him in recognition of his services in saving their property.

Notices were accordingly quickly nailed on all church doors and public buildings offering free transportation, provisions, and homes to all who would join the relief expedition the Governor-General was about to send to Guadeloupe. This liberal offer, coupled with the fact that the order forbidding the cultivation of tobacco had deprived many of their means of livelihood, had the desired effect, and in the middle of January,

1640, a band of 132 men sailed for Guadeloupe under M. de Sabouïlly. Not content with this small number, De Poincy took advantage of a peculiar situation to encourage the enlistment of a second detachment. A number of planters who had borrowed money to purchase expensive plantations found themselves unable to make payments because of the sudden curtailment of the tobacco industry. To obtain the services of these men De Poincy issued a proclamation canceling the debts of all those who would sail for Guadeloupe. Thus, shortly after Sabouïlly's departure a second contingent started out under La Vernade.

When these expeditions landed at Guadeloupe, the former at Capesterre, the latter at Basseterre, the leaders proceeded to assert their authority over all and sundry as though they were duly commissioned governors, quartering their men in the first houses they came to and appropriating the necessary supplies wherever they found them. Yet the inhabitants received the new arrivals with enthusiasm; anything was better than the continual attacks to which they had been subjected, and these men were sufficiently numerous to repel them.

Sabouïlly at once got down to business. Taking a boat with a detachment of sixteen men he started off to circumnavigate the island in the hope of locating the Indian stronghold. Having sailed northward along the Capesterre coast he came presently to the cul-de-sac formed by the junction of the two halves of the island, where he saw an Indian canoe lying just off the shore. His boat at once bore down on it under press of sail aided by the efforts of the rowers who added their power to the force of the wind. As they drew near two other war canoes, engaged in pursuing a small French boat manned by four fishermen, closed in on them. The fishermen, panic stricken at the approach of the Caribs, leaped overboard to escape, and Sabouïlly seeing their predicament felt obliged to alter his course to rescue them. While they were engaged in this work of mercy, the three Indian canoes surrounded him and the battle began.

The French had with them twenty muskets, which were at

once served out to the crew, four men being detailed to load them, while the others kept up a brisk fire. For more than an hour the battle lasted. The French, bringing to bear all the skill and coolness that frontiersmen are wont to acquire, fired with an accuracy that accounted for thirty Indians killed and a large number wounded, until the Caribs, completely outclassed, were obliged to seek safety in flight. The French lost only two men in the encounter.

Thus defeated, the Caribs disappeared for a brief while from Guadeloupe. But not for long, for their pride was presently restored by a raid on Antigua, where they captured the wife of Governor Edward Warner, and toward the middle of May they were back again in formidable numbers, determined to exact revenge for their previous humiliation. Sabouïlly, forewarned of the coming attack, made arrangements to join forces with La Vernade at a certain point near the southern extremity of the island, about midway between their respective headquarters. It happened that La Vernade was driven back by the weather and was unable to reach the rendezvous; and thus it was that Sabouïlly, while on his way there with a small force of only twenty-four harquebusiers, came face to face with thirteen large war canoes manned by six or seven hundred savages. Confronted by such odds the French commander at once turned and made for an island (probably one of that small cluster known as the Saints), where he landed and hastily threw up a barricade behind which his men could put up some show of resistance. The idea proved a wise one, for protected by this rude breastwork, the harquebusiers were able to pick off the Indians as they advanced over the sea. During thirty long hours of almost incessant fighting the French succeeded in holding off their foes until La Vernade appeared in the offing with his little fleet; then the savages, fearing that they were about to be attacked by a huge contingent, took to flight after uttering dire threats of vengeance. This victory had a lasting effect, and for six months no Carib war canoe dared show itself in the vicinity of Guadeloupe.

At this time there came to Guadeloupe a man to whom we are indebted for most of our knowledge of the early history of the French Caribbees. Father Jean-Baptiste du Tertre was born at Calais in 1610. He had led an adventurous life before entering the Dominican Order, for his wanderings had taken him to Greenland as a seaman in the Dutch marine, after which he had enlisted in the army. He was present at the siege of Maestricht in 1633. Shortly after his ordination to the priesthood he was selected to go with five other religious leaders to the Leeward Islands. The party which sailed from Dieppe on January 7, 1640, consisted of Du Tertre, Jean de Saint-Paul, Nicolas de la Mare, who acted as superior, and three lay brothers. They landed in Guadeloupe in the nick of time, for Father Breton, who had been ministering single handed to the spiritual needs of the colony for the past two and a half years, was nearly exhausted. "It was high time to assist him," says Du Tertre, "for he was reduced to such extremities that he had for clothing only a ragged garment. He was in absolute need of everything and was suffering from such fatigue that I wondered a thousand times how a man could endure so much without dying." Furthermore, the arrival of the clergy was timely for other reasons. An epidemic, the nature of which was unknown, had broken out among the soldiers, carrying off some three-quarters of them. During the months in which these wretched men lay sick and dying the fathers busied themselves with providing them with whatever comfort they could, administering to their physical as well as spiritual needs.

While Sabouïlly was thus battling valiantly to save Guadeloupe from the savages, Governor du Parquet, as we have pointed out, had been achieving considerable success in Martinique. His efforts elicited the praise of M. de Poincy, who wrote the directors of the company expressing hearty approval of the work of his subordinate, pointing out at the same time his immediate needs and requesting that supplies be sent him. "He has," so wrote De Poincy, "about 700 men capable of fighting, but if they were attacked they would not have enough powder to fire four rounds apiece. He has rebuilt the palisades of Fort Royal; all its guns are dismounted as they might well be, since the carriages are worthless. There is only one carpenter in the entire island, and considering other needs, this is not the least, and it is one which you should rectify and send over someone at once. So much for their material needs; as for their spiritual wants, they live very far from each other with only two secular priests to minister to them, who grossly deceive me, as do the two we have here (at St. Christopher), should they ever become chancellors of the Sorbonne, such is their incapacity."

The directors, seeing the prosperity of Martinique under M. du Parquet as compared with conditions in Guadeloupe, wrote him many suggestions, among which were plans for erecting a hospital, building a city, applying fines for the support of the sick and needy, and they urgently requested that he receive a judge for trying local cases. Du Parquet was inclined to smile when he received this communication, for the directors evidently thought that the island was literally swarming with planters and bursting with wealth; but he handled the situation with true diplomatic skill, arranging matters in such a way as to avoid putting unnecessary burdens on the planters and at the same time showing due regard for the suggestions of the company. He explained to the directors the difficulties that prevented him from complying entirely with their recommendations, at least for the time being, and requested them to send over as soon as possible a sufficient number of skilled workmen, bricklayers, masons, carpenters, and the like to permit him to undertake the building of a permanent settlement along the lines they had suggested. He vowed that he was ready to welcome anyone who could improve the plantation, but he drew the line at any official who might challenge his authority. The company had just sent over a judge to settle the various civil and criminal cases that might arise, and it was against this man that Du Parquet now protested, saying that he was the commander of an establishment that must be maintained on a military basis rather than the ruler of a settlement of burghers, and, moreover, that the colonists themselves would resent such an official. When the fortifications were completed it would be different.

When the judge did arrive Du Parquet took him to St. Christopher, where he renewed his complaint before Governor De Poincy, threatening to resign if the matter was pushed any farther. After much discussion the Governor-General finally persuaded Du Parquet to allow the judge to return to Martinique and to finish a criminal trial he had begun. The colonists objected strenuously to the presence of the jurist and were only held in check by Du Parquet's influence; but when the case was ended they drove the obnoxious official from the island.

Warned by the example of Guadeloupe, where there was so much trouble with the Caribs, Du Parquet determined to avoid such difficulties by extending the hand of friendship to these Indians. But they resented the presence of foreigners on general principles and were not so easily appeased. Matters came to a head when they carried off two of their own people from the plantation of a colonist named Lesperance. The Governor, who despite his conciliatory attitude knew when to be severe, promptly arrested their chief and threw him into prison, threatening to keep him there until the two men had been returned. Unfortunately the brave managed to escape during the night, and make his way to the jungle, where he died from the bite of a fer-de-lance. This sudden death, Du Parquet well knew, would at once be laid at the door of the French, and he accordingly wrote to De Poincy, begging permission to anticipate the coming attack by carrying the war into the enemy's territory. De Poincy saw the point and immediately issued an order, dated January 20, 1640, authorizing him to take whatever steps he deemed necessary for the protection of his colony and hinting that this might be the great opportunity to drive the Caribs entirely from the island.

Du Parquet, however, once he had received official permission to use his own discretion, contented himself with strengthening his defenses and bringing in the settlers from the outlying districts. These preparations had the effect of terrifying the savages, who, seeing that they had a determined foe to deal with, decided to return the men they had taken and sue for peace. De Poincy was immensely pleased at the outcome, so different from the continual uproars in Guadeloupe. To show his appreciation he appointed Du Parquet ranking captain of the militia at St. Christopher, a more-or-less-honorary post, since it did not oblige him to leave his work at Martinique. He also wrote to M. Fouquet, recommending the young man in flattering terms, with the result that the company continued to renew his commission and kept him in office until his death.

It was at this time, too, that the Jesuit fathers made their first appearance in the colonies. Du Parquet had written the company requesting them to send additional clergymen for the rapidly expanding settlement and suggesting that members of the Capuchin order would be particularly welcome. But M. Fouquet, who favored the Society of Jesus, sent two of its members: Jacques Bouton, who later wrote an interesting account of the French Antilles, and Father Hempteau. The Governor received them coldly; he resented their appearance in the place of his favorite Capuchins. But in the end, thanks to the excellent work of Father Bouton, he became their enthusiastic supporter.

Meanwhile, the Sieur Aubert had been carrying on his negotiations in France. As agent for Governor de Poincy he failed dismally in his mission, for the directors had no intention of giving up a colony on which they had spent so much money, no matter how attractive Guadeloupe might be, nor did they look with favor on the suggested appointment of M. de Sabouïlly to the governorship of that island, as they feared it would make De Poincy too powerful to have his henchman holding so important an office. But the directors were so favorably impressed with the emissary that they bestowed on him the coveted command, an action which, they said, gave them much pleasure, as they could thereby pay a compliment to the widow Duplessis, for whose husband they had always entertained a high regard. A commission was accordingly issued on April 4, 1640, appointing the Sieur Aubert Governor of Guadeloupe for the balance of the year and for three years thereafter.

Aubert sailed from Havre shortly after receiving his commission. He arrived the following September in Martinique, where he was hospitably received by Governor du Parquet, who gave him much valuable advice. He was told to make peace with the Indians as speedily as possible, and Du Parquet offered his services as mediator, an offer which was promptly accepted with thanks. Heartened by his cordial reception, Aubert left for Guadeloupe. On the way he stopped at Dominica, where he graciously received on board his ship a number of Carib chiefs, whose friendship he secured by means of ample good cheer and some presents. He also managed to convince them of his good intentions by promising that their arch-enemy, Sabouïlly, the man who had twice defeated them, would leave Guadeloupe as soon as he himself had taken over command of the island and that there would be no further wars between the Caribs and the French. Upon his arrival at Guadeloupe on the fifteenth of September he found to his surprise that his plans for peace did not meet with universal approval. The majority, it is true, were thankful, but there were many bellicose souls who regarded the proposal with deplorable lack of enthusiasm. Not that they were eager to fight, on the contrary they had had more than enough of these continual raids; but they put no faith in the promises made by Indians, who, they said, would quickly take advantage of any peace negotiations to descend upon them, accusing the savages of St. Vincent of being the actual perpetrators of the attack. It was these men who vowed they would shoot at sight any Caribs found lurking around Guadeloupe.

Unwilling to begin his administration by antagonizing a large part of his people, Governor Aubert proceeded to St. Christopher to pay his respects to the Governor-General, hoping that the colonists would undergo a change of heart during his absence. But he warned them that he would hold them responsible if they started any trouble with the Caribs. If De Poincy felt any resentment toward his erstwhile emissary over his failure to secure the approval of the company for his own plans, he concealed it carefully, for he received the new appointee cordially. He even advanced him a loan of 15,000 pounds of tobacco and permitted him to recruit settlers from among the colonists of St. Christopher. Cheered by the kind reception, Aubert returned to Guadeloupe in December, caused his commission as governor to be read to the assembled planters, and took office. Here, just south of the Rivière des Galions and north of Fort Royal, near the property given by L'Olive to the Dominican fathers, he built for himself a handsome residence.

As soon as he had been installed in office, trouble began. As usually happens in such circumstances, a clique was formed against the new arrival by the adherents of the old incumbent. Apparently Judge de la Rivière and M. de la Ramée were the leaders of the cabal, grumbling that Aubert, formerly a mere lieutenant under L'Olive, was now usurping the authority of a ruler. When De Poincy found that he could not seize the island for himself, he sent back the moribund L'Olive in the hope that he might rally some of his old followers. But L'Olive could not turn a sufficient number against the new Governor and soon returned to St. Christopher, leaving the irreconcilables, particularly Judge de la Rivière, to fight it out.

Strange to say, there occurred at this time a calamity which did much to heal the breach between the Governor and the old faction. M. Aubert had loaded a vessel with turtles and manatees to take to St. Christopher and had manned it with a crew composed chiefly of those who had been unwilling to declare peace with the Caribs. A squall struck the ship as she set sail, causing her to founder with most of the crew. Aubert, fortunately, managed to make his way to the shore, where he took refuge in the house of a poor planter. Here he was found by M. de la Ramée, who, touched by his misfortune, took him to his own house and cared for him. From this time on La Ramée became Aubert's devoted friend.

Again the Caribs made their appearance. They went first to Martinique, but Du Parquet advised them to proceed to Guadeloupe and make overtures to the new commander, who was eager to arrange for a permanent peace. Loading their canoes with pineapples, turtles, and pigs, suitable gifts for one of Aubert's prominence, they set sail for the southern part of Guadeloupe and hove to in sight of the Governor's dwelling. For a while they remained in their canoes, watching the French who had gathered on the shore to gape at the new arrivals, mistrustful of their mission. Then, seeing no hostile move on the part of their foes, the Indians dispatched one of their number to swim ashore and obtain an interview with the Governor. Aubert received the man so kindly he hastened back to advise his fellows that there was nothing to fear. At once they beached their canoes and marched in a body to the executive mansion. Here they were well received, and after a sumptuous meal copiously irrigated with liquor Aubert entered into negotiations with his guests and managed to conclude a treaty of sorts by means of the sign language—a treaty according to which the two parties agreed to remain friends. The hospitality shown the Caribs soon drew others to Guadeloupe, for the Indians always responded to the lure of alcoholic beverage, and soon the colonists were able to build up a lucrative traffic, as the savages brought them food and many articles filched from the English.

After the treaty was ratified the Indians, now filled to repletion, took leave, with many protestations of good will, and set out for Dominica. On their way they chanced to fall in with another contingent of braves under a chieftain known as Captain Baron. He inquired carefully about the reception given them by the French and was so pleased at what he heard that he decided to make a visit to Aubert himself. The Governor received him in such a friendly manner, that the chief, highly gratified by this condescension, was soon back again for a second visit. This time Aubert introduced him to one of Duplessis's sons, a young man of promising appearance, who at once struck the chief's fancy. In reply to a suggestion from Aubert that the savages should surrender some of their children as hostages he offered his own son and requested that young Duplessis be turned over to him. The Governor accepted the young savage as a matter of course; but when it came to parting with his stepson he drew the line. To save the situation, however, he persuaded Captain Baron that the lad was not strong enough to bear the Carib way of life, and he finally induced him to accept one of his servants instead. Baron, we are told, visited Guadeloupe many times after this to see his son. Pleased by the way he was treated, he showed his appreciation by turning over to the Governor one or two Frenchmen who had been for some time prisoners of the Indians. Free from the menace of invasion, the colonists now turned again with confidence to their fields, and plenty and prosperity gradually took the place of want.

News of the peaceful condition of the island was noised abroad throughout the archipelago and even across the ocean to France, giving a very favorable impression of the colonizing possibilities of Guadeloupe. Planters came there with their people, settled, and cleared additional acreage for cultivation; vessels put into its ports in greater numbers than before to get their share of the fast-growing trade; the population increased; and the island was soon able to rank with the better organized colonies of St. Christopher and Martinique.

The administration of Governor de Poincy was now beginning to cause dissatisfaction among many planters, who presently circulated a petition of their grievances which they forwarded to the directors at home. Their complaints were summed up under three headings: 1. The Governor had appointed a factor who had charge of the company's stores as judge to try M. de la Grange; 2. He had banished certain persons without trial;

3. He favored heretics against the expressed wishes of His Majesty. To counteract the unfavorable influence of this petition De Poincy felt obliged to compose a long letter to the directors justifying his conduct on these counts. In the main he seems to have been successful in vindicating himself, for whatever may have been the merits of the controversy he at least managed to impress them with his ability as an administrator as he presently received, under date of May 1, 1641, a document extending his commission as Governor of St. Christopher for three years, beginning the first of the following year, while the King also confirmed his reappointment as Governor-General of the archipelago.

When the new commission was placed in De Poincy's hands, he made the grave mistake of not reading it to the assembled planters, as was the custom when a governor took office. Perhaps he regarded the gesture as superfluous, since his commission merely confirmed him in office for another three years. But at any rate a rumor, assiduously fanned by the malcontents, quickly spread abroad that the new instrument actually curtailed his powers and for this reason he feared to make it public. To bolster up this wild tale, one of his enemies went to the length of forging a commission, which was circulated throughout the colony to prove that the Governor no longer enjoyed the powers he had formerly exercised. Enraged at this attempt to subvert his authority, De Poincy determined to find the culprit and make an example of him. His suspicions presently fell upon the Sieur des Marets, a former captain who had earned an unenviable reputation as a trouble maker; but as he had no direct evidence against the man, he decided to prove him guilty by a scheme that reflected little credit on his sense of justice. It appears, indeed, that he completely lost his head; for instead of setting suspicions at rest by the simple expedient of reading his commission to the planters, he sent one of his catchpoles to Des Marets's home with orders to "plant" a copy of the fake commission on the premises where it could easily be found. Faced with this incriminating evidence, Des Marets denied the charge, pointing out with perfect truth that he could not have been the author of this or any other document, since he could neither read nor write. Nevertheless De Poincy threw him into prison and ordered the charge to be pressed. Des Marets was in due time brought to trial before a court composed of a judge, specially imported from Guadeloupe, and nine assessors who could be relied on to carry out the Governor's wishes. The accusation was too transparent to deceive anybody, so the prosecutor was obliged to satisfy himself with a formidable array of witnesses, who testified that the defendant had frequently used blasphemous language and spoken about the Governor in a seditious manner, all of which was probably true. With this evidence the court expressed itself satisfied and promptly condemned the unfortunate man to death.

The crass injustice of the whole proceeding exasperated the Capuchin fathers, who had visited Des Marets in his cell and had become convinced of his innocence. They brought pressure to bear upon the judge to reverse his decision; they even persuaded him to call on De Poincy and urge him to view the case with more leniency. This protest unfortunately only threw the Governor into a towering rage—fairly conclusive evidence of the injustice of his position—and the terrified judge returned to the fathers, saying that he must carry out the sentence if he would save his own head.

Having failed to secure Des Marets's release by legal means, his friends now arranged for his escape, though it must be said that the Capuchins took no part in this proceeding. They brought a supply of wine to the guardhouse, with which they plied the guards, who soon fell asleep under its soporific influence. Then Mme des Marets cut her husband's fetters with a file. Freed, Des Marets lost no time in crossing the frontier and taking refuge with the English colonists.

When he learned of his prisoner's escape, the Governor's wrath knew no bounds. Hastening to the jail, he held a summary court martial, tried and promptly convicted two soldiers who had been in charge of Des Marets and had them beheaded on the spot. The two sergeants in command of the prison were sentenced to transportation to Guadeloupe and their property was confiscated. This done, the Governor took steps to capture his man. As soon as he learned that he had taken refuge in English territory, he raised an army of four thousand men and marched to the frontier, where he sent word to the British commander that he would seize the culprit by force if he were not at once handed over peacefully. The Englishman, unwilling to risk a war over a criminal case in which he had no interest, surrendered Des Marets, who was loaded with chains and taken back to prison. Preparations were immediately made to carry out the sentence; and despite the vigorous protests of the Capuchins, who maintained his innocence until the last, Des Marets was beheaded, after doing penance before the chapel at Basseterre for a crime he did not commit.

Needless to say, this high-handed action on the part of the Governor-General had sinister repercussions throughout the island. At first, discontent made itself manifest in murmurs of disapproval; then, as the feeling against him grew, it broke out in open insurrection. De Poincy now realized that he had lost the respect and the affection of his people and that his only hope of riding out the storm lay in a policy of terror. Therefore, chains and shackles were placed in all the jails, as well as instruments of punishment calculated to discourage those who might start any disorder, and preparations were also made to nip any disturbance in the bud.

While the Governor might by these means have prevented any disorder due to resentment against the Des Marets outrage, he had the bad judgment to take certain steps that struck a blow at the economic interests of the colony. He caused a warehouse to be built, in which he stored all goods brought to the island by French and Flemish traders, and he forbade the settlers from boarding their ships to purchase the goods themselves—all of which was done, he claimed, to protect the planters from the rapacity of the merchants. He then appointed seven factors to distribute the goods, exacting a profit of 40 percent[1] on all transactions. As a result of this scheme the Governor and his factors grew wealthy at the expense of the planters, who had no legal redress against the monopoly. It was far different from the days of Governor d'Esnambuc, when all could buy freely from visiting merchantmen. Matters came to a head at Pointe de Sable, where a planter named Clement Bugaud gathered a group of disaffected persons about him and threatened to instigate a general uprising throughout the whole island. The situation was beginning to take on an ugly complexion, when M. de Sabouïlly stepped into the breach and managed to calm the settlers by promising in the Governor's name to restore free trade with itinerant merchant vessels. This done, he had no difficulty in breaking up the little band of mutineers which had gathered under Bugaud. As for Bugaud and his followers, they were expelled from the island and went to South America, where they founded, so it is said, the colony of French Guiana.

During this time the affairs of the company were going from bad to worse despite all that could be done and despite the fact that St. Christopher was well colonized, that Martinique was producing excellent tobacco, and that Guadeloupe, thanks to Governor Aubert's wise management, was drawing hundreds of settlers from France. To get at the root of the trouble, the company decided to send one of their directors to study the situation on the spot. For this purpose they selected Charles Houël, whom we have previously mentioned in connection with the sugar industry. Houël, although carrying on duties as inspector, intended to choose for himself an island where he might later take up his residence. The directors, however, did not wait for his return to proceed with their plans for strengthening their position. This they proposed to do by obtaining further con-

---

[1] Du Tertre, I, 166, says 4 percent, but such a modest profit would not have caused resentment.

cessions from the government and greater powers over the islands, for inasmuch as the prosperity which their possessions now enjoyed would furnish them with the means for expansion, they hoped to extend the scope of their enterprise over a wider area, and thus make up for previous losses.

In the petition which they presented to the King, the directors grouped their demands under five heads: (1) confirmation of the charter granted them in 1635; (2) permission to enlarge their territory to include islands situated as far north as the thirtieth parallel (the previous limit had been the twentieth); (3) exclusive right to trade with their islands; (4) privilege to import products from the islands into France free from duty; (5) complete jurisdiction over the islands even to the exclusion of government authority. On the recommendation of Cardinal Richelieu the King granted the company in March, 1642, all they had asked, though he reserved for the Crown all islands that were not settled at the end of twenty years. To encourage colonization he offered four letters of ennoblement to be given to men who would transport to one of the uninhabited islands a band of at least fifty men and live there two years.

Meanwhile Houël was exploring the Caribbee Islands, keeping an eye open for a promising colony which he might appropriate. He landed at Guadeloupe, where Governor Aubert, who had no knowledge of his ulterior motives, took him at face value as a representative of the company making a tour of inspection, and entertained him royally, showing him the plantations and confiding to him his own plans for raising sugar cane for which he expected financial backing from the company. Upon his return to France, Houël made a complete report of his observations to the company with recommendations as to what should be done to promote the welfare of the fast-growing colonies. Through the influence of friends he caused pressure to be brought on his fellow-directors to appoint him governor of Guadeloupe with complete control over the proposed sugar industry, thus leaving Aubert in the subordinate position of lieutenant-governor. Considering the entire situation, this action may not have been so unjust as it seems to us. Charles Houël was an influential member of the board, one of those who had advanced money to promote the colonies; Governor Aubert, on the other hand, was a colonial of no particular importance, who had been given the governorship of Guadeloupe at a time when that island needed a commander and no one else seemed available to fill the position; moreover he would still be retained as Houël's lieutenant. M. Aubert quite naturally did not view the situation in this light, and when Houël reached Guadeloupe he complained loudly that he had been betrayed.

The year 1642 now drew to a close; but before leaving it we wish to mention an important event which had far reaching consequences for the colonies. On the fourth of December the great Cardinal Richelieu died. As Grand Master of Navigation and Commerce he had directed for sixteen years the fortunes of the budding French empire beyond the seas, supervising the colonization of Canada and the West Indies, organizing trading companies, furnishing men and money, ironing out difficulties, encouraging planters, moulding the colonial economic system to the needs of the French nation. At his death the foundation for colonization had been laid, and the impetus he had given the movement sufficed to carry it forward under the direction of his less able successor, the Marquis de Brezé. Five months later his master, Louis XIII, also died, and the government of France was placed in the hands of the Queen mother, Anne of Austria, as regent for Louis XIV.

When Houël landed at Guadeloupe on May 3, 1643, he found Fort Royal in a sad state of disrepair. The house he was to occupy had sheaves of hay as a palisade around it, while the garden had been ravaged by a hurricane and yielded but little in the way of vegetables. Half-a-dozen French servants and fifty-odd negro slaves comprised the staff of the establishment, and these poor devils were so weak from lack of nourishment that his first thought was to buy them some food. Disgusted by this situation, the new Governor ordered his men to carry his baggage to the Case du Borgne, located a long distance up the Capesterre coast at the mouth of the Rivière Ste. Marie, where he established the residence he was to occupy for several years.

Scarcely had Houël assumed his new duties, when there appeared on the scene a person whose influence soon equalled that of the Governor himself. The directors of the company had found it necessary, as they had at St. Christopher, to supply their colonists with wives, inasmuch as these worthy fellows had been obliged to leave their plantations when the spirit urged them and return to France in search of suitable helpmates. For this purpose a contingent of eligible girls had been rounded up from the Hospital Saint-Joseph in Paris, and were placed under the chaperonage of Mlle de la Fayolle. This lady appeared before the Governor with letters of recommendation from the Queen and several ladies of high standing at Court. The poor Governor, dazzled by such distinguished sponsorship, could do nothing but bow and scrape; but having no accommodations for so large a party, he hurried to Mlle Aubert[2] asking her to grant them quarters in her home until suitable ones could be provided. Mlle Aubert was not at all pleased; as a woman of somewhat austere disposition, she had little enthusiasm for the ladies of the Hospital Saint-Joseph as paying guests; but on being shown the letter of recommendation from the Queen she felt it her duty to comply with the Governor's request. Having thus made temporary arrangements for the prospective brides, Houël rushed the building of a home for them near his residence at Case du Borgne into which they moved on the twelfth of October. Mlle de la Fayolle, because of the great demand for her young ladies was courted by the officers of the island, who were all anxious to secure wives; being a person of proud and aggressive temper, she quickly took advantage of her position to become the center of intrigue.

[2] At this time the titles "Mademoiselle" and "Madame" were not used to distinguish between unmarried and married women as they are today. They denoted a certain social position, that of "madame" being applied to ladies of rank.

It was now high time for M. Houël to visit St. Christopher and pay his respects to his superior, Governor de Poincy. On landing at Basseterre, he had the misfortune to commit a breach of etiquette—whether accidentally or deliberately it is impossible to say—which augured ill for his future relations with De Poincy. There had recently arrived on the island a new official, one Claude Clerselier de Leumont, Counselor to His Majesty, who had been sent by the company in the capacity of civil and criminal judge to restore order to the finances of the colony, and put a stop to the depredations committed by the factors who had been filling their pockets at the settlers' expense, possibly with De Poincy's tacit approval. The company had found it increasingly difficult to check the rapacity of its agents at so great a distance, and needed a man on the spot with authority to deal promptly and vigorously with such irregularities. By a commission dated October 1, 1642, they had appointed M. de Leumont as Intendant of all the islands for a period of three years from the following January, a position which placed him in complete control of the factors throughout the archipelago. He was also to sit in the Governor's council, ranking above the ordinary judges. It was on this man that Houël had the bad taste to call first before making his official visit to Governor de Poincy.

When at last the Governor of Guadeloupe did present himself before the Governor-General, his reception was not particularly cordial. The interview started off with bickering. Upon showing De Poincy his commission, the latter declared it was not enough and that Houël would have to take an oath of loyalty to him as the other governors had done, since he was the representative of the King while they were merely agents of the company. Houël saw fit to argue the point, asserting that he, unlike the other governors, was a director of the company, and should therefore be exempt from any act of obeisance. The debate waxed warm, neither man being willing to yield, until De Poincy realized that he was dealing with a stubborn individual whom eventually he would be obliged to bring to heel if he expected to maintain his authority as Governor-General over him. When Houël offered to take the oath, with the reservation, of course, that he did so only for the sake of harmony and not because he recognized the validity of De Poincy's claim, the Governor-General still felt obliged to refuse such a compromise. "This struggle," says Du Tertre, "produced innumerable ills which exhausted the strength of the colonies, ruined entire families, caused the banishment of innocent people, and resulted in much slaughter and shedding of blood."

When Governor Houël returned to Guadeloupe after his bad start at St. Christopher, he immediately purchased the plantation of M. Aubert for 18,000 pounds of tobacco. But the place did not suit him, so he took up his residence at Ste. Marie. Years later he selected a site somewhat north of Aubert's plantation at Basseterre high up on a rocky cliff, hitherto regarded as inaccessible, on which he built a handsome residence which he called "Houëlmont." Hearing a rumor that a plot was brewing in France to remove him from his command, he caused the place to be fortified and guns mounted on the ramparts. The work was so difficult and was pushed forward with such haste that the colonists who were pressed into it were soon on the point of revolt. As for Aubert, he at this time appears to have been snubbed by Houël to such an extent that he was glad to escape from the island. He presently applied for, and obtained permission to visit St. Christopher whither his wife had moved.

After the departure of the unfortunate Aubert, Governor Houël took steps to ruin him completely in the eyes of the colonists and prevent him from ever returning to Guadeloupe. To accomplish this he adopted a mean and contemptible course of action. A report was presently circulated—at Houël's instigation, so it was believed—to the effect that Aubert had told the Caribs that Houël had come from France to seize their stronghold, Dominica, and massacre them. The purpose of this report was to convince the settlers that Aubert would stop at nothing to destroy the rightful Governor of Guadeloupe, even going to the extent of spreading false information about him that might lead to an attack on the colony by the savages. This wild tale, of course, gave the Sieur de Petit-Pré the excuse he needed to keep his rival from the island. To clinch the matter, he wrote De Poincy asking him to hold the ex-Governor at St. Christopher until the report could be verified, promising at the same time to sift the accusation to the bottom. The first act of his investigation was to arrest a man named Du Rivage who, so he asserted, was the one accused by the Caribs of circulating the report amongst them. After throwing the fellow into jail, the Governor kept him there for over two months, subjecting him to harsh treatment calculated to break his spirit and make him confess. At last worn down by his jailers and promised his liberty if he would talk, the man declared that he had spread the rumor about Governor Houël at Aubert's suggestion. This was all the Governor needed. Calling together his council, which included Father La Paix, the ranking clergyman of the colony, Houël had Du Rivage repeat his statement. No one, however, was much impressed, for it seemed questionable that Aubert would jeopardize the island where he owned so much valuable property; but the Governor was determined to press the matter and sent word by Father La Paix to M. de Poincy of the charges he was prepared to make against Aubert. Not wishing to appear vindictive in public, he wound up his complaint by assuring the Governor-General that he would be entirely satisfied if Aubert would sell his property and never return to Guadeloupe. At the same time he sent another letter by a separate messenger expressing himself in far different terms. In this communication he demanded the punishment of his victim, telling De Poincy that he had incontrovertible proof of his rival's guilt and enclosed Du Rivage's confession as evidence of his accusation. De Poincy, be it said to his credit, saw clearly that the whole thing was a plot to get rid of the unfortunate Aubert, and concluded that the easiest way to get at the truth was to send for Du Rivage and

DISCORD IN THE COLONIES

see if he would hold to his confession when no longer in Houël's power. For this purpose he appointed Nicolas Tostain as special judge to proceed to Guadeloupe, hear the evidence in person, and bring back a report of the proceedings together with the witnesses, particularly Du Rivage. Houël, however, took a high-handed view of the matter and refused to acknowledge the authority of the special judge, saying he would reserve his case for the Royal Council of France; but as a mark of respect for the authority of the Governor-General, he offered to send him a letter stating the reasons for his conduct. Thus there was nothing Tostain could do but return to St. Christopher without having accomplished his mission.

Governor de Poincy, needless to say, was deeply offended at the way the Sieur de Petit-Pré had flaunted his authority, and at once ordered a transcript of all the documents concerning the affair to be sent to the directors of the company. He also lodged a complaint against the Governor of Guadeloupe charging him with refusing to recognize his jurisdiction in the case after having invoked his authority against Aubert. In addition to this, he accused him of being too eager to ruin a former governor after having pledged himself to forget the matter if Aubert would leave the island for good, and furthermore, of using a man of questionable character (Du Rivage) to bear witness against a loyal servant of the King and the company. To give further proofs of the unsuitability of Houël for his post, he enclosed with his report two letters he had received: one from the Governor of St. Eustatius complaining that Houël had arrested a Dutch captain in Guadeloupe; the other from Sir Thomas Warner, stating that Houël had given asylum to Irish and English fugitives from the British islands and sundry bankrupt persons who were badly wanted at home, a course of action which might disrupt the friendly relations between the two nations and lead to a war between their colonies.

M. Houël now decided to take drastic action. He knew that De Poincy in his wrath was quite capable of coming to Guadeloupe in person to examine Du Rivage; thus to anticipate this move he determined to proceed to France with his witness, there to encompass the ruin of his rival. To make his case stronger, he caused the planters to sign a statement protesting that they were no longer safe in their homes through fear of the savages who, because of Aubert's activities, might attack them at any time. Those who could not write—and there were several of them—signed with a mark, according to custom, having only a vague idea of the contents of the document.

Houël sailed to France taking Du Rivage with him as a material witness, and placed his accusations before the Court. Aubert who had gone there also to tell his side of the story was warned by a friendly director that he stood no chance against the powerful friends and influential family connections of M. Houël, and that it would be safer for him to return at once to the West Indies. Aubert took the hint; and it was well he did so, for Houel, unhampered by any opposition, caused him to be condemned to death, while the wretched Du Rivage, now that he was no longer needed, was sent to the galleys for life. The sentence on Aubert was, of course, never carried out, for he had reached St. Christopher in safety, where he was protected by his friend Governor de Poincy, who promoted him to a captaincy in the militia.

VII

PATROCLES DE THOISY

DE POINCY's dual position as Governor-General of the Caribbees and Governor of St. Christopher was now beginning to prove burdensome. He therefore determined to resign from the latter post in order to devote his entire time to the duties of the former. Yet in tendering his resignation, he wished to keep an indirect hold on the affairs of the island, and for this reason requested the directors to appoint as Governor his nephew, the Sieur Robert de Lonvilliers Poincy (whom we shall refer to as Lonvilliers), a boon which the company expressed itself ready to grant in recognition of his five years' service. M. de Lonvilliers was accordingly given a commission on June 3, 1644, making him Governor for a period of three years from the following January with all the powers and privileges pertaining to that office.

The feud between Houël and De Poincy now broke out openly. Alarmed at the presence of his foe in France, who would be in a position to harm him greatly with the directors, the Governor-General wrote to an influential member of Parlement, giving the gist of his case against the Governor of Guadeloupe and referring his correspondent for further information to Lonvilliers, who was then in France. He accused Houël of showing disobedience to His Majesty by assuming the reins of government without first making obeisance to him as representative of the King, and of having left his post at Guadeloupe without permission to lay his complaints against the Governor-General before the Royal Council, after handing over command of the place to a man of his own choosing.

While awaiting the result of his accusations against M. Houël, De Poincy determined to send a representative of his own choice to take charge of Guadeloupe before some one else could get control of it. Furthermore, as an excuse for this rather highhanded action he professed to fear an attack by the savages who, he said, were withdrawing to Dominica in high dudgeon because one of their chiefs had drunk himself to death in M. Houël's home, an accident for which they apparently held the Governor responsible. For this purpose he selected the Intendant, M. de Leumont, and sent him forth to assume command of the island.

M. de Leumont landed in Guadeloupe on the third of November and proceeded to take up his residence in Houël's house at Ste. Marie in Capesterre, where the acting governor, Sieur Antoine Marivet, Houël's appointee, was living. His first act was to show his commission to the incumbent who, uncertain as to what to do, demurred about recognizing it and said he would have to consult with some of his colleagues. Accordingly a conference of fifty local officials was held a few days later, the members coming from all parts of the island to be present at the formal reading of the commission. The announcement that M. de Leumont was to be their Governor aroused no enthusiasm; on the contrary, it caused embarrassment. A strong faction questioned the right of the Governor-General, despite his position as the King's representative, to interfere with the affairs of Guadeloupe to the extent of naming its governor while the official duly appointed by the company was still in office and represented during his temporary absence from the island by his lieutenant. The point was a delicate one: on one side the authority of the King in the person of De Leumont; on the other, the authority of the company represented by M. Marivet. The assembled planters withdrew from De Leumont's presence in order to discuss the matter at their ease. It took some time to reach a decision; the pros and cons of the question were thoroughly aired; but in the end the principle of loyalty to Houël's administration prevailed. This decision was not to be wondered at, inasmuch as De Leumont was a stranger, the representative of the Governor-General at St. Christopher, while the Houël's appointee was a resident of the island. In presenting the decision to De Leumont, Marivet said: "I must also tell you, Sir, on the part of the Assembly that since you have accepted this commission, there is good reason to believe that you have the interests of the General [De Poincy] more at heart than those of M. Houël, and that is why they have no confidence in you and request that you leave the island in twenty-four hours." It was rather a brusque way of treating a representative of the Governor-General, but despite all the arguments he could bring to bear, they refused to recede from their position. Yet De Leumont could not believe that he would be summarily ejected and continued to remain at his post until a committee of habitans waited upon him and ordered him to leave the island forthwith. This he did the following day, and setting sail in Captain Volléry's ship arrived at Basseterre, St. Christopher, on the fifth of December to report his failure to Governor de Poincy.

Now that they were masters of the situation, Marivet and his fellow officials fell to quarreling among themselves. It appeared that Houël, when he appointed Marivet acting governor, did not have too great a confidence in his man and secretly detailed one Mathurin Hedouin, a former baker whom he had raised to the position of *procureur fiscal* during the difficulties with M. Aubert, to keep watch over him. Another rumor maintained that Mlle de la Fayolle had also been employed as a spy to watch the two of them. At any rate, so Du Tertre says, she was practically the ruler of the island; nothing was done by Hedouin and his crowd without her approval. It was she, therefore, who had been behind the movement to keep De Leumont from being installed as governor. A report was now started, presumably at the instigation of this precious pair of spies, that a traitor was plotting to sell the island to De Poincy. This rumor gave them the opportunity to step forward as the champions of M. Houël and promise rewards to all who would aid them in conserving Guadeloupe for their master. At the same time an incident occurred which brought matters to a head. Mlle de la Fayolle had come to grips with a woman named Petit Robert, whom she accused of spreading the report that she (La Fayolle) was posing as a widow, although her husband was still alive. Wild with rage at what she considered a serious slander, Mlle de la Fayolle appealed to Marivet for redress. The Governor evidently did not take the matter very seriously and strove to appease the irate lady, a proceeding which enraged her all the more, so that she ended by carrying the matter before the judge, who sentenced Petit Robert to be placed in irons in the guardhouse. This action caused a great scandal throughout the island, for the unfortunate woman was kept a prisoner for three weeks, despite the efforts of the clergy, to whose entreaties for clemency La Fayolle made answer that "she was not one of those fools who forgive everything for the love of God."

The colonists now took up the matter and marched to the guardhouse determined to set the prisoner free, and they would have done so had not Marivet, angered at what he considered a flaunting of his authority, liberated the woman on his own initiative. One can imagine the feelings of La Fayolle on being given this public snub. She at once called a meeting of her followers and together with Hedouin planned to imprison the presumptive commander. The plot was a simple one, but was carried out with a large force of men, evidently from fear that Marivet's friends might rush to his defense. The following morning as he was leaving his house for a stroll, the unsuspecting Governor was surrounded by a force of 150 men headed by Hedouin, sword in hand, who promptly arrested him and threw him into jail. Such a highhanded action against constituted authority had its natural reaction. A group of the more level-headed colonists rose to protest and held public demonstrations, enlisting the clergy on their side and urging them to use their influence with the fatuous Hedouin. But it all had no effect; Hedouin could not be reasoned with. He dispersed the assembled colonists with blows, and threatened the priests with banishment. At last, becoming somewhat apprehensive at what they had done, Hedouin and La Fayolle sent their version of the affair to the directors. Various officers did the same and thus gave the company a true, though unfavorable, picture of conditions on the island, pointing out that everything had become demoralized due to the actions of these two rebels. Yet, despite all they did, the unfortunate Marivet was kept in prison for eight months loaded with chains until he was released by Governor Houël.

While De Poincy's authority was being rebuffed in Guadeloupe by Marivet, his reputation as an administrator was being carefully undermined in France by the machinations of Houël. To reinforce the arguments of the Governor of Guadeloupe, there was an accumulation of complaints from the planters of St. Christopher, collected and sent over by De Leumont. The La Grange affair was dusted off and placed on exhibition, the persecution of Des Marets was revived, the various acts by which the Governor-General had injured the pocketbooks of the colonists were now put forth with renewed energy, until at last the directors became convinced of his maladministration and decided to have him replaced by a more satisfactory representative. M. de Poincy, it is true, was guilty of many arbitrary acts; but it is a pity that he was not in France to defend himself.

The directors now applied to the Regent for a successor to Governor de Poincy. The Queen, who had no particular interest in the Sieur de Poincy, was not loath to appoint some one in his place, particularly as it gave her an opportunity to reward an old and trusted servant, her equerry, the Sieur de Patrocles, by selecting for the post his son, Noël Patrocles de Thoisy. The choice was not a particularly fortunate one, for M. de Thoisy, though a young man of high principles and bland disposition, was scarcely the person to cope with the hard-bitten, aggressive veteran De Poincy, who had no intention of giving up his post without a fight. What the government needed, if it wished to displace the Governor-General, was a soldier capable of giving as good as he got. But the Queen-Regent had reckoned without her man when she moved to replace De Poincy. Evidently she expected him to bow humbly to her authority and recognize the representative sent to the West Indies out of sheer respect for the law. What actually happened was something far different.

De Thoisy accepted the position, but not with any great enthusiasm. He had heard of the trouble in the West Indian colonies and had no desire to let himself in for a fight; so he took the appointment provisionally, with the understanding that M. de Poincy would resign voluntarily. By a strange coincidence on the same day that he reached this decision, De Poincy was putting his signature to a letter in which he begged the company to permit him, in case it did not see fit to continue him in office, to remain in St. Christopher as a simple planter, at least until he had accumulated enough to pay his debts. When this letter reached France, it was shown to De Thoisy who put it in his pocket and promptly accepted the commission as governor-general which was tendered him on February 20, 1645. At the same time the company appointed him Seneschal of St. Christopher, a position which gave him control of the courts of justice throughout the island. Lonvilliers, as we have said, was made Governor.

In order to soften the blow, the Regent wrote De Poincy advising him of the change that had been made and ordering him to report to her as soon as he could get a ship for France, promising at the same time to provide him with another post. De Thoisy also wrote him a courteous note of no particular importance, expressing the honor he felt at having been chosen the successor of so distinguished a man. These missives were entrusted to M. de Lonvilliers who presently left for St. Christopher to take up his duties as governor.

M. Aubert, when he returned to St. Christopher after his unsuccessful attempt to defend himself against the charges of Governor Houël, had hastened to his protector, De Poincy, and poured into his ear an account of the attacks that had been leveled at him (De Poincy) in Paris by Houël; nor was he inclined to minimize their virulence for he was himself embittered by the treatment he had received at the hands of the Governor of Guadeloupe. Evidently he knew plenty, for he had argued vehemently in favor of his friend before the directors and had heard over and over again all the accusations against him. He also brought with him a letter from Lonvilliers who, alarmed at the possibility of his uncle's deposition, which of course would mean the loss of several remunerative emoluments he enjoyed in his capacity as Governor-General, warned him that he would be brought to trial on his arrival in Paris. De Poincy, therefore, on the urgent advice of his loyal nephew, ably seconded by his henchmen, determined to remain in St. Christopher and resist De Thoisy, by force if necessary.

Having decided on this line of conduct, De Poincy proceeded to make his preparations for defense. Many of the Capuchin fathers, whom he considered responsible for much of the criticism against him, were ignominiously expelled from the island. Overtures were made to Captain Giraud, ranking military officer and a judge to boot, to whom a flattering suggestion was made of a marriage between his daughter and Lonvilliers when the latter should arrive. De Poincy also made similar advances to his friend, Sabouïlly, offering him his niece in marriage, backed up by a handsome dowry. The latter offer, however, was spurned; Sabouïlly was not to be bought, even by an alliance with the house of De Poincy. He sent back word that he was a loyal servant of the King, unwilling to take part in a rebellion against the representative of his royal master. Ordered to leave the island within twenty-four hours under penalty of death, he replied with some spirit that his head was safer there than De Poincy's. De Leumont, whose reports to the company were largely responsible for the Governor-General's undoing, was driven off the island with a few other disobliging persons and took refuge in Guadeloupe. Aubert, of course, sided with De Poincy. Having thus rid himself of his enemies and strengthened himself with his friends, the Governor-General again turned his attention to Sabouïlly who this time took a less bellicose stand and fled to Martinique. Backed by a large following, De Poincy now proceeded to extend his influence by a liberal distribution of food and wine. He furthermore spread the report abroad that De Thoisy was coming solely to levy tribute in behalf of the company by means of fresh imposts on merchandise. Sir Thomas Warner was also approached, and agreed to an arrangement by which De Poincy was to help the English governor later on should occasion arise in return for his assistance in the present crisis.

Patrocles de Thoisy was now getting ready to sail for the West Indies. While making his preparations he received an unexpected visit from M. Houël. Houël had been vainly trying to secure the governor-generalship for himself, only to find the directors extremely displeased with his management of Guadeloupe, some even favoring his dismissal from the command of that island. Blocked in this direction, he now presented himself to De Thoisy and by his insinuating manner managed to secure the new Governor's confidence, even going so far as to obtain his consent to be the bearer of his commission so that he might precede his superior to St. Christopher and prepare a reception worthy of the new Governor-General. With this document in his pocket he went to La Rochelle to embark on his journey.

It was while waiting at this port for his vessel to sail that Houël received a long letter from M. Fouquet telling of the impression made upon the directors by the startling events that had recently taken place in Guadeloupe, that is, the refusal of the planters to receive De Leumont and the subsequent imprisonment of Marivet. Evidently these troubles had reconciled the colonists to their Governor, for they were now anxious to get him back to Guadeloupe. To meet this situation, Fouquet suggested to Houël that he land at Martinique where he could learn how matters stood in Guadeloupe and dispatch there an advance guard of colonists who could send him a detailed report of conditions. After the disturbances had quieted down, he could go to the island, release Marivet, arrest Hedouin with his colleagues, and revoke their commissions, as it was the company's intention to make an example of men who without proper authority laid violent hands on a superior whose actions had obviously been for the best interests of the Governor.

When Houël's ship anchored off Grande Anse on May 29, 1645, the colonists of Guadeloupe were impatiently awaiting the arrival of their Governor who, it was firmly believed, would speedily release Marivet from prison and liberate the inhabitants from the oppressive exactions of the self-appointed rulers. Houël had not seen fit to follow M. Fouquet's rather old maidish advice of staying in Martinique until the situation had cleared. On seeing the ship, Hedouin knew that the game was up. Entering Marivet's cell, he vented his rage on the helpless prisoner by threatening to kill him, and would probably have done so had it not been for the sudden appearance of two officers who had rushed in to learn the cause of all the uproar. Houël landed at once and proceeded to his residence. His first act was to release his acting governor; but, strange to say, he showed him no particular mark of friendship, and far from punishing those who had maltreated him he called them together, blandly announcing that since it would be difficult, if not impossible, ever to find out just who was to blame, he would grant pardon to all, an action which, he said, he took out of respect for the Jubilee which the Pope had proclaimed that year. This reason was too farfetched to carry conviction, and the many who had suffered from the abuses of Hedouin and his faction were loud in their complaints at this miscarriage of justice, even voicing the opinion that the whole business of the revolt against Marivet had been carried out under Houël's secret instructions. The truth of the matter was that the Governor plainly saw that trouble was brewing throughout the French possessions and wished to have the good will of Hedouin and his powerful clique. On the second of June Houël presented De Thoisy's commission as Governor-General of the islands to be registered by the local notary, a formality he repeated at Martinique on the twenty-second of August. What happened at St. Christopher was far different and will be told later.

M. de Thoisy now made ready to sail for the West Indies to take up his new duties. Among the members of his party was Jean-François Parisot de Boisfaye, captain of his guard. M. de Boisfaye also held another far more important position which was to bring him into considerable prominence under the new administration. He had been given a commission as lieutenant to the Grand Provost of France, the Marquis de Souches, who had jurisdiction over the King's household and acted as a court of last resort in criminal matters. It was the intention of the Marquis to give his subordinate similar powers in the West Indies.

As De Thoisy was collecting his company at Havre, a rumor got about that De Poincy had no intention of surrendering his office peacefully, but was prepared to resist by force of arms any attempt to oust him. Somewhat alarmed, De Thoisy approached the directors and obtained from them permission to treat with De Poincy should the latter's objections to the proposed change in administration be based on fears for his property on the island, which fears could probably be dispelled by some friendly compromise. He also secured from them a letter to Houël ordering him to allow the new Governor-General to establish his capital in Guadeloupe pending the outcome of the situation at St. Christopher.

Arrangements having been completed, De Thoisy, accompanied by his wife and a retinue of servants suitable to his station, embarked at Havre on the thirteenth of September in the ship commanded by Captain Bontemps, carrying with him, among other things, a letter from the Queen of England recommending him to the friendship of Sir Thomas Warner. Two weeks later the vessel stopped at the island of Madeira, where De Thoisy spent a few days exchanging civilities with the local governor. On the sixteenth of November the lookout saw the towering height of Mt. Pelee, and a few hours later the ship anchored in Cul de Sac Royal. De Thoisy at once sent officers ashore to notify Governor du Parquet of his arrival; on their return they brought the ominous news, told them by MM. de Leumont and de Sabouïlly who had just arrived from St. Christopher, that De Poincy had raised the standard of revolt. The following day the new Governor-General landed to make his formal entry in the style demanded by his exalted position as representative of the King. He was met at the shore by Du Parquet with the militia, and conducted to what with considerable stretch of the imagination might be called the executive mansion, where he was entertained during the day. He held a long interview with Du Parquet at which the situation at St. Christopher was thoroughly discussed. In the end it was decided that he should proceed there, as soon as he had visited Guadeloupe, and force the issue. He returned to his ship that night with Sabouïlly to assist him in his plans, and at once gave orders to set sail. Two days later he anchored off Basseterre, Guadeloupe, where several officials boarded the vessel to pay their respects to the new commander, explaining that M. Houël was absent at the time, but would be back the following day to receive his superior in the proper manner. Meanwhile, would the Governor-General come ashore? M. de Thoisy would and did. Preceded by his guards he landed and went to the company's building, where he was royally entertained. The next day Houël arrived and the ceremony was repeated, this time the Governor leading the militia in person to welcome the new incumbent at the landing. After the customary exchange of courtesies a council was called to discuss the situation at St. Christopher. The conversations had barely begun when Sabouïlly developed a grievance. He had been told, so he claimed, that the company had promised to give the governorship of St. Christopher to one of his protégés, a M. de Guinant, and he now refused to take part in any further deliberations until the matter was settled to his satisfaction. Evidently De Thoisy had been given power to depose Lonvilliers in case of rebellion, and now that De Poincy and his faction were preparing to resist him, Sabouïlly saw fit to claim the post for his man. De Thoisy very tactfully managed to overcome his resentment and agreed to carry out the company's promise in case De Poincy and his nephew offered any resistance.

On the twenty-second day of November, M. de Thoisy sailed for St. Christopher with MM. de Sabouïlly and de Leumont as his chief advisers, leaving behind his wife and daughter in the care of Governor Houël, and three days later anchored off Basseterre. The time had now come for a shown-down between the legitimate representative of the King and the rebellious Governor-General. As De Thoisy was determined to act with the utmost caution and a strict regard for proper legal procedure in his attempt to enter his capital, for it would not do for him with the law on his side to put himself in the wrong, he opened the proceedings by sending ashore M. de Boisfaye to look over the situation. This officer, on approaching the landing place, saw on the dock ready to receive him M. Aubert with a company of militia drawn up behind him. If any thoughts still lingered in De Boisfaye's mind as to De Poincy's intention to submit peacefully, they were dispelled immediately when Aubert bluntly told him that the men of St. Christopher wanted no other representative of the King. Nevertheless, Aubert offered to call a meeting of the planters to discuss the matter and promised to be ready with a final answer on the morrow. The following day saw De Boisfaye again at the landing place where he was met by Aubert. As word of his arrival had spread through the settlement, a large crowd was gathered on the shore to hear what he had to say. The captain saw his chance, and quickly drew forth the King's commission to read to the multitude which as quickly pressed forward to hear him. Aubert, fearing the effect a letter written by the Sovereign might have on the people, drove them back, at the same time ordering De Boisfaye to return to his ship. There was nothing the captain could do in the face of such opposition but to comply, so with a parting warning to Aubert that he was guilty of lese majesty he stepped into his boat and returned to report to De Thoisy.

De Thoisy now held a council of war. After much wrangling it was decided to sail to Pointe de Sable where Lonvilliers resided, in the hope that the nephew might prove more amenable to reason than the uncle. Orders were given to that effect, and by two o'clock in the afternoon the disconsolate Governor-General was gliding swiftly along the coast. On approaching the English section of the island, the idea occurred to him to stop and deliver to Sir Thomas Warner the letter from the Queen of England. It also occurred to him that with this imposing introduction he might come to some arrangement with the English governor, a sort of treaty, perhaps, in case of a serious clash with De Poincy. The idea was not a bad one, but unfortunately it had also occurred to De Poincy who had dispatched La Vernade as his ambassador extraordinary to secure the friendship of the English commander. Thus when the Sieur de Guinant came ashore with the letter, thinking that here, certainly, he would meet with a friendly reception, he was stopped at once by an officer and a file of men who, after questioning him, grudgingly gave him permission to land. But scarcely had he stepped ashore when another officer rode up and roughly asked the reason for his visit. Briefly explaining his mission, the Frenchman requested to be led to Governor Warner; but to his amazement he was coldly informed that the English commander acknowledged no representative of the King of France save M. de Poincy. The reason for this strange attitude was quickly revealed to him when the officer after a hurried consultation with La Vernade, who was holding himself in the background among the crowd of curious persons gathered from nowhere in particular, stepped forward and informed De Guinant that the colonists would have nothing to do with his master. He ordered De Guinant to leave the island at once, an order which he emphasized by firing a volley at the retreating Frenchmen as they rowed hastily back to their ship. Thus repulsed, there was nothing for De Thoisy to do but to sail back to Guadeloupe since he did not have an army sufficiently strong to attack so large a body of colonists; and this he did, arriving there on the twenty-eighth.

While De Thoisy and Houël were cudgelling their brains as to the proper way to compel the recalcitrant De Poincy to toe the mark, there arrived in Guadeloupe two gentlemen, cousins of Du Parquet, MM. Jacques de Saint-Aubin and Jean Le Comte, who had recently fled to Martinique to escape the injustices they had suffered at the hands of De Poincy while residing at St. Christopher. M. du Parquet accompanied them. They were eager for revenge, and their eagerness took form in a scheme to establish De Thoisy in his rightful position as commander of the archipelago. They arrived just in time, for on landing they found Houël, De Leumont, and Sabouïlly violently discussing ways and means for attaining this desired end. Among the schemes suggested and seriously considered was one to land four hundred men at Basseterre who would entrench themselves and be in readiness when, and if, the colonists should rise against their governor. But the plan which Du Parquet and his kinsmen brought to the conference did not take into consideration the possible uprising of De Poincy's colonists; it was less optimistic and more practical; it was nothing more or less than the kidnapping of De Poincy's nephews, MM. de Lonvilliers and de Treval, who at that time were in command of Pointe de Sable. They furthermore assured De Thoisy that nearly every one in Capesterre would side with them once they had carried off their coup. The boldness of the idea caused Houël's advisers to gasp, but in the end their confidence in Du Parquet overcame their fears and they gave their consent to the audacious plot. On January 17, 1646, De Thoisy issued a commission to the Governor of Martinique ordering all officers and inhabitants of St. Christopher to submit to his orders and appointing him to the post of Governor of the island, made vacant by the rebellious conduct of Lonvilliers. The appointment was, of course, a temporary one, for the position had been promised to M. de Guinant. Armed with this instrument, Du Parquet turned over the government of Martinique to Jerome du Sarrat, Sieur de la Pierrière, and went ahead with his preparations. Houël showed his good will by furnishing a ship with a suitable supply of provisions, while Sabouilly joined the expedition with enthusiasm.

The start was made at once. The day after he had given the commission to Du Parquet, De Thoisy boarded his flagship and led the undertaking to Nevis, where he proposed to remain while Du Parquet and his cousins proceeded to Pointe de Sable. On reaching the Pointe, the adventurers seem to have met with a more cordial reception than that accorded to De Guinant at Basseterre, possibly because De Poincy's influence was not so strong in the northern part of the island. At any rate, they encountered no opposition on landing and marched to the guardhouse, where, being a stickler for legal technicalities, Du Parquet read the King's commission to those assembled. This he did with such telling effect that he was greeted with cries of "Long live the King and M. de Thoisy." Pleased with this promising beginning, the French commander proceeded to rouse the countryside. He dispatched messages to the leading colonists, particularly to two captains, Haussier de la Fontaine and Antoine Camot, urging them to gather at the Pointe and pledge their loyalty to the King. During the night, some three or four hundred men assembled ready to do Du Parquet's bidding. While this was going on, Du Parquet, accompanied by his cousins, went in person to Lonvilliers's dwelling, broke in the door, bound the Governor and Treval, loaded them on the backs of their own slaves, and had them carried down to the boat. This done, he left them and returned to the guardhouse to see how matters were progressing.

The news of Du Parquet's landing had spread like wildfire over the island; and by the next day De Poincy had succeeded in raising an army of two thousand English colonists whose plantations lay adjacent to Capesterre, and who were obliged to come to his aid in just such an emergency as a result of the treaty he had signed with Governor Warner. De Poincy advanced at once on the guardhouse, where the forces of Du Parquet were collected, and opened fire. In the skirmish which took place, some sixty Frenchmen were killed and the rest surrendered, seeing themselves hopelessly outnumbered, while Du Parquet escaped into the forest. La Fontaine and Camot were likewise put to rout and sought refuge with some three hundred followers on the woody slopes of Mt. Misery.

For three days and three nights Du Parquet wandered helplessly through the dense undergrowth, living as best he could on the wild fruit he chanced to find and vainly trying to join the band commanded by La Fontaine. At last rendered desperate by privation, he decided to make his way to the house of the Capuchin fathers, the only place on the island where he could hope to find refuge. Fearing that soldiers might be on guard there in anticipation of such a move, he waited till midnight and then made his way cautiously to the window of Father Gardien and tapped on it gently. His knock was heard. Father Gardien came to the door and quickly spirited his visitor inside. Here where they could talk freely, the priest told his guest that his arrival at the convent had been expected by De Poincy who had stationed soldiers around the main building ready to seize him. With many expressions of regret, Father Gardien informed him that it would be impossible to grant him asylum. He suggested that the safest course of action would be to appeal to Governor Warner who might be persuaded to shield him for the time being and facilitate his escape from the island. In an evil moment Du Parquet accepted the advice—though we must absolve the priest of any suspicion of bad faith—and went to Sir Thomas's headquarters where he was received with all marks of good will. But while he was entertaining his unbidden guest, Sir Thomas sent word to De Poincy who hurried up to Fort Charles, surrounded the Governor's house, burst in upon the unsuspecting Frenchman, and placed him under arrest. Enraged at this treatment, Du Parquet seized a knife and lunged at the treacherous Governor, who quickly fled from the room, leaving his victim in the hands of De Poincy's men. Du Parquet was promptly thrown into prison.

Meanwhile, Saint-Aubin and Le Comte had taken their prisoners to Nevis where they turned them over to the Governor-General. They also brought with them a letter from Du Parquet, written in the first flush of success, urging his superior to send him reinforcements to Pointe de Sable, for he felt confident he could easily get control of the northern part of the island. De Thoisy, ignorant of the true state of affairs, naturally saw fit to comply with this request and wrote Houël, ordering him to send a strong body of men under MM. de Sabouïlly and de Leumont. Houël obeyed with alacrity. He gathered a force of about three hundred men from the various divisions of Guadeloupe, rushed them down to the waiting fleet, which consisted of two ships commanded by Captains Volléry and Bontemps, and personally led the little army to Nevis. M. de Leumont excused himself from accompanying the expedition on the grounds of age and illness. At Nevis, Houël learned from an English vessel anchored in the roadstead that De Thoisy had gone to Pointe de Sable. On reaching the Pointe, he was met in the offing by a messenger sent by the Governor-General to tell him of Du Parquet's capture. Astounded at the news Houël hastened on board the flagship to consult with De Thoisy; and after careful consideration of the situation urged him to return to Nevis where he would presently join him to discuss further plans.

M. de Thoisy agreed to this in principle; but before leaving he decided to make at least an effort to secure the release of Du

Parquet. Asserting his authority as governor-general, he requested De Poincy, through a lieutenant, to surrender his prisoner at once, an order which never reached its destination, as the messenger was not even allowed to land. Blocked in this direction he then induced Lonvilliers and Treval to send La Vernade an urgent request for a peaceful settlement of the matter; but the only response was a sardonic reply that Du Parquet was being treated with as much consideration as his own prisoners. Thus rebuked, he bethought himself of a plan to attack the rebellious governor in his stronghold at Basseterre. Accordingly a reconnoitering party was sent out to survey the possibilities of landing in hostile territory; although they succeeded in getting ashore, they found the place so well protected by troops that it would have been impossible to make any impression on the town with the small force at the Governor-General's disposal. De Thoisy now again had recourse to the mediation of his prisoners, for he regarded them, not as men he had kidnapped, but as disobedient colonists lawfully placed in custody for revolting against his legitimate authority, while he considered Du Parquet as a man illegally detained. This time he was more successful, for De Poincy relented to the extent of allowing his prisoner to receive letters and a visit or two from the Governor's lieutenant. De Thoisy was obliged to be satisfied with this concession for the time being; realizing that he could make no further progress, he returned to Nevis where he met Governor Houël with whom he joined forces and sailed back disconsolately to Guadeloupe, arriving there on February 3, 1646.

While De Poincy had won the contest so far, all was not going well with him at St. Christopher. He had made enemies, as an arbitrary man will, and now that he had placed himself in the wrong by sowing the seeds of rebellion against his lawful sovereign, he could retain his position only by acts of repression directed against those who had stood loyally by the King. The Capuchin fathers were his first victims. Shortly after the capture of Du Parquet these worthy men were placed under arrest. From his prison Father Hyacinthe spoke out boldly against the usurper, reproaching him for his violence, and pointing out the evils of the monopoly he had created in business. What was even more offensive, he reminded the people that De Poincy had been lawfully deposed and that those who abetted him against De Thoisy were guilty of lese majesty. After three days' imprisonment the entire order was driven from the island and took refuge in Guadeloupe where they were charitably received.

Having rid themselves of the clergy, De Poincy and his gang now began to organize a reign of terror against their foes. Threats were made—but happily not carried out, perhaps it was not intended that they should be—to drive into the sea the wives and children of those who had fled into the woods after the unsuccessful defense of the guardhouse at Pointe de Sable. A price of 10,000 pounds of tobacco was placed on the heads of La Fontaine and Camot. A wretched boy, the servant of M. Camot, believed to be in communication with his master, was barbarously tortured to make him disclose his hiding place, but died without uttering a word. All those suspected of being in sympathy with De Thoisy were maltreated and driven from the island. The goods belonging to Camot's men were confiscated and given over to pillage. The men themselves were hunted like wild beasts by negroes and dogs, until despairing of ever again enjoying peace on the island, many put to sea on hastily constructed rafts and made their way as best they could to St. Martin and St. Eustatius. The rest surrendered to De Poincy who spared their lives on condition that they would leave St. Christopher at once.

However, inasmuch as La Fontaine and Camot, the leaders of the anti-De Poincy party, were still at large with a handful of followers, every effort was made to apprehend them. Knowing them to be running short of provisions, one of De Poincy's henchmen hit upon the idea of setting a trap baited with a supply of food which would surely attract the half-starved men. He placed a keg of meat beside a path leading from the forest with a man hidden in the shrubbery beside it. As one of La Fontaine's men approached, this fellow killed him with a blow, cut off his head, and carried it to M. de Poincy who paid him a reward of five hundred pounds of tobacco. Efforts were also made by the usual methods to force confessions regarding La Fontaine's whereabouts from his slaves, for they had been discovered carrying provisions to him; but repeated floggings and threats of death by fire could not shake the fidelity of these poor men, and De Poincy was obliged in the end to release them after clipping off their toes to prevent them from rejoining their master.

La Fontaine and Camot were by this time nearly exhausted. For days they had remained hidden in the branches of a huge banyan tree, safe from dogs and treacherous negroes, until the Sieur Camot became seriously ill. In desperation they decided to make their way to the seashore where La Fontaine could swim out to the nearest vessel and implore assistance. Fortunately a Dutch ship commanded by one Captain Breda, a native of Flushing and an intimate friend of La Fontaine happened to be in the roadstead. When he saw this craft in the offing, the Frenchman plunged into the water and struck out boldly. After a long, exhausting swim, he reached the vessel's side. As he clambered aboard Breda gazed at him with tears in his eyes, for the wretched man was a frightful sight, his half-naked body was shrunken from exposure and lack of nourishment, while his matted hair and feverish eyes gave him the appearance of a savage rather than a civilized man.

As soon as La Fontaine had rested enough to tell his story, he made his request for help. The captain proved sympathetic. "My dear M. La Fontaine," he said, "it will be necessary then that I risk for the love of you my life, my property which is now in St. Christopher, as well as that of my merchant friends, for M. de Poincy has forbidden all ship captains, whether Frenchmen or foreigners, from having any dealings with you on pain of death, and your head as well as that of the Sieur Camot has a price on it of 10,000 pounds of tobacco. If my men who are now sleeping below deck should awake, we are both lost; so hide yourself in my cabin so that no one can see you and tomorrow I shall weigh anchor, abandon all I have in the island and take you to Holland." La Fontaine was deeply touched by this generous offer, but he was forced to explain that his fortunes were linked inseparably with those of his companion and rather than desert him he would return to land and share his fate. Captain Breda was not proof against such a demonstration of loyalty. He leaped into his gig and quickly rowed La Fontaine to the spot where he had left Camot. As soon as he had the two Frenchmen safely on board and locked in his cabin, Breda informed his crew that he had pressing business which compelled him to leave at once for St. Eustatius. Those on shore were promptly recalled, and in a few hours he was under way, leaving his property to the mercy of M. de Poincy who, be it said to his credit, made no attempt to seize it. When La Fontaine and Camot eventually reached France, they presented themselves before the Queen Mother and gave her a complete account of the rebellion at St. Christopher. At the request of Mme de Patrocles, mother of M. de Thoisy, Her Majesty gave them a present of 2,000 francs to tide them over until the affairs of the island could be straightened out.

When De Thoisy returned to Guadeloupe, he found Governor Houël in a somewhat unfriendly mood. The representative of the company was beginning to realize that the continued presence of the King's Governor-General on the island would place him (Houël) in a subordinate position in his own bailiwick. He had been willing to tolerate De Thoisy's company for a while and even to assist him, for he considered his stay but a temporary one, lasting only until matters could be straightened out at St. Christopher, the real capital of the French West Indies. But now that De Poincy had proved himself so firmly entrenched, it seemed as though De Thoisy would make his headquarters in Guadeloupe for some time to come. Furthermore, his friendly disposition was bound to make him popular with the colonists, many of whom nourished grudges against the Governor. M. de Thoisy sensed all this—in fact Houël's jealousy was quite apparent—and did his best to smooth things over by ignoring many of the touchy Governor's acts of insubordination; but, as often happens in such cases, this method only served to aggravate the situation, and from now on we find M. Houël looking for an opportunity to rid himself of his unwelcome superior.

M. Houël started to make trouble immediately after De Thoisy's return. His first overt act took place in the Governor-General's residence, and was a piece of insolence meriting prompt disciplinary action. Marivet, who now held the position of judge, had come before De Thoisy to present a case. Something in his conduct of the business annoyed Houël who was constantly on the lookout for an occasion to make trouble; he hurled himself on the unfortunate Marivet and gave him a sound thrashing in the Governor-General's presence. De Thoisy chose to overlook the affront to his dignity, even going so far as to put the blame for the fracas on Marivet. Emboldened by this pusillanimous attitude, Houël pushed the matter farther and demanded the immediate expulsion of Marivet from the island.

The affair naturally caused much comment. M. de Guinant, who had no patience with Houël, announced boldly that if he had been in the Governor-General's place he would have known how to make himself respected. Houël, on hearing this, showed his displeasure by taking advantage of every occasion to speak out against De Guinant. To make matters worse, De Guinant wrote a friend asking him if he could give any information about the remarks Houël had made, and the recipient of this communication had the bad taste to show it to Houël. The Governor, enraged at what he considered a slight on his authority, rushed at once to De Thoisy and demanded the immediate expulsion of the writer, saying he did not feel safe with such a dangerous character loose on the island. The Governor-General, with a sigh of disgust, sent for De Guinant and questioned him as to his intentions. As these proved to be of the most harmless kind, he offered to guarantee personally the good behavior of the villain. The entire incident shows that M. de Thoisy, whatever his good qualities may have been, was hardly the man for the place. Under peaceful conditions he might have made a good administrator, but in times of stress he was utterly unable to control the situation. He was no match for Houël, still less for De Poincy; he tried to placate, when he should have used force.

Yet despite his policy of appeasement De Thoisy still failed to satisfy the Governor of Guadeloupe. At last realizing that this state of affairs would end in the ruin of the colony, he wrote MM. de Sabouïlly and de Leumont setting forth at length the unreasonable actions of Houël, and requested them to formulate some plan to settle these dissensions. These two loyal assistants were willing to help, but the stubborn Houël refused to meet them and discuss matters. The Governor-General then turned to Captain Bontemps who managed, much to everybody's surprise, to arrange a meeting on board his ship. Houël, strange to say, had become unexpectedly amenable, from ulterior motives, it may be surmised, feeling confident that inasmuch as M. de Thoisy was so anxious to meet him, he could turn the interview to his advantage and secure a concession he had long desired. De Thoisy had brought with him from France a decree signed by the King on August 1, 1645, which purported to rectify an alleged defect in the edict of 1642 by which Louis XIII had confirmed and enlarged the charter of the company. By this document His Majesty had given the company supreme jurisdiction over the archipelago; but, as the directors pointed out, in order to fulfill the charter's provisions, it was necessary to establish a judicial system in the islands which would enable litigants in both civil and criminal actions to obtain final decisions on the spot instead of being obliged to carry their cases to France, an expensive proceeding which many could not afford. The decree of 1645 aimed at remedying this evil. It provided that the Governor of each island, assisted by a council of his own choosing, should be the supreme judge within his own jurisdiction. It was Houël's purpose, therefore, in agreeing to a reconciliation, to secure from De Thoisy a promulgation of this edict.

M. de Thoisy, as usual, favored conciliation. As guests of Captain Bontemps, the two men met and embraced with true Gallic fervor; all was forgotten—at least by De Thoisy. They dined together and parted with assurances of everlasting friendship. Two days later on April 28, 1646, the Governor-General, despite the earnest advice of his friends, published the King's proclamation making the Governor of Gaudeloupe also its chief justice. Defeated by De Poincy, De Thoisy was now outwitted by Houël.

～ VIII ～

GOVERNOR-GENERAL VERSUS GOVERNORS

ONCE MASTER of the situation, Houël proceeded to comply with the terms of the edict by selecting the required number of men for his council. From among the leading inhabitants of the island he chose eight, well known for their hostility to the Governor-General, and added to them MM. de Sabouïlly and de Leumont who were then residing in Guadeloupe, a clever trick calculated to wean them away from their allegiance to their rightful master. Houël did not have long to wait before putting his council into action.

On returning to Guadeloupe, De Thoisy had instituted proceedings against Lonvilliers and Treval who, as relatives and adherents of De Poincy, were naturally implicated in his rebellion and therefore guilty of lese majesty. The prosecution of these young gentlemen was, as a matter of course, turned over to M. de Boisfaye who had been appointed to deal with just such cases. At the same time another case arose which came under the jurisdiction of this prosecutor. Captain Bontemps had just returned from Martinique bringing the startling news that M. de Poincy, angered at the kidnapping of his nephews, had determined to carry the war into the enemy's territory. For this purpose he had persuaded Boutain, the commander of a vessel from La Rochelle, to act as the bearer of a letter to one Auvray de Lesperance, an old friend of D'Esnambuc then living at Martinique, urging him to organize an uprising against De Thoisy's authority. Bontemps had obtained a copy of this letter, which appears to have been a sort of seditious manifesto, and on reading it had strongly urged La Pierrière, Du Parquet's righthand man, to place the captain under arrest. His advice was promptly taken, and the representative of M. de Poincy was thrown into jail, there to await the pleasure of the Governor-General. The evidence against Boutain was too strong to admit of any hesitation, and De Thoisy with the advice of Houël sent word to La Pierrière ordering him to bring his prisoner to trial at once and to seize his vessel with its entire cargo.

At this point De Leumont appeared in the role of troublemaker, stirring up difficulties for the benefit of Houël while appearing to act in the interests of De Thoisy. No sooner had the Governor-General given orders for the trial of Boutain than De Leumont wrote him a letter strongly urging him to send Boisfaye to Martinique to conduct the case, as the charge, one of lese majesty, would bring it under his jurisdiction. M. de Thoisy in his usual naïve way accepted the suggestion. He did not see that such an action would be taken as a slight by La Pierrière and the judges at Martinique, who would feel themselves snubbed at having the case taken from them and placed in the hands of a stranger. It did not, however, take Houël long to see the point; like a wise man he immediately seized the opportunity to make himself solid with the authorities at Martinique. Summoning his council, he secured from it an order forbidding Boisfaye from exercising his powers and questioning the validity of his appointment.

It was a bold move thus to defy regularly constituted authority, but Houël was ready and eager to go even further. From his residence in Capesterre he encouraged the habitans of that section to protest against paying yearly dues to the company, and surreptitiously caused a petition to be circulated among them asking for a remission of these obligations as well as those due him as governor. When the signed petition was formally presented to him, he passed it on to De Leumont, as the dues collected by the company came under the jurisdiction of the Intendant and he alone could decide what could be done about them. Regarding the taxes due the Governor of Guadeloupe, Houël promised to take the same attitude towards them as De Leumont did toward those of the company. Thus without directly committing himself to any definite policy, he appeared before the people as one who would be as liberal as the directors, and the entire responsibility for the outcome of the affair was placed squarely on the shoulders of the unfortunate Intendant.

The situation now took on a more alarming aspect, one that caused De Thoisy to fear for his own personal safety. News reached him that Captain La Bazilière, a member of Houël's council, had been seen going mysteriously from house to house during the night, preceded by a torchbearer, asking the inhabitants which governor they would side with in case of a break between them. When asked for an explanation of his seditious activities, the captain put off De Thoisy with evasive answers, refusing to disclose the identity of the person under whose orders he was acting. It was, of course, easy enough to guess who was behind it all. Convinced that he must do something to protect himself, De Thoisy had the fortifications of his house at Basseterre strengthened and a palisade thrown around it, for he feared not only the colonists of Guadeloupe but a possible attack from St. Christopher, as he had received word that De Poincy was also on the move.

But there was more to be feared than actual violence. The unlucky Governor-General could scarcely close his eyes to Houël's efforts to discredit him and drive him to commit some overt act that might lead to his expulsion from the island. To meet this emergency he appointed a council of war composed of the principal officers of the militia to offset the council recently named by the Governor. The ordinance announcing this plan was made the occasion for clearing up a number of controversial points, particularly those connected with the status of M. de Boisfaye. On August 1, 1646, the Governor-General read his proclamation. Like most of De Thoisy's pronouncements, it began in a conciliatory tone. For the benefit of doubting Thomases who might question his position, he announced that he had caused his commission from the King to be read a second time at Basseterre, and proposed to have the same done also at Capesterre so that those who heard might believe. He then proceeded to explain carefully the position of Boisfaye whose judicial activities had given rise to so much criticism. This official had been sent over, he assured his hearers, not to supplant the existing judicial system, but solely to try those accused of lese majesty, particularly De Poincy, as there was no judge in the archipelago armed with the proper powers to try such a crime. Whether these statements convinced anyone or not, it is impossible to say, but they probably eased De Thoisy's conscience and fortified him in his determination to hold his ground.

Since the Governor-General evidently meant business, Houël decided it would be best for him also to elucidate his position in regard to Boisfaye; and this he proceeded to do. The appointment of a provost's lieutenant, he pointed out, was contrary to the King's edict of March, 1642, which gave comprehensive powers to the company which would be seriously marred by the presence of a judge responsible to the King alone. It was not a convincing argument, perhaps, in view of what De Thoisy had said, for even if the appointment violated the edict it was for the King and the company to settle the question, not for M. Houël; but it was the best argument he could offer. As for a second reading of the Governor-General's commission at Capesterre, Houël thought wise to humor his superior; but he took care to mar the force of it by reading a letter the directors had written, placing a time limit on De Thoisy's stay in Guadeloupe, deliberately omitting a subsequent communication dated August 26, 1645, which granted him permission to remain on the island as long as he saw fit.

M. de Thoisy, having carefully explained the position of Boisfaye, proceeded to grant him the necessary protection for the discharge of his duties. He issued an order forbidding the members of Houël's council from placing any stumbling block in his way while engaged in prosecuting De Poincy and his adherents. This order was endorsed by Boisfaye himself, who assured the Governor's council that he had no intention of using his power for any other purpose than prosecuting those accused of lese majesty.

The following week De Thoisy, always anxious to conciliate and smooth things over, decided to open negotiations with the Governor. He sent De Leumont as emissary with a memorandum stating his position and emphasizing the points he deemed essential to maintain it. This communication embodied his minimum claims, the ones he would insist on in any agreement he might make with his adversary. First, he said, Boisfaye must be permitted to try De Poincy and his followers; secondly, the Governor-General should have the right to preside over Houël's council during his stay in Gaudeloupe (though De Leumont was instructed to say that he would not use it); thirdly, the orders given Houël by the company instructing him to obey De Thoisy should be read in public to the planters.

So reasonable were these demands that Houël at first could think of no valid reason for rejecting them, and wrote at once tendering his submission; but a few days later he evidently had a change of heart for he formally withdrew his acceptance of the terms. In fact, on thinking the matter over, he decided it would be best for his peace of mind to rid himself entirely of his superior. He felt himself the stronger of the two, as indeed he was, and would brook no higher authority than his own on the island of Guadeloupe. Thus he became a co-belligerent with De Poincy against the Governor-General, if not an actual ally. But before describing the occurrences that led to the final outcome of the struggle, we shall turn for a few moments to record the events in Martinique.

The seditious manifesto brought to Martinique by Captain Boutain quickly spread its virus through the island, and would have caused a serious revolt had it not been for the prompt and determined action of a man named Le Fort, who knew instinctively how to handle a desperate situation. The purpose of the manifesto was to rouse the colonists against the company and prevent them from accepting De Thoisy in place of the former Governor-General. This was done by describing the dues paid the company as an intolerable burden, and representing De Thoisy as a tool of the directors sent out to impose new and vexatious taxes on the already overburdened settlers. The propaganda was successful. On the twenty-sixth of June a tumult broke out in the Quartier du Prêcheur where a number of habitans massed about the residence of La Pierrière and raised an uproar, crying out they would make no more payments to the company. The sudden arrival of two men from Guadeloupe, agents of De Poincy, it was said, with news that the colonists there had refused further payments and consequently had been exempted from the customary dues, capped the climax. The entire island rose in rebellion. The more radical element, led by a man calling himself General Beaufort, a former glovemaker from Paris, decided to make a thorough job of it and refused to recognize even Du Parquet as their commander, accusing him of working solely for the company's interest. The more conservative rebels contented themselves merely with repudiating the authority of De Thoisy.

Faced by a divided citizenry, La Pierrière tried to preserve a neutral position between the two factions, though he was believed to favor that of General Beaufort. The leader of the moderates, those who wished to retain Du Parquet, was Mlle Saint-André. This lady, whose maiden name was Marie Bonnard, had recently secured an annulment of her marriage, and had wedded Du Parquet on November 21, 1645, though for various reasons the affair was kept a secret. True to the interests of her absent husband, she sided with the conservatives; but more anxious for his return than for anything else, she constantly besieged the leaders of both parties, urging them to offer the nephews of M. de Poincy in exchange for their rightful governor. Disorders now broke out. The mutineers of the Quartier du Prêcheur attacked the stores, both those of the company and those of the merchants, and stole all they could find in them. In one instance they attempted to kill the factor in charge, a brave fellow who had the courage to put up a show of resistance against the marauders. General Beaufort at the head of his rabble meanwhile set fire to the house of Lesperance, one of those who had been foremost in the rebellion and was De Poincy's righthand man.

There happened to be in the colony at this time, a man called the Sieur Le Fort, whose real name was Yves Le Cercueil, a friend and partisan of Du Parquet. Becoming alarmed at La Pierrière's irresolution, he went to Mlle Saint-André with a plan to eliminate the leaders of the radical faction and also La Pierrière, if he did not declare himself at once against these mutineers. The lady does not appear to have been troubled with any scruples as to the means if only the end could be attained (which is not particularly surprising since Father du Tertre is not critical) and readily gave her consent to the scheme. On the fifth of August Le Fort proceeded to La Pierrière's house with a small group of seventeen picked men, and boldly asked him if he did not have a commission from Du Parquet as commander of the island, and, if so, what steps he proposed to take to rid the island of a gang of rascals who had cast off the authority of their masters and set up their own officers and tribunals. The Governor replied in a somewhat De Thoisian manner saying he felt unable to cope with the superior numbers of the rebels, nor could he think of a better course of action than to let them do as they pleased. This was too much for Le Fort.

If you will give me your word to do as I say [he said] I will give you mine to rid you of this rabble. Tomorrow they are coming to get you to sign their proclamation. Think up some excuse for a delay, but yield to their request and sign anything they present. After this leave the house, call for a glass of wine to drink the health of the King, keeping your musket pointed upward. Then lower it quickly and fire point blank at General Beaufort's head. Don't worry, I shall have enough men to rid you of the others.

It was a vile plot, but La Pierrière agreed to it. After all these men were rebels, and no one could think of a better scheme. The following day when General Beaufort appeared with his staff of twenty men at Fort St. Pierre, all armed in true buccaneer fashion with muskets in their hands and pistols at their belts, La Pierrière was ready to receive them while Le Fort and his men stood in the background ready for action. General Beaufort stepped forward and presented the Governor with his ultimatum, a rather lengthy document of twenty articles, the gist of which was that Du Parquet, when he returned to the island, should break off all relations with the company and govern in the name of the King alone, while local affairs would be arranged under a system of self-government. When the document was presented to him for his signature, La Pierrière demurred a little according to plan, then signed a long-drawn-out hypocritical statement expressing his approval of the articles, even going so far as to declare the habitans who had opposed the radical party guilty of lese majesty and threatening them with dire punishment if they did not sign the declaration within eight days. His duty done he stepped from the house to let Le Fort do his part. Wine was brought out and all filled their glasses. Then as the Governor raised his glass to drink the King's health he lowered his musket and discharged it squarely at Beaufort. Instantly Le Fort's men opened fire, each having selected his man, and thirteen fell at the volley. The rest, seeing themselves hopelessly outnumbered, fled precipitately, closely followed by their attackers who quickly caught up with them and dispatched them without mercy.

All this was bad enough, but La Pierrière proved himself a precious sort of scoundrel by launching an attack on certain members of the rebel faction who had taken no part in the insurrection since Beaufort had issued his manifesto. Going to the Quartier du Prêcheur, he deliberately killed four or five men in cold blood, including a mere lad of fifteen years of age guilty of having carried some letters for General Beaufort. This done, he sent a report of the affair to M. de Thoisy expressing considerable pride in having rid the island of seditious spirits, but showing no compunction about the methods used to accomplish this result. To prevent any action ever being taken against him for what might be considered an unwarranted usurpation of authority, he nevertheless requested from the Governor-General a formal pardon for himself and his men. At the same time Mlle Saint-André seized the occasion to send a representative to press the scheme always uppermost in her mind, namely, the return of M. du Parquet. Though pleased at the loyalty of the La Pierrière-Saint-André faction, the request of Mlle Saint-André embarrassed the Governor-General, for he felt that a mere exchange of prisoners would leave matters between him and the rebellious De Poincy just as they were, and he could not afford to surrender the only hold he had over his adversary unless the latter was ready to make complete submission. Thus with a feeling of deep regret, he explained his position in the matter to the loyal colonists at Martinique; but he sent the pardon without any hesitation. This pardon was no mere brief word of approval; it was a long-winded document reciting the trials of Martinique, caught in a wildly raging conflagration, until La Pierrière gallantly came to the rescue. De Thoisy gave his unqualified approval to La Pierrière's acts, so much so as to appoint him Governor of Martinique until De Parquet should return. As good measure, he also granted an amnesty to all who had taken part in the revolt in the hope that the warring factions would settle down in harmony. This edict was taken to Martinique by M. de Boisfaye who read it on the second of September to the militia drawn up in formal array to hear it.

The suppression of the revolt and the blessing sent La Pierrière had greatly strengthened De Thoisy's position as leader of the anti-De Poincy group, as it bound Martinique for a time more closely to him, though the tie was one that snapped at the first test. Such a situation not being at all to his liking Houël redoubled his activities to drive the Governor-General from Guadeloupe. He called various meetings to foster dissatisfaction and ordered members of his party to arm themselves. De Thoisy, when he heard of this, took the opposite course, as might be supposed, forbidding his followers to bear arms, and even reducing the number of his guard. But setting a good example was not enough for De Thoisy; he must follow it up by showing the rebellious Governor the error of his ways. He wrote a letter, as he had done many times before, gently rebuking him, but announcing this time that he would presently call in person to deliver his sermon. And so the representative of the King prepared to undertake the wearisome journey to Fort Ste. Marie in Capesterre to plead with his recalcitrant subordinate. Fortunately, as he was about to start on this humiliating expedition, Judge Le Normand arrived from Houël's settlement, and hurrying to De Thoisy told him of the ambush placed along the road by the Governor for the purpose of assassinating him. M. de Thoisy, however, was not a man to be easily frightened. He may, or he may not, have considered the judge an agent of Houël sent to scare him; but he rose at once, vowing he would leave for Capesterre instantly with only two guards and a companion, and furthermore, to show how little he feared the machinations of his enemy, he sent word to Houël telling him what road he would take.

Warned of the Governor-General's impending journey, Houël sought to ward off the unwelcome visitor by writing him a letter in which he began by posing as the one persecuted and ended up with threats. Several persons had told him, so he said, that M. de Thoisy had boasted that it would not be long before he (Houël) would be forced to leave the island. These reports he had the magnanimity to disbelieve, "but," he went on, the terms of your ordinance of the first of August of this year state that those who form the council of this island over which I preside, have struck a blow against the royal authority which obliges you to take action against them with all your power. This compels me to inform you with all the respect I owe you that I cannot guarantee the safety of your person until the King has rendered his decision in the matter, and that is why I humbly beg you not to come here.

When De Thoisy received this letter, which was scarcely more than a thinly veiled threat, he was about halfway to Ste. Marie. He saw the folly of continuing the journey with only the meager protection of two guardsmen so he contented himself with dispatching his companion, M. des Martineaux, to Houël to calm him down. Des Martineaux did not succeed in this mission, but had an exciting time, presently returning to report that there was no hope of ever reaching an agreement with the stubborn Governor of Guadeloupe. During the interview, it seems, Houël had put on quite a show. He had bellowed with rage to the edification of all present, swearing he would rather come to an understanding with the devil himself than with the Governor-General; he laughed at the company, called himself the real master of the island, and vowed the directors already owed him more than the whole place was worth.

Houël now threw off the mask to embark on a course of action which even De Thoisy could not fail to understand. He gave his officers secret instructions to incite the colonists to take up arms for a march on Basseterre, where he hoped to bring together enough men to force the expulsion from the island of the unfortunate Governor-General. These officers were given verbal orders, as Houël did not wish to appear openly in the affair until he felt certain that the habitans were with him. Hearing rumors of what was going on, Father du Tertre, who at this time ruled a parish in Capesterre, started out on a survey to take the temperature of the neighborhood. Always a strong partisan of De Thoisy, he was anxious to forestall any move against the Governor-General. He found to his dismay a deep-seated hatred of the King's representative—fostered no doubt by Houël—

permeating all classes of society. Some would have burned him in his house, others would have his head and also that of Boisfaye, to make drinking cups of their skulls, while the more moderate would be satisfied with running him off the island.

Du Tertre remonstrated with these people, pointing out that such actions were in direct violation of their oath to the King's lieutenant, and that even should they succeed, they would have to answer for such a crime. In his attempt to combat this mob spirit, the priest first asked who was stirring up all the trouble, and learning that it was the work of certain officers in Capesterre, quickly saw through the entire scheme. To counteract it, he urged his people to force the agitators to show them written orders from the Governor; pointing out that if they refused, it was positive evidence they had none and were acting on their own responsibility. In that case, no one would be obliged to obey them.

While Du Tertre was going his rounds, Houël heard of it and sent his lieutenant, Charles de la Forge, to put a stop to such activities. La Forge found the priest in the home of a planter talking to an excited group of habitans, and placing a pistol at his head took him to the house of Captain Le Roy du Mé where the leaders of the pro-Houël party were gathered. Here he was subjected to a none-too-courteous questioning. Brusquely told to mind his own business, he quietly replied that his business was the care of his flock, and he intended to see to it that nothing was done to dragoon them into rebellion against their lawful master; furthermore he requested to see the order of M. Houël authorizing the officers of the militia to rouse the countryside against the representative of the King. Incensed at such language, the rebels seized the priest, tore his cassock, and literally kicked him out of the building into a nearby puddle where he landed flat on his back. Nothing daunted by this reception, Father du Tertre rose and continued his exhortations, crying out that they were merely troublemakers who, not content with committing the crime of lese majesty, were encouraging others to do the same. Angered at these accusations, especially as the people present were beginning to side with the priest, Du Mé sent out two musicians to silence him by the unpleasant method of blowing their trumpets loudly in his ears.

Captain du Mé's plantation was located near the Rivière d'Orange, which he and his fellow-conspirators were planning to cross in the hope of rallying to their standard the settlers living on the other side. Father du Tertre, who had heard this as he crouched beneath a window, decided to swim the river at once and frustrate the plan. But the water was high and it was not until the following morning that he was able to get across and make his way to the house of M. d'Orange. Here a large number of people were accustomed to gather when there was anything extraordinary afoot, for d'Orange, whom the reader will recall as the man who made the preliminary survey of the island for M. de l'Olive, had for years maintained a plantation where he welcomed all comers. Aided by his saintly wife, he fed the hungry, nursed the sick, and was acclaimed patriarch of the community. These people now gazed in open-mouthed astonishment at Father du Tertre as he appeared dripping wet from his early morning bath, and their astonishment increased when they learned the purpose of his coming. He explained to them the strange situation; a governor sending out his officers to carry out orders which he did not openly acknowledge; and he gave so many good reasons for his opposition to the proposed uprising that over a hundred men volunteered to join him in a march to Du Mé's headquarters, promising to refuse to follow the captain if he could not show them a written order from the Governor.

Captain du Mé was ready to start when the crowd reached his house. Du Tertre opened the interview in an ironic vein. "You see, Monsieur," he said, "I am bringing you some people. I am going with you. It is only a question of your showing the order you have to lead them, for they wish to see it and have charged me with asking you for it." Trapped, Du Mé could give no answer. He merely buckled on his sword belt and cried: "Let whoever loves me follow me. No order will be shown until we get to Basseterre." But Du Tertre's people stood firm, and the captain started off with a squad of only ten men, leaving the priest master of Capesterre.

When Du Mé reached the Governor-General's residence, he found it already surrounded by a force of 250 to 300 men under Captain La Bazilière. De Thoisy thus trapped in his own house now at last realized he would have to adopt a more aggressive attitude. The time for conciliation was over; it was for him to strike if he wished to be spared the humiliation of being driven from the island. Yet even so, he could scarcely bring himself to use violence. He first wrote a note to Houël, more peremptory in tone, it is true, than his previous communications, warning him of the dire consequences in store for one who thus persisted in defying the authority of the King. While waiting for an answer, he led a sortie with twenty-five men which, strange to say, struck terror into the hearts of La Bazilière's followers. Doubtless they were none too confident of their own position, since they were in arms against the King's lieutenant, and were ready to abandon the enterprise on the slightest provocation; in fact, La Bazilière could not hide from himself the fear of being seized as a rebel and turned over to De Thoisy. Uncertain of the loyalty of his men, he therefore wrote the Governor-General begging him to take no further action as he would call on him in a short while to talk over the situation.

Meanwhile, Houël was pondering over De Thoisy's letter. The business had not turned out as he had expected. The Governor-General, instead of fleeing from the island, had barricaded himself in his house, a well-fortified building protected by eight pieces of artillery, where he had stored a plentiful supply of food and ammunition. Furthermore, La Bazilière's besieging army was made up largely of men who had gone into the affair unwillingly, ready at any time to desert to De Thoisy. Casting about for some means to save the situation he suddenly thought of Father du Tertre. He sent for him; and much against the advice of his friends, who felt it might be a trap, the priest presented himself before the Governor in obedience to the summons. He found M. Houël in an anxious mood, nervously pacing the floor of his office. Acknowledging Du Tertre's greeting with a curt bow, he started off with a mild rebuke criticizing him for his actions in dissuading the colonists from following Du Mé. Then pleading ignorance of the entire business, he said: "Now the Governor-General's residence is besieged without my knowing anything about it, yet he holds me responsible for everything as though I had been the author of the uprising." Turning abruptly to Du Tertre he begged him to carry a message to the besiegers ordering them to disband.

Amazed at such a request, the priest did not hesitate to express his feelings on the subject. "Monsieur," he said, "I will not go, for if your officers, who had only water to drink here treated me so roughly, what will they do when they have enjoyed the Madeira wine of Basseterre? If you really want peace send M. de Sabouïlly, who is loved and respected by all the habitans and is the only man I know of here who is able to restore peace." Unable to shake the priest in his determination, Houël finally persuaded him to accompany Sabouïlly if the latter could be induced to undertake the mission. Sabouïlly at first refused, then yielding to the priest's eloquence grumblingly agreed to go. Embarking in a canoe, Sabouïlly and the priest set sail that night and landed at Basseterre the following morning.

They arrived just in time, since the firing had already begun; but the sudden appearance of Sabouïlly at once put a stop to hostilities. Sabouïlly would stand for no nonsense. He ordered the mutineers to lay down their arms and disperse, threatening to go to De Thoisy's house, call out the little band of men quartered there and give them a taste of what well-disciplined soldiers could do with a mob. This was enough: the rank and file fled, while the leaders made a formal submission to the Governor-General. As for Father du Tertre, he presently sought refuge in Martinique.

The peace thus established was scarcely more than a temporary truce, for opposition to the Governor-General and his party soon broke out afresh. Threats of disorder became so alarming as to compel La Bazilière to write Houël urging him to come to Basseterre and use his authority to suppress a possible outbreak. Even De Thoisy felt obliged to write him in a similar vein. When Houël received these communications, he began to doubt his ability to control the situation. Instead of replying frankly, he adopted a vacillating policy towards the authorities at Basseterre, keeping them in suspense by promising to come, then putting off his departure from time to time, until at last he refused to move. To satisfy his conscience for this pusillanimous attitude, he informed De Thoisy that the same reasons which had induced him to request the Governor-General not to come to Capesterre now prevented him from going to Fort Royal. He made matters even worse by coolly informing De Thoisy that he was sending him the prisoners taken in St. Christopher for him to look after. Angered at this attitude, for he now clearly saw that Houël was back of all the disturbances, De Thoisy wrote him a stinging reply, upbraiding him for having dared to send him prisoners who would now become a burden to him and his people, while he, the Governor of Guadeloupe, had the power and means to erect prisons for their safekeeping.

Fortunately there arrived at this time a communication from the King that brought matters to a head. M. de Guinant who had sailed for France the previous summer in Captain Bontemps's ship with letters from De Thoisy, had given the government a complete account of the situation in Guadeloupe and Martinique, stressing the controversy over the exchange of Du Parquet for De Poincy's nephews. On learning this, the authorities felt that the first step toward the restoration of peace would be to arrange for the return of the nephews with their people in exchange for Du Parquet and Saint-Aubin. This was to be followed up by a general amnesty for those who still roamed the jungles of St. Christopher as a result of the fracas at Pointe de Sable.

GOVERNOR-GENERAL VERSUS GOVERNORS 165

De Thoisy was immensely pleased by these suggestions as he foresaw a speedy adjustment of the principal differences between De Poincy and himself, and looked forward to enjoying the rest of his administration in peace. But in this he was speedily undeceived, for sedition broke out with greater virulence than before. A report quickly spread about the island that the Governor-General was to be murdered on New Year's Day, or, if this plan could not be carried out he was to be lured on board a ship commanded by Captain Grégoire and there dispatched. Fortunately for De Thoisy, the rumor reached his ears in time, and when he received Captain Grégoire's kind invitation to dine with him on his ship, he returned a polite refusal, pleading the obligation of a previous engagement.

By this time De Thoisy had had enough, and decided to leave the island. On New Year's Eve he loaded his possessions on a Portuguese caravel he had chartered for the purpose, and set sail for Martinique. Before leaving, however, he took a parting shot at Houël, setting his pen to a letter breathing dire threats against him should he dare to disobey the orders of his superior, knowing full well the communication would not be delivered until the writer was out of sight of Guadeloupe.

Although you have told me [he wrote] that you took orders from no one on this island I command you by the orders of the King, which I received in the ship of Captain Béliard, that you send me the Sieur de Treval; and if you foil me you shall see that I know how to make you obey. I shall say nothing more, save that I await your answer in order to decide what to do.

Brave words; Houël did not pay the slightest attention to them.

On January 3, 1647, De Thoisy arrived in Martinique where he was enthusiastically received, and took up his residence with the Jesuit fathers. From this point of vantage he began to issue orders to De Poincy and Houël, asserting his position as representative of the King, and again demanding the surrender of M. de Treval whom he hoped to use as a pawn in his dealings with the rebellious commander of St. Christopher. No notice was taken of this command. He also forbade Captains Béliard and Grégoire from taking their ships to St. Christopher; but Houël at once sent the former there with dispatches for De Poincy. Far from inspiring the respect due him by virtue of his position, the Governor-General appears to have been consigned to oblivion by both De Poincy and Houël, who went about their plans for ridding the islands of his presence without any thought of what he might have to say about it.

Governor Houël, however, by this time had raised a storm in Guadeloupe which he could quell only with the greatest difficulty. In arming the colonists to expel De Thoisy, he had roused the disorderly element which now overran the settlements, pillaging right and left. Those who had sided with De Thoisy were, of course, the special objects of attack. M. de la Ramée, well-known for his loyalty to the King's representative, was severely beaten, his house was looted and burned, his slaves driven off, his cattle destroyed, and he himself finally expelled from the island without a bale of tobacco to pay his passage. He was reduced to poverty after having been one of the most prosperous habitans; all he had accumulated in fifteen years was confiscated.

A reign of terror now broke out on the island. Houël, obliged to keep order, went about his job with a ruthlessness that seems more severe than the circumstances justified. Men were flogged, branded, and banished from the colony; some were hanged, including no less a person than Captain La Bazilière. Even those who had been most conscientious in carrying out the Governor's wishes in the struggle against De Thoisy were seized and summarily punished, the most celebrated case being that of Guillaume d'Orange. M. d'Orange, who was picked up for some trifling remark which the ill-disposed interpreted as a wish for the return of De Thoisy, was placed under arrest in his own house. He had merely said, a few days after Christmas, that Noël had gone but would soon return, and as De Thoisy's Christian name was Noël, a political construction was placed on a perfectly innocuous remark. Feeling he could get no justice in Guadeloupe, D'Orange decided to write Houël for permission to go to France to plead his case. Being illiterate himself, he requested the services of a clerk, a favor readily granted him. But the person sent to write his letter was in reality a creature of Houël's who wrote out a bitter diatribe against the Governor, hoping D'Orange would sign it in ignorance of its contents, thus giving the authorities written evidence of his disloyalty. Fortunately, before affixing his signature to the paper, D'Orange had the good sense to show it to one of the priests who at once threw it into the fire; but Houël thinking he had signed it had him arrested. Brought before the Governor, he was asked for the letter, and being unable to produce it was given a severe thrashing.

Having vented his spleen against his prisoner, Houël now remanded him to jail at the same time forbidding the clergy to visit him. D'Orange's clerical friends, however, were quite equal to the occasion. It being the Lenten season, one of them seized the opportunity to preach a pointed sermon dilating upon the injustice which occurs when the weak are tyrannized by the strong. Houël, of course, saw the point; but unable to take any official notice of it, he proceeded to wreak his vengeance on the unfortunate D'Orange whom he brought to trial for an alleged plot he had made with the priests to drive the Governor from the island. The case was tried before a packed court; even the judge sent to examine the priests apologized to them for the role he was forced to play.

At the close of the Lenten season Houël found himself in a quandary. He was obliged to present himself at communion on this great day of obligation or be considered an atheist by the people. In this predicament he sought a reconciliation with the clergy. He began his overtures by praising them, particularly those he had previously vilified. Thinking the time propitious for obtaining the release of D'Orange the priests broached the subject to Houël, but he imposed such insolent conditions on their request (conditions are not stated in the narratives) that they could make no headway in their conversations.

When the negotiations fell through Houël pressed his attack on the clergy with renewed vigor. He sought to harm them in other ways, being unable to do anything through the tribunals. Gangs were sent out to trample down their gardens, beat their workmen, kill their poultry; people were discouraged from speaking to them or having any communications with them. At Pentecost when their tithes, payable in tobacco, were due them, the people were forbidden to make payments on the specious plea that the priests were not missionaries but merely almoners with no authority save what the Governor was pleased to delegate to them. When they protested that they had a duly signed and sealed commission as missionaries, Houël attempted to get hold of it by requesting to see it, but his request was, of course, refused. Checked in this direction, he secured from his council a resolution authorizing him to deport the priests; but this plan had to be abandoned at the last moment inasmuch as the vessel chartered for the purpose was stolen as she lay at anchor in the harbor by a Portuguese freebooter.

At about this time Governor Houël was stricken with the plague which was then raging on the island. During his illness he sent for Father Breton, head of the mission, and effected a reconciliation with him. How much of this was due to sincere repentance is a question, for De Thoisy was by that time in France pressing his charges. The Governor, in preparing his defense, therefore believed it to be to his advantage to be able to prove the genuineness of a letter he had formerly received from Father La Paix acknowledging receipt of instructions from him to act as mediator in arriving at an understanding with De Thoisy. This bit of evidence, so Houël thought, would show him as a man ready, even eager, to smooth over misunderstandings and make peace with the Governor-General. For this reason he approached the priests and asked them in the name of charity to forget the past, as his enemies were seeking to encompass his ruin. Hoping to placate the Governor and secure peace, they extended him this favor and signed an affidavit vouching for the genuineness of the letter.[1]

While engaged in this controversy with the clergy, Houël did not neglect his action against D'Orange. Unable to extract a single compromising admission from him, the subservient court nevertheless sentenced him to pay a fine of 2,000 pounds of tobacco and ordered him to surrender to the Governor, without compensation, a slave he had recently bought from him. Still not satisfied, Houël decided to rid himself of his victim's obnoxious presence. For this purpose he organized a military expedition against the English colony at Barbuda which he placed under the command of D'Orange, appealing to his pride as a soldier to lead the undertaking. The expedition was poorly organized from the start—perhaps the Governor would not have regretted if it had never returned; a mere handful of men was placed in a small bark and sent out to conquer the island. D'Orange did his best. He reached Barbuda, fought successfully, and presently returned with nothing save his wounds to show for his efforts. Instead of praising him, the Governor now attacked his reputation, confiscated his property, and made life so miserable that at last he was only too glad to leave the scene of his misfortune and, after a brief sojourn in Mariegalante, take refuge in Martinique where he was cordially received by Governor du Parquet.[2]

Meanwhile, Captain Béliard, whom, as we have said, M. Houël had sent to St. Christopher, arrived at his destination. He proceeded at once to the residence of De Poincy and handed him a letter from his master announcing the departure of the Governor-General for Martinique. What the exact contents of this letter were, we do not know, nor do we know what verbal

[1] An elaborate account of the struggle between Houël and the clergy is given in Mathias du Puis, *Relation de l'etablissement d'une colonie française dans la Guadeloupe.* 1652. Du Tertre tells us but little about it.
[2] Accounts of D'Orange's trouble are to be found in several documents which are cited in H. R. du Motey, *Guillaume d'Orange.*

message the captain delivered; but from the course immediately adopted by De Poincy we can make a fairly shrewd guess, for no sooner had Béliard left the house than the Governor gave orders to embark a detachment of eight hundred men under the command of La Vernade and sail for Martinique.

La Vernade reached Martinique on January 13, 1647, and made his debut by a little indiscriminate gun practice that killed one of the colonists. News of this was quickly relayed to De Thoisy, who immediately ordered the island to be placed in a state of siege; but his and his officers' splendid resolution to defend it at all costs went by the board when a number of habitans, who had received permission to visit the fleet, allowed themselves to be drawn into a plan to exchange the Governor-General for Du Parquet. This in reality was the purpose for which De Poincy had organized the expedition, for with Du Parquet as bait he knew he could induce the Martinicans to make the exchange; but if they refused, La Vernade had orders to land and seize his man by force. The offer was one the habitans could not well decline. They longed for the return of their rightful governor, and now that he could be obtained in exchange for one who was little more than a stranger, they found it difficult to resist the temptation. At the call of La Pierrière, the leaders drew up a resolution to request the coöperation of De Thoisy on the ground that a ready compliance with De Poincy's suggestion would save much bloodshed. This resolution was a mere matter of form; the colonists had no intention of passing up this opportunity no matter what stand the Governor-General might take; and even while he was drafting an elaborate reply protesting his inability to do anything not in keeping with his exalted position, they were busy drawing up a treaty with La Vernade pledging themselves to make the exchange.

When the time came to carry out the provisions of this arrangement, La Pierrière felt somewhat ashamed of the part he was called upon to play; so he delegated the unpleasant task of arresting the Governor-General to Captain Le Fort, a man not overburdened with delicate scruples. Le Fort proceeded to the house of the Jesuit fathers, threw a detachment of musketeers around the place, then boldly marched in and seized his prisoner as he was walking peacefully in the garden with Father du Tertre. He was immediately taken on board one of the vessels together with Boisfaye, and the entire fleet set sail for Guadeloupe. Here the commander signed an agreement with M. Houël fairly bristling with provisions, showing clearly that neither party trusted the other. Houël was to surrender Lonvilliers and keep Treval as hostage until La Vernade had gone to St. Christopher, picked up Du Parquet and conveyed him to Martinique. La Vernade was then to take Treval to St. Christopher, exchange him for all the inhabitants of Guadeloupe held in durance there, and send them wherever they might wish to go.

Returning to St. Christopher on the twenty-fourth of January, La Vernade anchored off Basseterre amid salvos from the fort, while the fleet riding in the roadstead echoed the salute. He was regarded as a sort of hero since he brought back both Lonvilliers to resume his duties as governor and De Thoisy, archenemy of De Poincy. The distinguished captive was brought ashore the following day and placed in a prison near that of Du Parquet where he was left to reflect on the vicissitudes of fortune in the company of his *fidus Achates*, M. de Boisfaye. Here he was kept incommunicado for nine days, visited only by servants who brought him food and departed without uttering a word. Being a devout man he sought the consolation of religion, spending much of his time in prayer and in turning over the pages of a little copy of the *De imitatione* he kept about his person. Indeed, it was a situation that called for the greatest philosophical resignation; for here he had been cast into jail like a common felon, not even treated with the respect due a distinguished prisoner of war, which was the least De Poincy might have done, and all for no other reason than that he had tried to exercise the authority vested in him by the King in the most tactful and forbearing manner possible. Despite his congenital unfitness for the task of coping with the two tough, unscrupulous men who ruled the archipelago, his sufferings redeem him from the somewhat pathetic position in which his lack of forcefulness had placed him, and compel us to grant him a certain amount of sympathy.

While these events were taking place, the ministers of Louis XIV were pondering over the reports brought them by De Guinant. Unable to come to any definite conclusion as to the merits of the case, though it is difficult to understand how they could have failed to back De Thoisy to the limit, unless they felt it was impossible to act, they reached the following compromise. De Poincy was to be King's lieutenant in St. Christopher for a period of one year only, while De Thoisy remained in command of the other islands; then at the end of the year he was to be given St. Christopher also, and De Poincy was to assume the status of a private citizen. The King issued a proclamation embodying this arrangement and sent *lettres de cachet* to the officials concerned, ordering them to conform to his wishes. But with De Thoisy in his power, De Poincy had no intention of letting him resume his authority; and the only evidence we have that His Majesty's orders were not tossed into the waste-basket is that we find them reproduced in the pages of Du Tertre.

It was now high time for De Poincy to fulfill his part of the contract with the inhabitants of Martinique and release M. du Parquet. The unfortunate Governor had been held prisoner for about a year, and it was doubtless with a feeling of relief that his captor unlocked the door of his cell, for after all he was a fellow-governor of the French West Indies, held only as a hostage. Anxious to earn his good will, now that he was about to resume his duties at Martinique, De Poincy placed him on board a ship with orders to show him every courtesy, and sent him away with protestations of friendship. At Martinique Du Parquet was welcomed with the wildest enthusiasm by the inhabitants. His first act was to show his gratitude to the woman who during the time of his captivity had given such proofs of her unflagging devotion to his interests. On the last day of April his secret marriage to Marie Bonnard, the erstwhile Mlle Saint-André, was publicly acknowledged, and was blessed by Father Techenel in the Chapel of St. Jacques.

The imprisonment of De Thoisy soon began to have unpleasant repercussions throughout St. Christopher. Reports of the kindness he had shown the colonists of other islands began to circulate, to the extreme annoyance of De Poincy, whose severity toward his own people showed up in an unpleasant contrast. A few bold spirits led the movement, and soon a formidable army of twelve hundred people arose with the cry: "Vive le Roi et M. le General de Thoisy." Alarmed at this outbreak of popular feeling, De Poincy hastily summoned his counselors, who after deliberating for some time came out with the helpful suggestion that the object of this popular adulation be put to death. Wiser counsel, however, eventually prevailed, and it was decided to place De Thoisy immediately on board a ship and send him back to France. That evening a detachment of three hundred men surrounded the prison to guard against any possible uprising of the colonists, and on the stroke of midnight a squad of twenty men entered and seized the Governor-General. He was taken to the shore, an officer walking by his side ready to blow out his brains should any attempt be made to rescue him. Here he was carried out to a boat and rowed during the night to Pointe de Sable where he was placed on board a ship commanded by Captain Mansel. By good fortune he found as traveling companions La Ramée and La Fontaine, who had been driven from Guadeloupe by Houël and were therefore inclined to regard him as a companion in misfortune, struck down by the same hand that had wounded them. He derived considerable comfort from the society of these men. He also managed to secure decent treatment from Captain Mansel—one of De Poincy's creatures—by posing before him as a friend of the rebellious governor with whom he had been acting in concert to destroy their common enemy, Houël, sole cause of all the disorders in the islands. The crew were also inclined to favor him, as they had no taste for the activities of their captain in supporting De Poincy. In this manner the Governor-General, turning one face to the captain and another to the crew, found the crossing not altogether unpleasant.

On the seventeenth of May the ship anchored off St. Malo where De Thoisy remained for six weeks to bring action against Captain Mansel as an accomplice of De Poincy. Later he proceeded to Paris where he instituted suits against the leaders who had remained in the West Indies. They were long-drawn-out affairs lasting about six years; but in the end he won two richly deserved verdicts: one of 90,000 pounds of tobacco against De Poincy, the other of 61,715 pounds against Houël. Thus in a sense justice was done.

IX

THE FRENCH EXPAND

THE DEPARTURE of M. de Thoisy from the West Indian scene did not, as one might suppose, inaugurate an era of peace. On the contrary, the rebellious commanders thought it necessary to follow up their victory by a sort of pogrom against all who had been faithful to the representative of the King. It is difficult to understand why this was so, for deprived of their leader the loyalists had no reason for prolonging the struggle and might have been expected to quiet down; but De Poincy, and to a less extent Houël, had by their policies and methods made many enemies—as the uprising in favor of De Thoisy just before his departure clearly showed—and they felt it necessary to eliminate all who had opposed them. Besides, they were suffering from a bad conscience. They were rebels against royal authority and as such did not know whether the King might send over another governor-general backed up this time by a sufficiently large force to command respect, consequently they did not want any tongues left that could wag in the witness-box. In St. Christopher the adherents of De Thoisy were called "Patrocles," and woe betide those to whom this name was fastened, for they were driven from pillar to post, beaten, thrown into jail, ruined, and banished from the island. Even those who fled to the woods found no safety there, and were glad to seek refuge on neighboring islands.

In Guadeloupe Houël carried on similar activities. An incident occurred which shows the methods he used to rid himself of persons who incurred his displeasure. There was a certain lieutenant in Capesterre named La Fontaine (not to be confused with Camot's partner) who at first had strongly favored him in his struggle against De Thoisy and later had shifted his allegiance, taking sides against his former commander. One day he happened to meet Mlle Trezel, wife of the merchant who had introduced sugar manufacturing in Martinique, who was on her way to pay the Governor an early morning visit. La Fontaine saw fit to stop her and make some impertinent observations regarding her intended visit which cast unpleasant reflections on her character. Angered at the insult, she complained to her husband who at once hurried to ask Governor Houël's permission to beat up the impertinent lieutenant. Whether or not Houël gave him the coveted permission it is impossible to say, but at any rate, Trezel boasted that he had received it and was going to administer to La Fontaine a sound and well-deserved thrashing. Badly frightened at this, particularly as he was a cripple unable to defend himself, the terrified lieutenant begged Houël for protection, saying he would certainly use his musket if attacked. We do not know what the Governor's reply to this request was, but after the interview La Fontaine told his friends he had been given permission to kill Trezel if attacked by him. Trezel, so Du Tertre hints, was in disfavor with Houël, and if this is so, the Governor may not have cared to put too great a damper on La Fontaine's enthusiasm. At any rate the opportunity to test the value of these permits for mayhem and manslaughter soon presented itself. A few days after his interview with Houël, La Fontaine was standing in front of his house and saw Trezel coming at him cane in hand ready for business. Seizing a gun he threatened to shoot him on the spot if he made another move. Trezel, laughing at the cripple's threats, closed in on him determined to administer corporal punishment on the spot, but as he did so La Fontaine pressed the trigger, stretching the unfortunate man dead on the ground.

Terrified at his deed the lieutenant fled to the woods. Perhaps, after all, his claim to immunity was a fabricated story calculated to frighten Trezel, and again, perhaps not, for a few days later he decided to surrender himself and take his chances at a trial. His decision was an unfortunate one, as Houël refused to interfere with the workings of justice, and the wretched lieutenant was speedily condemned and as speedily executed. In this manner, so the gossips said, the Governor managed to rid himself of two persons whose presence in Guadeloupe he considered superfluous.

There was one man, however, who refused to bow his head to the ruthless Governor. That valiant major-general, M. de Sabouïlly, stood high in the opinion of everyone, and had been warmly recommended to the directors of the company by both De Poincy and Houël as a man worthy of the utmost confidence. Fearing that the directors might select him as the man to restore order in Guadeloupe and, perhaps, succeed M. de Thoisy, Houël suggested in a friendly manner that he might find it wise to return to France. When Sabouïlly declined to take the hint, the Governor formally ordered him to leave, and after his refusal to obey threatened his life. Sabouïlly shrugged his shoulders at this, but kept his eyes open. One day as he was strolling down a narrow path he chanced to meet the Governor surrounded by his bodyguards, and mindful of a rumor that these men had orders to slay him, he called to him one who had previously been his valet and engaged him in a long conversation. The others stood at ease, thrown off their guard by this unexpected move. Suddenly the Major-General marched straight at Houël who, dumbfounded at this maneuver stood meekly aside to let him pass, not daring to utter a word of protest, and from that time on Sabouïlly did pretty much as he pleased in Guadeloupe remaining there until he returned to France to spend his last years.

It must not be assumed, however, that Houël was an evil man devoted entirely to evil works. In our narrative we have followed Father du Tertre, practically the only authority of any importance for the period we are describing, and he for obvious reasons was unfriendly to the Governor. Perhaps Houël may have undergone something of a change after defeating De Thoisy and crushing his enemies in Guadeloupe, for Antoine Biet, who came to the island five years later, speaks highly of him. He tells of his sympathy for the indentured servants, a class which certainly deserved commiseration. They were often people of bad habits, who being unused to labor, quickly fell ill when called upon to exert themselves, and it was for them Houël built the hospital at Rivière aux Herbes. The truth of the matter is that Houël received Biet kindly and was unfriendly towards Du Tertre, thus each described the Governor as he had seen him. It is interesting to note also that Biet is the only contemporary writer who is hostile to M. du Parquet.

While the situation in Martinique was not so bad as on the other islands, yet it also had its share of trouble after the disturbances quieted down. The turmoil created by the De Thoisy affair was one that could not easily be quelled. The example of rebellion given the colonists by the struggle between the governors and their superior, a struggle in which the subordinates incited the inhabitants to rise against the supreme commander, was not conducive to a respect for authority on the part of the masses, and even after the bone of contention had been removed, the disorders continued. Du Parquet threw himself into the work of restoring discipline with commendable zeal. Agriculture had suffered during his absence, and as this was the colony's only source of wealth, he devoted his entire energies to building it up. New *quartiers* were established by enlarging the acreage under cultivation, encouraging planters to develop their fields, and increasing the number of homes. It was a serious undertaking to organize a new *quartier* and make it a self-sufficient unit independent of the others for it was necessary to provide a fort, a guardhouse, a church, a storehouse for the factor, and a public weighing-scale. Du Parquet was also fearful of foreign invasion, and made elaborate preparations to sustain an attack. At important points along the shore and in the interior, he organized a permanent guard composed of all men capable of bearing arms, and compelled them to do guard duty at all times. When hostilities seemed imminent, hunting was forbidden, all powder and shot being carefully husbanded against the coming attack. Foreign traders were encouraged to supply munitions, and the sums due in payment therefor were given preferential treatment over other debts. The custom of bearing arms which nearly everyone followed had the unfortunate effect of encouraging the duel, a disastrous practice for a colony that could ill afford to have its man power reduced. Du Parquet, partly by persuasion, partly by threat of punishment, strove to break this vicious practice; but his efforts, as usually happens when a government goes counter to the popular trend, met with little success, and probably accomplished no more than did the efforts of Cardinal Richelieu along the same lines in France.

A curious situation was created at this time in the affairs of the island by the immigration of a large number of Jews. They had come there from France, probably because of some minor persecution, and, as might be expected, devoted their energies to trade and not to planting. Soon their many stores at St. Pierre made them the principal merchants of the island. Though their presence in such numbers was deplored by the clergy, they were held in high esteem by M. and Mme du Parquet, and soon obtained enough influence to change the routine of business. It had been the custom of the planters to bring their produce to town on Saturdays to be weighed at the public scales where the Jewish merchants congregated to make their purchases. As this important business day came on the Sabbath, they persuaded Du Parquet to change it to Friday when both they and the Christians could trade with a clean conscience. Even seventeenth-century Martinique had its Jewish problem.[1]

The reader will doubtless recall MM. de la Fontaine and

[1] Biet, *Voyage de la France Equinoxiale*.

Camot who had escaped from St. Christopher in the hold of a Dutch merchantman at the time of Du Parquet's capture. On reaching France these two gentlemen, still smarting from the treatment they had received, hurried to the directors to plead their case. They told them of the terrible persecution visited by De Poincy on people of substance who had sided with De Thoisy, and how they had been dispersed, some to Holland, others to France, but most of them to the neighboring Dutch and English islands. They wished to bring together these people, who were all skilled colonists, and found an independent settlement on the little island of Mariegalante, just south of Guadeloupe.

The plan appealed to the directors, for here was an opportunity to reward a group of worthy persons without its costing the company a penny. A meeting was accordingly held on February 8, 1647, at which a charter, based on the King's edict of March, 1642, was granted the two officers, permitting them to found a colony on the island they had selected, which they were authorized to govern for a period of four years. Colonists settling there were to enjoy exemption from the usual dues for the first four years and to pay for the next four only half those levied at St. Christopher. These privileges were to apply only to persons emigrating from France and to those who had been driven from St. Christopher, not to settlers coming voluntarily from other islands, as the company had no desire to have the population of Mariegalante built up by a general exodus from the larger colonies. The same day the patent was signed, La Fontaine and Camot received their commissions; but the poor exiles had no money to finance the venture, nor could they borrow any, and the two thousand francs procured them by Mme de Patrocles were soon exhausted. Unable to do anything about their colony, Camot eventually returned to Martinique where he was heartily welcomed by Du Parquet, while La Fontaine took part in an expedition to the Orinoco with Father Pacifique de Provins where he landed and was never heard of again.

M. de Poincy now began to receive letters from France telling him of the Queen Regent's displeasure at his treatment of her representative. He had expected trouble, of course, but he hoped the Order of Malta could smooth things over with the government and make some arrangement with De Thoisy. Pending the outcome of negotiations, he thought it wise to rid himself of certain eminent people who had favored the Governor-General. But it would not do to send them to France where they would be sure to testify against him, nor was it advisable to drive them from the island like common criminals as he had done with the humble folk, for such action would be sure to hurt his cause, so he made arrangements to send them to the Virgin Islands under the pretext of founding a new colony. For this purpose he selected sixty of the most obnoxious, some of whom held prominent positions.

They left St. Christopher in September, 1647, in a bark commanded by Jean Pinart. No sooner had they sailed than the true purpose of the venture became apparent to all who had remained behind. It was easy enough to see that De Poincy had not sent them forth to found a colony, but to be dumped on some desert island, as the man selected to lead the expedition was a boorish lout named Le Verrier who had barely escaped hanging for the part he had taken in the Bugaud mutiny, scarcely the person to be entrusted with a serious undertaking. Moreover, if any had lingering doubts as to the Governor's intentions, they were speedily dispelled when the property of the emigrants was confiscated as soon as they were beyond the sight of land. Fortunately for the pioneers, Captain Pinart had cruised the islands and knew of one, recently taken by the English, where quantities of sweet potatoes and other edibles could be found. Father du Tertre does not tell us which island it was, but from the hints he gives it was probably St. John.

Landing on the island, the colonists, if we can call them such, hung their cotton hammocks between the trees, and attempted to get some sleep after their exhausting voyage despite the violent attacks of mosquitoes. The following morning the more venturesome started out on a reconnoitering expedition. They had scarcely passed beyond their camp when they came upon a row of corpses lying on the sand, frightful remnants of a band of Englishmen who had come there to found a settlement. This horrible spectacle, mute evidence of a recent massacre, made the French fear they had landed at a spot where the same fate awaited them, for they now remembered that they were not far from Spanish Puerto Rico. Indeed, their fears were well founded as the Spaniards had heard of De Pioncy's policy of expelling undesirables from St. Christopher, and had no intention of permitting foreign exiles to colonize in their neighborhood. When news of Pinart's landing reached them—we have no way of knowing by what means—they quickly armed five vessels, loaded them with men and munitions, and dispatched them to give the French the same reception they had given the English. As the fleet drew near the island, the French, both colonists and crew, rushed to arms. At the first clash they more than held their own, driving the enemy back to the harbor's edge where both parties halted, but after a few moments' respite the Spaniards returned to the charge, rushing the French with such violence that they broke and fled to the mountains where they remained until the Spanish fleet returned to Puerto Rico.

For three or four months the miserable refugees eked out a wretched existence on such odds and ends as the island afforded, as all they had brought with them, including Pinart's ship, had been destroyed by the Spaniards. Several had died of want, others were on the verge of death, when five of the most robust determined to escape at any cost. By good fortune they found an axe someone had left behind at the foot of a tree, and with this one tool managed to cut some logs which they bound together with creepers in the form of a raft fourteen feet long by eleven wide. On it was erected a short mast bearing a rough sail made from a couple of shirts torn into strips and held in a semblance of unity by means of thorns. It was a crude affair, very crude indeed, one on which only desperate men would think of venturing to sea; but these were desperate men determined at all cost to reach some place where they could get assistance.

On the day set for leaving, those who were to stay behind dragged their starving bodies to the shore. All knelt in prayer, and then partook of a last meal together. It was difficult to say which felt the parting more keenly. Those who were about to leave wept for those who remained behind, destined, perhaps, to die of starvation, while the latter in turn could not believe the venturesome travelers would ever survive the dangers of the sea. Nor, in truth, were the adventurers themselves unduly confident. The raft they now embarked on was scarcely a first-class example of ship-building; but they really had no choice; it was either reach an inhabited island or perish. With a last farewell they shoved their raft into the water and climbed aboard. Two men sat in the stern steering the contraption by means of a sweep which acted as a rudder, while the other three took positions forward to ply their paddles.

Towards evening, after a heartbreaking passage, they landed on a little island near Virgin Gorda where they found the grave of a former inhabitant from St. Christopher who had been driven from the island some time before. This man's name, so it appeared from the headstone, was La Violette and they called the island after him. A fire was built, some crabs were thrown into a kettle, and the group sat down to dinner. The following day the raft was again put in motion, the refugees paddling vigorously until they came to the fertile island of St. Thomas where they remained five days refreshing themselves with the generous supply of bananas, oranges and figs that grew here in great abundance. From St. Thomas they proceeded to the southern shore of Puerto Rico. Here they landed and made their way inland for a couple of leagues to find herds of wild cattle; but fearful of attacks by the Spaniards, they did not linger long, only long enough to repair the raft and put to sea again.

Heading to windward they paddled for three days until they came to a little island, the nesting place of wild fowl. The presence of a few huts showed the place to be inhabited, so the wanderers decided to build themselves a house where they could live until the inhabitants returned. Here the wretched castaways remained for three months, hoping against hope for the arrival of someone who could assist them. Then one Sunday morning, as they gathered on the beach for prayer, they saw in the offing a Spanish vessel running before a northerly breeze. By making frantic signals they succeeded in attracting the attention of the captain who at once furled his course, lowered his topsail, and sent a boat ashore to see what was going on. The shocking appearance of the Frenchmen, half naked, emaciated, and heavily tanned by the sun moved him to compassion, and he received them on board with every consideration possible. By means of a Walloon interpreter who happened to be among the crew the French gave the skipper an account of their sufferings which touched him deeply. He offered them a supply of clothing, fed them with bread and wine, promised to take them fifteen days hence to Puerto Rico after he had done his fishing. He was as good as his word. Two weeks later he again stopped at the island, picked up the Frenchmen, now somewhat recovered from their privations, and sailed boldly for San Juan, capital of Puerto Rico, with the raft lashed to his bowsprit as a trophy for the Governor, Francisco Maldonado.

And now occurred the strangest part of the story. As they were heading for San Juan the pilot, sweeping the horizon with his glass, saw a league to windward a strange object bobbing up and down on the ground swell that resembled the device attached to his bowsprit. The helm was put over and the ship headed for the object. On reaching it the Frenchmen saw with amazement a raft similar to their own to which clung six men, all that remained of the castaways they had left months before on St. John and hardly hoped ever to see again. Yielding to their pleas, the Captain hauled the wretched beings on board, furnished them with clothing, and carried the entire band to San Juan where he presented them to the Governor who, touched by their sufferings, gave them the freedom of the city. The hardships they had undergone, their miraculous rescue on the point of death, made them objects of charitable interest to the inhabitants. Work was provided for those who knew a trade, while one of them presently earned enough for himself and to spare by playing a violin. When at last they had accumulated sufficient funds to leave the island, they took passage on a ship (all but one who had married and settled down) and sailed back to France.

The year 1648 saw the beginning of a policy of expansion on the part of the French governors reminiscent of the settlement of Martinique and Guadeloupe in 1635. It began with the acquisition by De Poincy of a part ownership in St. Martin, one of the lesser jewels of the Caribbee archipelago, situated north of St. Christopher. The Spaniards had taken possession of it some ten years before, and had erected thereon a fort manned by a suitable garrison; but the venture had proved unprofitable, as little was to be obtained there to offset the yearly expenditure of 100,000 *écus* borne by the Spanish government. The establishment was, therefore, to be destroyed and the place abandoned to the first comer. In the detachment sent out from Puerto Rico to undertake the work of dismantling the place, there happened to be a French prisoner named Fichot and three companions who on landing fled to the woods, where they remained in hiding until the Spaniards, their business finished, returned to San Juan. Coming forth from concealment, the fugitives wandered down to the shore where they were astonished to find five Dutchmen who like themselves had been prisoners and had used the same tactics to escape. Pooling their resources the two groups decided to notify the nearest French and Dutch governors of the opportunity to seize the abandoned island, so the two nations could occupy it simultaneously, as the French and English had done at St. Christopher.

The general plan having been agreed upon, it became necessary to devise ways and means for carrying it out. As the Dutch island of St. Eustatius was the nearest of any to St. Martin, the Hollanders offered to make their way to it on a raft, notify the governor, Abraham Adriensen, then proceed to St. Christopher and carry the news to Governor de Poincy. No sooner said than done. All fell to work with a will; the raft was quickly built, and in a short while the Dutchmen were standing before their governor telling him of the golden opportunity. Adriensen acted at once. In the name of His Highness the Prince of Orange, he issued a commission to Captain Martin Thomas on February 14, 1648, authorizing him to take command of the island.

When Captain Thomas came to St. Martin with a band of prospective settlers, Fichot became suspicious, since he had received no word from De Poincy. At the first opportunity he slipped away to St. Chrisopher, made his way into De Poincy's presence, and told him the entire story. It was news to the Governor. The Dutch had played Fichot false and kept the secret to themselves. Eager to obtain another island, De Poincy did not hesitate, for he felt, from what Fichot had told him, that the French had a valid claim to St. Martin, and also recalled that the Sieur de Saint-Martin had taken possession of the island ten years before on the basis of a commission given him by the King. With two such good titles to possession, De Poincy prepared to assert the French claims. He dispatched the Sieur de la Tour with thirty men, a small force, it is true, but one he deemed sufficient, as he did not expect the Dutch to raise any objections to a French settlement in view of the agreement with Fichot. But in this he was doomed to disappointment, for the Hollanders had no intention of sharing the prize with any rival nation and would not allow a single Frenchman to set foot on shore.

When this was reported to De Poincy, he decided to make a show of force that would impress Governor Adriensen. On the sixteenth of March he issued a commission to his nephew,

Lonvilliers, appointing him Governor of the island; but fearing that the Dutch had some legal claims which might cause trouble at home if an attempt was made to expel them, he cautioned Lonvilliers not to be aggressive but to fight only if he were attacked. Accompanied by La Tour as lieutenant-colonel, M. de Lonvilliers arrived at St. Martin a few days later with a force of three hundred men. On landing he sent a messenger to the Dutch with offers of friendship. Seeing the French had come with too powerful a force to be resisted, they replied with many professions of good will. A week later Lonvilliers and Thomas met to draw up a treaty of amity similar to that signed years before between Warner and D'Esnambuc. By its terms the French were to occupy the northern part of the island, the Dutch the southern. Both nations were to enjoy in common rights to hunt, fish, collect minerals, salt, and dye-woods anywhere on the island, and all harbors were to be thrown open to both. Mutual aid was pledged in case an outside enemy attacked either. In short the agreement greatly resembled the Warner-D'Esnambuc treaty, after which it was presumably modeled.

Once the colony on St. Martin had been established, M. de Poincy thought it well to seize the island of St. Bartholomew (St. Barts) between it and St. Christopher. It was held by no one and would make a good addition to his growing empire. Furthermore it had a good harbor. Jacques Le Gendre was accordingly sent there with fifty men to take possession. A few planters of St. Christopher helped in the business, sending settlers and slaves; but as they did this more to please De Poincy than with any expectation of profit the venture was never successful. Eight years later the Caribs slaughtered the inhabitants, and for three years the place remained deserted; then De Poincy sent out men to establish a colony which, though a small one, proved permanent.

Two years after the seizure of these islands, De Poincy decided to annex the important island of St. Croix, today the southernmost possession of the United States in the Virgin group. For several years it had been inhabited jointly by English and Dutch colonists, but of late the English had increased greatly in numbers, driving away the Dutch settlers who had been there for some time. The close proximity of such a large foreign colony to Puerto Rico was not relished by the Spanish authorities. They accordingly raised a large force of twelve hundred men in August, 1650, and made a surprise attack on the island, killing a large number of the inhabitants. The survivors took refuge in the woods where they were presently found by two of their number who had been taken prisoners by the Spanish commander. They presented his offer to leave the English unmolested for three weeks if they would arrange to quit the island during that time. There was nothing for them to do but accept, for the Spanish army far outnumbered them, so they quickly sent a messenger to the English governor at St. Christopher, Colonel Roland Rich, who had succeeded Sir Thomas Warner upon his death in 1648, asking him for ships to transport them and their household goods. This assistance was promptly given them.

When the Dutch at St. Eustatius heard of these events, they jumped at the opportunity to recover their lost colony. Thinking the Spaniards had returned to Puerto Rico after driving out the English, they loaded two barks with soldiers and set sail for St. Croix in the expectation of taking it without a struggle. In this they were quickly undeceived, for on landing they were met by a volley from the little fort where some sixty men had been left for just such an emergency. The little band of Dutchmen could do nothing but surrender.

It was at this stage that De Poincy entered the picture. Like Governor Adriensen he had heard of the expulsion of the English and regarded it as a heaven-sent opportunity to annex the island. He had, fortunately, no illusions about finding the place undefended; unlike the Dutch governor, he gave the Spaniards credit for holding it after they had expelled the English. A band of 160 picked soldiers was therefore selected for

THE FRENCH EXPAND

the job and dispatched under command of the Sieur de Vaugalan. On reaching the island Vaugalan decided to land at a spot about a league from the fort where he could assemble his men to march on the place in proper military formation; but by misfortune one of the vessels, which contained some forty men, missed the landing place, sailed into the harbor, and came to anchor under the guns of the redoubt. Seeing this strange bark the Spaniards guessed its errand, and to protect themselves against a sudden attack posted their men in an ambuscade to hold off a landing party. The Frenchmen, on the other hand, jumping to the erroneous conclusion that Vaugalan and his men had already arrived at the scene ready to support them hurried ashore to join them in the attack. No sooner had they landed than they were met with a volley from the Spaniards in ambush. Being good soldiers they faced the enemy, giving as good as they got, but in the end, numbers and advantage of position told, and all were killed save three or four who made their escape.

Three days later Vaugalan, tired of waiting for the ship that never came, decided to attack. He had a force of 120 men, all experienced fighters on whom he could rely. He set out for the fort, and after a brief march came to the harbor where he took up a position about eight hundred paces from his objective. Here he summoned the garrison to surrender. The Spaniards, of course, played for time; they sent back word they needed three days to think the matter over. Vaugalan, however, moved up his men to within two hundred paces of the fort, placing them behind a little hill where they would not be seen; at the same time he left a handful of men at his former position with orders to keep up a constant fire to cover the maneuver. Twice again Vaugalan summoned the Spaniards, and when at last they perceived the French army drawn up in front of them, they realized the game was up and promptly surrendered, asking only to be allowed to return to Puerto Rico, a favor at once granted them. On entering the fort, Vaugalan's first care was to set free a handful of wretched Dutch prisoners he found there and send them back with his compliments to Governor Adriensen.

Immensely pleased at the speedy capture of St. Croix which added another island colony to his rapidly expanding dominion, Governor de Poincy sent out three hundred men under the Sieur Auger to found a permanent settlement. This proved such a blow to Vaugalan, thanks to whose enterprise the island had been captured that he presently died of grief, according to Du Tertre. This statement, however, is not to be taken too seriously as the island proved unhealthy and took a heavy toll from its colonists, including three governors sent out during the following year. Yet St. Croix was the apple of De Poincy's eye. He swore it was the most beautiful of all the French islands, extolled its virtues, spent large sums on its development, and sent his closest friends there as officials; if one wished to get into his good graces, it was advisable to speak highly of its possibilities, and plan to send colonists there, even if the plan was never carried out.

While De Poincy was thus engaged in expansion to the north, Governor Houël saw fit to follow his example by adding to his possessions the little cluster of islands just south of Guadeloupe, known as the Saints. On October 18, 1648, Captain du Mé, accompanied by Father du Puy, landed there with thirty men, erected a cross and took possession with the customary ceremonies. It was a barren achievement, for a drought soon drove the pioneers back to Guadeloupe; but the islands had been formally annexed. Four years later M. du Buisson le Hazier took up the burden of settlement and founded a permanent establishment.

Having taken the first step, Houël decided to continue his policy of southward expansion and proceeded to colonize the island of Mariegalante which, like the Saints, was a natural dependency of Guadeloupe. The charter given the previous year to La Fontaine and Camot appears to have lapsed, since neither of the two grantees ever attempted to enforce the claim. There being no one to oppose him, Houël accordingly dispatched the

Sieur le Fort, hero of the mutiny at Martinique, who had come thence to Guadeloupe because of some misunderstanding with Du Parquet, to colonize the place with fifty men. He landed there on the eighth of November, erected a fort, labored assiduously for eighteen months, then returned to Martinique with a few of his followers, leaving the rest to shift for themselves. He was well received by Du Parquet who later used him in the colonization of Grenada.

Five years later Mariegalante received a severe blow. The Caribs of the Capesterre section of Dominica, returning from a raid on Antigua, stopped for a few days at the island where they were well entertained by the commander, being even invited to sleep in the fort. On reaching Dominica they were horrified to find that their homes had been pillaged during their absence by a gang of white marauders from Martinique. Eager for revenge they determined to raid a white settlement, and selected defenseless Mariegalante, since Martinique, though responsible for the outrage, was too strong for them. After all it was all part of the continual war with the white man. Naturally the inhabitants of the little island were unsuspicious when they saw the war canoes approaching, for were these not the savages they had entertained a few days before? The Caribs drove their boats up on the beach and immediately fell to work without a word of warning. They killed every last one of the inhabitants, looted the houses, and set fire to the entire village. From nearby Guadeloupe Houël saw the conflagration, and probably suspected its cause. As he was awaiting definite news, a canoe-load of savages came from the Basseterre part of Dominica to tell him of the massacre, strongly protesting their own innocence and blaming it all on their Capesterre neighbors, even volunteering to join a punitive expedition against them.

Before undertaking the chastisement of the Indians, Houël rebuilt the ravaged colony. He sent his brother, the Chevalier Robert Houël, with a hundred men to take charge of the work. The Chevalier landed in October and proceeded to repair the damage as best he could. His first task was to bury the dead whose mutilated corpses had been left on the shore where they fell, the heads crushed by war-clubs and severed from the bodies. This gruesome duty done, he started work on a fort (a more substantial structure than the former one), which he erected at a spot called Pointe du Fort at the southern extremity of the island. After three months of continual labor it was completed. It was built of stone with four large buildings within its walls, capable of giving shelter to the entire colony. After the Chevalier had returned to Guadeloupe to make his report, the Governor sent Captain du Mé with a band of soldiers to administer a well-deserved punishment to the savages of Dominica. Needless to say, nothing was done to the French brigands who had first attacked the Carib settlements and started all the trouble.

X

GRENADA AND ST. LUCIA

IT WAS now Du Parquet's turn to expand the dominion of France in the archipelago, and he proceeded to do so in the grand manner, annexing within the space of a year and a half the large and important islands of St. Lucia and Grenada. In doing so he was not actuated solely by a desire to increase the domain of the company—neither, indeed, were Houël and De Poincy—for the company was now seriously considering a plan to divest itself of its none-too-profitable proprietorship by selling the various islands to the governors who ruled them. The details leading up to the final transactions cover a considerable period of time and will be fully discussed in the following chapter. Meanwhile, we shall take up the story of the colonization of Grenada and St. Lucia.

The island of Grenada, one of the largest of the Lesser Antilles, is also the southernmost of the archipelago. One might say that it is the last stop before reaching Trinidad, and as such was regarded as particularly important by the Caribs who used it as a port of call on their journeys to the mainland. Governor de Poincy was the first to cast a covetous glance at it. In 1638, after listening to the glowing reports of its possibilities brought him by M. de Bonnefoy, he decided to take formal possession by planting a settlement on its shores. He abandoned the plan, however, on further consideration, as the large number of hostile Caribs inhabiting the island, and its distance from St. Christopher made colonization impractical. Five years later that unfortunate governor of Guadeloupe, M. Aubert, when he saw himself about to be superseded by Houël, dispatched an agent to look the place over, and was on the point of undertaking its settlement when the sudden arrival of the new incumbent took all his attention from extraneous affairs. Two years after this on July 10, 1645, the company gave the Sieur de Noailly a commission as governor of the island, and when he was unable to found a colony there, transferred it to his lieutenant who, like his superior, let it die on his hands. Such was the state of affairs concerning Grenada when Governor du Parquet turned his attention to it.

Shortly after his return from St. Christopher, that is towards the end of 1648, or perhaps in the early part of 1649, Du Parquet took the preliminary steps towards establishing a colony in Grenada.[1] Selecting a captain named La Rivière, who commanded a bark which he frequently used for fishing excursions near the island, the Governor sent him to build a house at some suitable spot along the shore near one of the native villages, a house wherein arms and munitions might be stored until a permanent fortification could be built to receive them. La Rivière acquitted himself well in this job. Skirting the western shore of Grenada, he landed in the harbor known today as St. George, and erected a small building at the foot of a nearby hill. To the Indians who flocked about him in a hostile manner, he pointed out the advantages they would gain by forming an alliance with the French against the predatory English. His arguments, reinforced by generous draughts of whiskey distributed to his listeners, had the desired effect, and he was able to return to Martinique fully confident that his mission had been successful.

[1] An account of the early events in Grenada is to be found, of course, in Du Tertre, but an anonymous account, entitled *Histoire de l'Isle de Grenada*, gives greater detail and is considered by Pierre Margry more reliable. He uses it in his article, "Origines françaises des pays d'outre-mer" in the *Revue maritime et Coloniale*, vol. 58, pp. 283-305. 1878.

Having heard his agent's report, Governor du Parquet bestirred himself to equip a suitable expedition. To make the undertaking attractive, he offered exemption from the payment of taxes to those who volunteered, an inducement so alluring as to give him the pick of his colonists. From the multitude that came to enlist, he selected 145 of the ablest and placed them on board the ships he had chartered for their transportation. This little armada consisted of two vessels, the one commanded by Jean Lepelletier, known as Captain Le Pas, the other by Captain Lorimer; and two barks, one of which belonged to La Rivière. The vessels were plentifully supplied with cassava bread, salt meat, pork, peas, and beans, enough to last several months, and Du Parquet also placed on board some timbers and planks already cut in sections for a house, so the building could be thrown together in a few days. There was also a supply of arms, munitions, and agricultural implements, and last, but not least, three kegs of whiskey and two pipes of excellent Madeira wine. Never before had an expedition for the colonization of a West Indian island been so well fitted out; even its personnel was carefully considered for it numbered several masons, carpenters, locksmiths, and artisans of various kinds. Thus equipped the expedition was ready for any emergency.

The fleet sailed on March 14, 1649, from Fort St. Pierre and entered St. George's Harbor three days later. The site selected for the settlement was an isthmus separating the southeastern part of the harbor from a small lagoon. Here the pioneers fell to work with a will. In a remarkably short time the ground was cleared, the house erected, and a stout palisade built around it pierced by loopholes for cannon. Because the fort was completed on the twenty-fifth of March, the day of the Annunciation, it was called Fort Annunciation; and Du Parquet seized the occasion to take formal possession of the island with the usual ceremonies. As he expected to return presently to Martinique he named his cousin, Jean Le Comte, a man fifty-five years of age, as the first governor of Grenada.

Meanwhile, the Caribs who had been watching the proceedings from the neighboring hills with some misgivings came fifty strong in a war-canoe, led by their chief, Kairouane. They were armed with bows and war-clubs, adorned in barbaric splendor with feathers, but otherwise, as a shocked missionary observed, they were in *puris naturalibus*. Captain La Rivière, who was the first one to sight the canoe, rushed down to greet the invaders, and as he understood their dialect he persuaded them to come ashore. With La Rivière as interpreter, Du Parquet explained the reasons for his coming and induced them to accept him as an ally against the English who might at any time come to seize the island. To make himself solid with them, he gave presents in the shape of axes, scythes, and various tools, topping off his munificence with a splendid red coat strewn with silver and a gray hat ornamented with feathers as a personal gift for Kairouane. It was hoped that in this manner the basis for future friendly relations might have been laid. On the sixth of April, Du Parquet left for Martinique in La Rivière's bark, while Captain Le Pas sailed for San Domingo.

The first few months passed quietly for the new colony. Land was cleared, houses erected on the shore of the lagoon near the fort, and the settlers went peacefully about their business of tilling the fields. But in the nearby island of St. Vincent, stronghold of the Caribs, grumblings of discontent were beginning to make themselves heard. The savages resented the presence of white men on this hitherto uninhabited island despite the friendly relations they had formed with the natives dwelling there. Matters were brought to a head when three Frenchmen from Martinique, while engaged on a fishing expedition among the Grenadines, looted a Carib canoe and made off with considerable booty. With the hearty approval and backing of the Indians at Dominica, the Caribs of St. Vincent decided to drive the French colonists from their possessions or massacre them on the spot.

An expedition was accordingly organized which reached

Grenada in November. Eleven canoes containing five hundred warriors armed to the teeth and ready for business descended on Fort Annunciation. Fortunately the French had been warned of the coming attack by a friendly Carib chief called Duquesne. Provisions were hastily stored inside the fort and all the inhabitants ordered to seek refuge within its walls. The Indians at once laid siege. For eight days the French remained within the palisade suffering greatly from lack of water, while the savages roamed around outside destroying everything they could lay their hands on. For some reason or other they did not venture a direct assault on the fort—perhaps the battery of guns deterred them—but contented themselves with setting fire to some dry shrubs to windward, hoping in this manner to destroy the palisade. The scheme failed when a torrential rain suddenly poured down from the heavens extinguishing the flames and thoroughly dampening the military spirit of the attackers. In a few days they decided to give up the attempt, and left as quickly as they had come.

This attack opened the eyes of Governor Le Comte to the true state of affairs behind the Indians' protestations of friendship. What had just taken place might occur again at any time, and perhaps with fatal results. Furthermore, the Caribs of Grenada, fired by the example of their fellow-Indians from St. Vincent, were becoming extremely hostile, murdering several colonists who had wandered off from the settlement. To protect his little colony, the Governor decided to carry the war into the enemy's territory, attack their village, conveniently situated on a nearby mountain, and drive them to some other part of the island, if he could not destroy them entirely. In order to accomplish this it would be wise to have assistance from Martinique, and he was about to apply to Governor du Parquet when an incident occurred which brought the desired help. A young savage named Thomas had sought the daughter of Chief Duquesne in marriage, and having been repulsed by the girl's brother, slew him and sought refuge in Martinique from the father's vengeance. Presenting himself before Du Parquet, he assured him that the Caribs sought his (Thomas's) life because he had always been friendly to the French, adding that if the Governor wished to save the colony at Grenada, now was the opportunity, for he would show him where he could surprise the Indians at a council they planned to hold on a mountain near Fort Annunciation. Du Parquet at once accepted the offer. Getting together a force of three hundred men, he set sail from Martinique on May 20, 1650, arriving at Grenada six days later.

Du Parquet landed his men and was immediately joined by Le Comte. The place where the savages were ensconsed was the summit of a hill which rose precipitately from the water's edge in such a manner as to form a perpendicular drop to the sea. That night a detachment of sixty men, led by the Governors, made its way up a rough path on the land side of the mountain to a place where the Caribs, some forty in number, were peacefully gathered, blissfully unconscious of the approaching enemy. A volley from the French, fired point blank into the camp was the first notice of an attack, but before the Indians had time to prepare for battle Du Parquet's men were on them. They were completely surrounded; wherever they turned they were met by musketry fire from men concealed behind rocks and trees. It was a massacre rather than a battle. At last, unable to break through the enemy's line, they turned in the only direction left open to them: the cliff overlooking the sea. Here they paused, for there was no way of escape. Then seeing only a choice between death by drowning and death at the hands of their foes, all that remained of the band, one by one leaped over the cliff into the sea. In a frenzy of victory, a victory won with the loss of only one man, the French set fire to the huts, destroyed the gardens, tore up the plants, then, happy in the belief that the Caribs would never have the heart to attack them again, they made their way back to the fort. The mountain from which the Indians had leapt was ever afterward called the Morne des Sauteurs.

His work done M. du Parquet bade farewell to Grenada on the

seventh of June, after authorizing the construction of a little fort, completed two weeks later, to be erected about a quarter of a league from the first one. It was named Fort St. John. For a garrison he left seventy men under the command of the Sieur Le Fort.

Du Parquet had hardly returned to St. Pierre when he undertook the colonization of St. Lucia, just south of Martinique. This island, well-known today for its rugged beauty, shares with Dominica the claim to being the most picturesque of the Caribbee chain. It is mountainous and wild, thrusting a jagged outline against the sky, yet it offers considerable acreage for cultivation, though its agricultural possibilities have never been fully exploited. It is known for its scenery rather than for its produce. The English were the first to attempt its settlement and sent out two expeditions at separate intervals which attempted to found a colony on its shores; but their efforts were fruitless, and it remained for the French to establish a permanent settlement which gave them title to ownership. The efforts of the English are interesting and well worth telling, particularly the first venture which took place before any of the Caribbees were settled.

In the year 1605 Sir Olive Leigh, "a worshipful knight of Kent," dispatched a ship, the "Olive Branch," under Captain Nicholas St. John, to carry a band of settlers to his brother, Charles, who had recently established a colony in Guiana. The expedition left Woolwich in April and headed south, but due to the master's lack of skill made a poor landfall, striking the South American coast, a considerable distance west of its objective, which meant a long beat against the prevailing easterly trade winds to reach its destination. As the supply of food was limited, the officers decided to put in at St. Lucia where additional provisions could, it was hoped, be obtained. The island, as we have said, is indeed a beautiful one, and one cannot blame Captain St. John and his sixty-seven passengers if they decided to give up the original plan of joining Charles Leigh's colony and found a settlement of their own. On the twentieth of August the party landed, bringing with them swords, muskets, gunpowder, and a curious assortment of beads, knives, and fishhooks, but only one barrel of biscuit. The following day the ship sailed, leaving the pioneers to their own devices.

Life went along pleasantly for a while. Game was abundant, and the settlers were able to obtain fruit and vegetables from the Caribs in exchange for their trifles, as well as some cloth and jars of oil the natives had salvaged from Spanish vessels wrecked on the coast. For several weeks they lived in this quiet manner until one day the captain chanced to notice on the arm of a native chieftain four square plates of a metal that resembled gold. To the white man's inquiries as to where he had got them, the Indian pointed to a high mountain in the northern part of the island. Nothing would satisfy St. John now but to lead a detachment in search of whatever might be the source of the precious metal. For this purpose an expedition was organized to proceed northward by sea, a much easier mode of travel than marching over the rough, mountainous ground, and a far safer one, too. As many as could safely be squeezed into the ship's boat, started northward, promising to be back in a week's time, saying hasty farewells to those left behind in charge of the captain's son, Alexander.

For several days those remaining in camp kept to the even tenor of their daily life, until a large force of Indians, some two or three hundred strong, had gathered about them. These men showed no signs of hostility; on the contrary, they smoked placidly and drank freely of their hosts' whiskey; then after a brief stay they started for their villages, leaving behind a chief named Augramert, Captain of the island of St. Vincent. Augramert proved friendly enough. He invited the colonists to make an excursion into the interior, and even led them in person a long distance inland through gardens planted with cassava and other native fruits. Having thus won their confidence, he urged a number of his white friends to make a further expedition, this time along the seashore. To this they willingly agreed, and the following day saw them tramping along the shore, joking with their guide in friendly fashion, until they came in sight of a group of native cabins. Then suddenly Augramert drew his sword and slashed at young St. John, while from a neighboring wood came a volley of arrows fired by a host of braves concealed in ambush. The Englishmen fled headlong from this savage attack until the youthful leader, recovering from the blow dealt him, rallied his men behind a point of land and attempted to put up a spirited resistance. But the Indians were too strong for them. Surrounded on all sides the white men took a terrific punishment from the volleys of arrows hurled on them. In despair they turned to the woods only to be met by another division that attacked them with swords and knives. Young St. John fell at last and with him all the band, save one, John Nichols, to whom we owe our narrative. "I only," he says, "with three arrows in me by running into the woods and swimming over a standing lake escaped home, giving them [the English] warning before they [the Caribs] came to assault them."

Three days later the Caribs arrived, a great host some thirteen or fourteen hundred in number, coming by land and sea from the further parts of St. Lucia and neighboring St. Vincent, in a final effort to drive out the obnoxious white men. For a space of seven or eight days the gallant band of Englishmen, now reduced to a meager nineteen, held off this army, barricading themselves behind their seachests, piled up to form a rude breastwork. When the huts were destroyed by flaming arrows, they salvaged what they could from the conflagration and reinforced the ring of chests with stakes and thatch, piling up earth over them to form a solid protection against the assaults of the enemy. The siege lasted a full week, then the Indians departed as suddenly as they had come, leaving the little garrison sadly reduced in numbers and almost without food. Later, a few Caribs returned, and to their credit be it said furnished the half-starving men with a supply of potatoes and plantains in exchange for a few beads and trinkets.

When these meager provisions were exhausted, the English cast about for means to leave the island. The ship's boat had been lost or destroyed; but by dint of persuasion, they induced the Caribs to give them a canoe in exchange for whatever beads and utensils they had left, and at once fell to work cutting a mast and shaping a sail. They worked under pressure for they were warned that Augramert would soon return from St. Vincent where he had gone to raise an army to finish the job of extermination. At midnight, the twenty-sixth of September, everything was ready, and the entire band, nineteen in number, embarked in the canoe. They had no card or compass to guide them nor did the leaders understand the art of navigation; but they "sailed by the sun in the daytime, and by the stars in the night, going always betwixt south and by west." The rest of the story does not come within the scope of our narrative, for it deals with the adventures of the explorers after they reached the Spanish Main. Suffice it to say that most of them eventually reached England. What became of the men who set out in search of gold in St. Lucia is not told us; doubtless they were all killed by the Caribs.[2]

It was towards this island of St. Lucia, where his fellow-countrymen had met with such remarkable adventures in the days before his arrival at St. Christopher, that Sir Thomas Warner directed his attention when planning his schemes of expansion over thirty years later. Whether St. John's expedition gave the English any valid title to the place is extremely doubtful; but at any rate, no one else had a better claim. Accordingly in the year 1638, Warner issued a commission to a planter of St. Christopher, named Captain Judlee, authorizing him to take possession of the island and found a colony there. Judlee collected a following of some three or four hundred people. Among these were 130 ambitious pioneers from Bermuda who had en-

[2]Purchas, *His Pilgrimmes*, edition of 1906, XVI, 324-37.

listed enthusiastically for St. Lucia despite the efforts made by the Bermuda authorities to restrain them by securing from the Commissioners of Foreign Plantations a grant of land in Virginia where life would be more pleasant than in this far-off island of the West Indies. Judlee's venture, despite its auspicious beginning, was not much of a success. He managed to found the colony, but two years later the settlers were in such want that Captain Philip Bell, later Governor of Barbados, applied for and obtained a permit allowing him to transport thither a huge supply of provisions together with 140 men to reinforce the stranded colonists. But the settlement was beyond assistance. Before Captain Bell could get his relief expedition under way, an incident occurred which settled the fate of the infant colony. An English ship becalmed off Dominica had welcomed on board some Indians who had come out on a friendly visit. They were well entertained, too well in fact, for while they were busy drinking the captain weighed anchor and put out to sea, hoping to carry off his guests to some port where they could be sold as slaves. Seeing themselves caught, they rushed to the vessel's side and dove overboard, all but four who were quickly grabbed by the crew and clapped into irons. On reaching land, for they were all powerful swimmers, these men complained loudly of the treachery of their hosts, and calling together a council of war induced the chiefs to send a message to Martinique and Dominica summoning all the braves for a raid on St. Lucia, the nearest of the British islands. The summons was promptly answered, and in August 1640, the savages landed on the island with fire and sword, killed the Governor together with most of the inhabitants, burned the houses, uprooted the meager crops, and caused such damage that the survivors were only too glad to escape. They blamed the attack on Du Parquet, asserting that he had been the instigator. Their leader even brought this preposterous charge to De Poincy's attention, but the Governor of Martinique gave ample evidence of his innocence, showing that far from having incited the Indians, he had sent warning to the Englishmen as soon as he had heard of the proposed attack.

When a period of ten years had elapsed after the expulsion of the English, Du Parquet saw no reason why he should not seize the island. He was at this time contemplating a voyage to France for the purpose of negotiating the purchase from the company of the islands under his jurisdiction, and it might be well, while he was about it, to add St. Lucia to his expanding domain. Busy with preparations for his coming journey, he could not spare the time to lead an expedition in person, and therefore selected Louis de Kerengoan, Sieur de Rosselan, a citizen of the Quartier St. Pierre who stood very high in the good graces of the Caribs because of a marriage he had contracted with a woman of their tribe. To the Sieur de Rosselan the Governor gave a detail of thirty-five or forty men well equipped for the business, and sent him forth on his errand some time in June, 1650. Rosselan made his way to the harbor on the western coast where the modern town of Castries now stands, and erected a fort at the mouth of the stream then called Rivière du Carenage, surrounded by a strong double palisade, well protected by a moat and some first-class artillery; for the Governor, despite his deputy's influence with the savages, did not trust them entirely. Rosselan was successful from the start. He immediately had his men clear the land for a tobacco plantation. The little colony prospered, and its governor lived there in peace and contentment until his death in 1654.

∾ XI ∾

GOVERNORS BECOME OWNERS

THE QUARRELS between the governors and their respective factions on one side and the representative of the King on the other, with their attendant periods of anarchy and confusion, could not fail to have a depressing effect on the finances of the company. M. de Poincy, intent on his own aggrandizement, cared little for the interests of those who had financed the undertaking, and when the planters of St. Christopher, during the quarrel with De Thoisy, refused to pay the taxes due the proprietors, he took no measures to compel them. Charles Houël was even more independent, stating boldly that inasmuch as he had used his own money prodigally in developing the island he owed the company nothing; on the contrary, the company was indebted to him. Only in Martinique do we find a governor who had some sense of the obligations due the backers of the colonial enterprise.

By 1648 the company was virtually bankrupt. A special meeting of the directors was called in May of that year to consider the situation and decide what course to pursue in order to remedy it, if a remedy was possible. It was disclosed at this meeting that a criminal action which had been instituted against De Poincy for his activities in resisting De Thoisy had been suffered to lapse, which had resulted in a complete loss of revenue from St. Christopher. A resolution was therefore passed to press the suit relentlessly until a verdict had been obtained.

The Queen Regent was also notified of the state of affairs and urged to bring her authority to bear on the culprit. A circular letter was sent out to all the stockholders calling a special meeting for the first Friday of June and setting forth the sorry state of the company's finances. The letter carefully explained how the disorders in the islands had cut all revenues, how it had been necessary to borrow money at usurious rates in order to meet the bills of exchange drawn by M. Houël for his establishment, how the wages of officers and servants had been allowed to accumulate until they reached a burdensome total, and how it would be necessary, if the business was to be saved, to have each stockholder contribute four thousand francs for each share he held in the business.

As might be expected, the stockholders showed no enthusiasm for this assessment. Not only had they received no returns on their investment for some time, but now they were expected to put in more money; to make matters worse, a letter was received at this time from Governor Houël in answer to complaints from the directors over his expense account in which he informed them somewhat haughtily that they need expect nothing in the immediate future. Stern necessity, he said, had caused him to run into debt; and, moreover, he himself had fared no better than the company for he had been obliged to buy some sixty slaves—for which he still owed fifteen thousand pounds of tobacco—to purchase foodstuffs, and pay the wages of workmen engaged in making repairs on the company's property. He concluded his letter by suggesting to the directors that since they were in his debt they might cede to him the island of Marie-galante on the same terms they held it from the King, and allow him to transport thither the sixty slaves for which they had never reimbursed him.

From this letter, and from other sources of information, the company saw the handwriting on the wall. The governors had made themselves masters of their islands, while the officers representing the directors no longer exercised any authority over them. The more interest the directors took in the colonies, the more they would be called upon to spend with little chance of ever getting any of it back. For this reason they decided to listen to proposals for the purchase of their island possessions by the governors ruling them, or by others who might be interested in their acquisition. The idea was not a new one, for during the previous year (1647) a proposition to sell St. Christopher to De Poincy's father had been seriously considered, and a committee had even been appointed to open up the negotiations. The directors fearing, however, that M. de Thoisy would seize the proceeds in payment of the damages he was claiming, decided to abandon the idea for the time being. Finally, it became necessary to liquidate the property to meet pressing debts. Mlle l'Olive, widow of the founder of Guadeloupe, had just won a suit against the company entitling her to a considerable sum, and there were also other creditors.

Fortunately for the company the governors were in a mood to buy. They knew the value of their colonies and the way to make them a paying proposition. Houël, as soon as he heard of the company's intentions, sent word to his brother-in-law, Jean de Boisseret d'Herblay, authorizing him to enter into negotiations for the purchase of Guadeloupe, Mariegalante, Desirade, which Houël had recently settled, and the Saints. The Governor urged Boisseret to buy the islands at any reasonable price, with the understanding that they be held in joint ownership by them both and the profits be divided equally between them. So great were the possibilities of Guadeloupe that Houël promised to deliver fifty thousand pounds of sugar, and also a considerable quantity of tobacco as early as 1649, with twice that amount the following year, a consignment easily worth thirty thousand francs. Thus, if arrangements could be made to extend the payment for the islands over a period of three or four years, the property could be acquired without putting up any cash.

Dazzled by the prospect of such wealth, M. de Boisseret hurried to the directors, and finding them as ready to sell as he was to buy closed the deal on September 4, 1649. But the company was unwilling to have Houël appear in the transaction, for some reason or other, and the bills of sale—there were two separate contracts—were accordingly made out to Boisseret alone. The prices agreed upon in the first contract were sixty thousand francs with the addition of six hundred pounds of sugar a year for the ownership of the four islands. The second document covered the property on the islands, both real and personal, that is, the houses, cattle, guns, munitions, and machinery which belonged to the company and were now turned over to the purchasers for eleven thousand five hundred francs to be paid to M. Rosée, merchant of Lyons, while at the same time the sum of fifteen hundred francs in cash was paid to cancel the annual payment of six hundred pounds of sugar. In addition to this Boisseret assumed the company's debts for wages etc. incurred in the islands.

Governor Houël, on learning the terms of the sale, was of course greatly displeased. As his name was not included in the contract, he jumped to the conclusion that his brother-in-law had tricked him to secure the property for his own family. Houël, as we know, was not a man to let himself be imposed upon. He showered Boisseret with letters breathing dire threats of vengeance until the unfortunate man at the urgent request of his wife, who was Houël's sister, made a separate contract associating the Governor of Guadeloupe in joint ownership with himself.

Now that he had rid himself of the company's yoke, Houël took measures to force Boisseret to sell him his share of the islands, for he had no intention of stopping until he was absolute master of Guadeloupe and its dependencies. By various methods, such as making large expenditures for which the co-owner had to bear half the burden, he seemed to be succeeding in his plan when he received the startling news from France that two powerful personages, the Prince d'Aubigny and Mme de Guébriant, were negotiating for the purchase of Boisseret's share. If unsuccessful, they planned to appeal to the King to have themselves substituted for Boisseret in the deal with the company, for, be it remembered, he had paid no cash for the property, but was to pay with the sugar to be sent from Guadeloupe. Houël bent every effort to prevent the consummation of this scheme. He urged his mother to obtain an order from the Royal Council forbidding the Prince or any other person from taking any action contrary to the edict of 1642, which, as the reader will recall, was the document confirming and enlarging the company's original charter. He also suggested that she spread a rumor describing military preparations in the archipelago made for the purpose of resisting by force any claims put forth by outsiders. These schemes evidently had the desired effect, for neither the Prince nor Mme de Guébriant pushed the matter any further, and Boisseret remained in possession of his share of the property.

The directors of the company who had always been well pleased with the administration of Du Parquet, far more so than with those of Houël and De Poincy, now desired to show their appreciation for his services by giving him the first opportunity to buy the property under his jurisdiction. On receipt of their letter granting him the option, Du Parquet sailed for France and promptly closed the deal on September 27, 1650, purchasing Martinique, St. Lucia, Grenada, and the Grenadines for 41,500 francs.[1] While in France he seized the occasion to present himself several times before the King who, pleased with the services he had rendered the Crown, appointed him in August, 1651, Governor-General of the islands he had acquired. Thus he became the sole proprietor of these islands and the King's representative in their government. By taking advantage of the Crown's edict of 1645, the one De Thoisy had brought with him to Guadeloupe which permitted the governors to create councils with the power to administer high justice, Du Parquet was able to exercise an almost complete control over the affairs of the islands he had purchased.

[1]This is the figure given by Margry in "Origines françaises des pays d'Outremer," *Revue maritime et coloniale*, LVIII (1878), 291.

With the sale of these two groups to their respective governors, the directors again turned their attention to the business of disposing of St. Christopher. The negotiations to sell the property to De Poincy's father had, as we have seen, been suffered to lapse, and now in taking up the business anew the Order of Malta, to which De Poincy belonged, appeared as a prospective purchaser. Evidently this powerful order considered the island a good investment, especially as it could be administered by one of their number. The business was placed in the hands of the order's representative, a M. de Souvré, who on May 24, 1651, purchased the property for one hundred and twenty thousand francs. St. Martin, St. Croix, and St. Bartholomew were also included in the bill of sale. Anxious to show its appreciation for the way in which he had built up the colony, an achievement now of great benefit to the order, the Grand Master confirmed M. de Poincy in his position as Governor with the title of bailiff. Shortly after this the Chevalier de Montmagny was sent to St. Christopher to succeed him. It was scarcely to be expected that De Poincy would grant the new arrival a hearty welcome, and Montmagny had the tact to see the point. He therefore took up his residence in Cayonne where he lived in retirement, patiently awaiting the demise of the Governor. But fate willed otherwise, and Montmagny himself died in 1657 leaving De Poincy master of the situation.

Having thus obtained the ownership of St. Christopher and its adjacent islands by buying out the company, the order sought to secure the right of eminent domain over them by obtaining an edict from the King. M. de Souvré was entrusted with the mission. He appeared at Court and urged that the many services rendered the Faith by the Knights of Malta made it desirable for them to have a post besides the one in the Mediterranean where they could carry on their work. As De Poincy had frequently drawn funds from certain properties of the order which he controlled, for the purpose of building up his colony, it would not be out of place to put the colony under

GOVERNORS BECOME OWNERS

the jurisdiction of the Knights in order to reimburse them. To this the King agreed, and in March 1653, he ratified both the edict of 1642 and the recent sale by a document in which he decreed that the Grand Master was to enjoy direct lordship and proprietorship over St. Christopher and its dependencies, including the ownership of all fortifications, the rights of lay patronage over the Church, and the royal right to appoint judges and officers to judge criminal and civil cases. The King reserved for himself only the right of sovereignty to be acknowledged by the payment of a crown of gold worth one thousand *écus* to each future king at his accession to the throne. It was understood that the command of the island was never to be given to any one save a subject of the King of France. With the cession of St. Christopher to the Knights of Malta, the Company of the Isles of America divested itself of the last shred of property it held in the West Indies, and the three groups of islands were now each under a different proprietor who ruled his domain subject only to the authority of the King.

During 1654 the island of Guadeloupe was benefited by the influx of a large number of Dutch Protestant colonists, driven to its shores by the loss of their colony at Pernambuco. The Portuguese, who considered this place within their domain, had besieged it successfully and insisted that all its inhabitants leave at once, though they permitted them to take away their portable property including their slaves. This, of course, made them valuable additions to any settlement, for they were experienced pioneers and had the wherewithal to set themselves up and add to the wealth of the colony. Sailing northward from Pernambuco, they eventually came to Martinique. The leaders went ashore to pay their respects to the Governor and requested permission to settle on the island with the same privileges as the French planters. Du Parquet saw clearly how valuable such people would be to his colony, and was on the point of acceding to their demand when the Jesuit fathers pointed out that by admitting these people, many of whom were Jews, he would be encouraging heresy and Judaism in the colony in contravention of the King's orders. It was, unfortunately, too true, and Du Parquet felt obliged, with many protestations of regret, to forbid their landing.

Undaunted by this rebuff, the migrants set sail for Guadeloupe where they met with a very different reception, for Governor Houël knew the value of these people and intended to profit by their misfortunes. Thus it was that when the first shipload anchored off the shore and the leaders asked permission to land, he gave them a royal welcome and acceded to all their requests. Other vessels came the following day, one of them a huge ship which saluted the fort with a salvo of guns, setting fire to her magazine and blowing off her stern, killing nearly everyone on board and destroying one hundred and fifty thousand francs worth of property. Several other ships now brought their quotas until as many as nine hundred persons, including slaves, had landed, bringing with them immense riches in the shape of gold, silver, precious stones, and silver plate which they used to buy supplies.

M. du Parquet was by no means pleased when he learned of the wealth he had let slip through his fingers and was inclined to take it out on the Jesuit fathers. To appease him the superior proceeded to Guadeloupe, hoping to persuade Governor Houël to dismiss his guests as Du Parquet had done, thus preventing Guadeloupe from benefiting from the opportunity Martinique had lost. But Houël was not to be intimidated. He suggested politely to the priest that it was none of his business and sent him back to Martinique. Shortly after this a ship that had fallen behind appeared at the latter island with three hundred refugees. This time there was no hesitation on the part of Du Parquet. He gave them a concession around Cul de Sac Royal and put them to work. Scarcely had they settled there, however, when they were raided by the Caribs who destroyed their houses and drove them to seek shelter in the French settlements.

The advantages to be derived from the addition of these new

arrivals in Guadeloupe were enormous, at least so they appeared at first. Du Tertre puts their number at twelve hundred of whom nine hundred landed on the island. Among them were three hundred experienced Walloon and Flemish soldiers, the rest skilled planters who brought with them two hundred women and three hundred slaves. Furthermore, many of them understood the sugar business which proved to be a godsend to the colony. Houël brought the leaders to Capesterre to show them the soil, and after giving it a careful examination they pronounced it to be excellent for purposes of sugar raising, an opinion that in the long run was well justified by the results. The Governor thereupon made arrangements with a planter, skilled in handling the machinery for this sort of work, to organize a large sugar plantation, advancing him ten oxen, twelve cows, two horses, two wagons, and promising him twelve slaves from the next batch brought to the island. In addition to this, he also allotted the planter one-half his lands at Ste. Marie for twenty years and a plot of ground adjacent to it in perpetuity. The recipient of these bounties obligated himself to keep a certain amount of this land under cultivation, retaining three-fifths of the produce in return for his labor, while Houël and Boisseret received two-fifths. At last it seemed as though prosperity had come, despite theological differences. But the outcome was far different from what Houël had expected. Gradually the leading Dutch planters withdrew, not only from Guadeloupe but from Martinique as well, while the others, including the Jews, set up cheap eating establishments where they sold food for cash only, that is, for gold or silver instead of tobacco, the common medium of exchange on the islands, and were thus able to make a clean sweep of Guadeloupe and Martinique, recapturing all the precious metal they had brought with them in the fleet.

The year which saw the arrival of the Dutch refugees also witnessed a prolonged and savage war with the Caribs, waged on a larger scale than any heretofore. The cause of the uprisings lay in the resentment of the Indians toward French expansion in

Mariegalante, St. Lucia, and Grenada. The almost simultaneous seizure of these important islands gave them a feeling of insecurity; perhaps, they thought, the day was at hand when they would be driven from the islands forever. The outbreak of hostilities took the French by surprise, for they believed the chastisement inflicted by Houël on the Indians of Dominica for their attack on Mariegalante would keep them quiet for a while; but at this moment an incident occurred for which the French were entirely to blame that gave the savages their *causus belli*.

A sea captain, laboring under the impression—whether true or false we cannot say—that a Carib of St. Vincent whom he had on board his vessel was responsible for the death of one of his men, caused him to be lashed to the mast and given a fearful flogging. The fellow managed to escape and rejoined his tribe where he displayed his wounds, demanding vengeance for the sufferings he had undergone and for the insult offered the tribal honor by this assault on his person. Already angered at the French, the Indians needed but such an outrage to set them in motion; and, when at the same time a band of them killed a Frenchman who had attempted to shoot one of their number, all rushed about the island shouting that war had actually begun and every man must see it through.

Once the decisive step had been taken, the Caribs went to work. First they destroyed the local missionary settlement, then, there being no other Frenchmen at St. Vincent on whom they could vent their feelings, they gathered together in a goodly number, jumped into their canoes, and headed for Grenada. Here they roused the natives to join them in a war against the French settlers, who by this time had spread northward from St. George's Harbor and were living on plantations scattered over the countryside. The first blow fell on the fourteenth of April, when a colonist named Sieur Imbaut was attacked and murdered. The following day the Caribs surrounded the house of M. de la Mare where a number of people had taken refuge, and set fire to the roof with flaming arrows. The inmates managed to escape, but as they fled southward to Beausejour, they were caught in an ambush at Rivière de l'Anse-Noire and suffered heavy losses.

News of the invasion spread quickly throughout the island and all hastened to seek shelter in well fortified places, while the Caribs followed them up, burning their houses and pillaging their plantations. A month later the savages invaded Beausejour, and using the same tactics, scattered the inhabitants, driving them back into the forests where they nearly perished of hunger. Only the providential arrival of a ship from Cayenne which carried some three hundred soldiers saved the colonists from utter destruction. Glad to earn a little honest money, the new arrivals agreed—for a consideration—to serve as guards, and took up their position on the Morne des Sauteurs in a little redoubt named Fort d'Esnambuc after Du Parquet's young son, whence they made sorties from time to time in the line of business.

Meantime Governor du Parquet heard of the uprising. Anxious to secure peace on what he hoped would be a permanent basis, he wrote Governor Le Comte urging him to take as many men as he could without weakening his defenses, march northward to Capesterre, and drive out those Caribs who came from St. Vincent, taking care, however, not to harm those of Grenada who, so he thought, would never have given trouble had they not been stirred up by outsiders. If the situation had been less serious, Le Comte would have been amused. "How," he asked, "can I attack the savages of St. Vincent without touching those of Grenada when they are always together and have the same complexions, manners, and language?" Nevertheless, he decided to carry out his orders as best he could, without too much regard for the nice distinctions drawn in Martinique. Leaving Beausejour with a small squad, he sent the Sieur Le Marquis with fifty men by another route so as to catch the enemy between two fires. The maneuver was successful; the Caribs, domestic as well as foreign, were destroyed to the number of eighty, their houses were burned, and their property confiscated. The return to St. George's Harbor was to have been one of triumph, but at an unfortunate moment Le Comte gave orders to proceed by sea to Fort d'Esnambuc despite the advice of his officers who saw a storm brewing. Scarcely had they gone a couple of leagues when the storm broke, driving their little vessel on a rock where she foundered. M. le Comte and several of his companions were drowned.

The victory, as subsequent events proved, had its unfortunate repercussions. Had Le Comte been able to carry out Du Parquet's orders and attack only the natives of St. Vincent, there might have been no evil consequences, but the Caribs of Grenada were now fully determined to seek revenge. Gathering together a sizable flotilla of twenty-four war canoes, they proceeded down the coast to the Grande Anse, south of St. George's Harbor, where they landed and began to lay waste the countryside. A month later they returned to attack the redoubt of a planter named Sieur Mariage, but despite their success in wounding the owner, his place was too well guarded for them to take it. After another month they suffered a decisive defeat at Fort d'Esnambuc and abandoned the enterprise.

It was at this time that Du Parquet sent out Louis Caqueray de Valmenière to replace Le Comte. M. de Valmenière used excellent judgment in handling the situation. He brought together in places of safety the colonists who lived on scattered plantations, for the Caribs were now masters of the sea, pursuing French boats whenever they could find them, making sudden raids on the coastal settlements, and carrying off the inhabitants to St. Vincent where they were held as slaves.

In St. Lucia a similar event took place. M. de Rosselan at his death had been replaced by Captain La Rivière who had commanded one of the vessels that brought the first French settlers to Grenada. He was well liked by Du Parquet, but the Caribs who had been extremely friendly with the former governor because of his marriage to an Indian woman, felt no special interest in La Rivière. He had taken up his residence at some distance from the fort, where he lived with his family in a handsome residence. Here the Caribs saw their opportunity to get rid of him and began to make friendly advances to lull him into security. Eager to please his savage neighbors, the Governor invited them to his home where he entertained them with great hospitality. One day as they were drinking together, they hurled themselves on him and quickly dispatched him with ten of his people. He was succeeded as governor by M. Haquet, a relative of Du Parquet, who lasted but two years when he was severely wounded in an attack by the natives and forced to retire to Martinique where he soon died.

M. du Parquet now made a curious appointment: he selected for the successor of Haquet a man who had formerly served his wife in the capacity of valet. Why he did this is difficult to say, unless it was because the position of governor of this savage island did not appeal to any one else; at any rate the choice was an unfortunate one, as the officers there, feeling it beneath their dignity to serve under such a leader, presently fled and took refuge on an English bark that happened to be in the harbor and set sail for home. The cause of this sudden exodus cannot, however, be laid wholly to snobbishness on their part, inasmuch as the Sieur Le Breton, for such was the valet-governor's name, had proved to be a haughty man who enjoyed giving orders in a loud voice and comported himself with all the arrogance of a parvenu. Though there is no reason to suspect that he tried to abuse those under him, the soldiers tried to kill him before embarking in the English vessel, but he made his escape to the woods, leaving the fort deserted. A few days later a French vessel chanced to enter the harbor and was hailed by Le Breton who asked to be taken to Martinique. The captain, seeing the fort in excellent condition, placed four sailors there to guard it while he made a report on the situation to Du Parquet. At Martinique Le Breton told his story to the Governor, who suspecting the true reason for the desertion of the island by his men, determined to send someone better suited socially to command officers. He selected the Sieur Coutis, to whom an allowance of two thousand pounds of tobacco a year was made, and dispatched him with forty men to re-establish the colony of St. Lucia.

The attacks on Grenada and the massacre at St. Lucia made Du Parquet fear that the storm would presently break on Martinique itself. Realizing that the best defense would be a vigorous offensive, he decided to carry the war into the enemy's stronghold at St. Vincent. For this purpose he equipped a small fleet consisting of a ship of twelve guns, a bark of four guns and two *pierriers*, or mortars used for throwing stone projectiles, another of two guns and four mortars, and a small boat of two mortars. The flotilla was used to transport one hundred and fifty picked men under the command of La Pierrière who was given strict orders to do a thorough job, sparing neither women nor children. It is somewhat of a shock to hear Father du Tertre calmly mentioning such a barbarous order as though it called for no disapproving comment, and to learn that it was issued by the generous Du Parquet who is lauded by more than one writer for his humane character. The attitude of white pioneers toward savages is one that cannot be clearly understood today, and the more we delve into it, the more puzzled we become. Zealous missionaries devoted their lives to the salvation of these backward people yet laymen slew them with little compunction. Whatever may have been their Christian ideals, the pioneers lived too close to nature to be troubled by theories; to them the Carib, whatever the Church might say about his soul, was a savage belonging to a race inferior to the white men. When he attacked them, even though it was with justification, the French knew instinctively that they must destroy him or perish themselves. It is all very well to speculate on what might have been the result if Europeans had at all times been governed by a humane and enlightened policy in dealing with the savage. The rank and file of colonists did not come from the better class of people. Many were persons who had few principles and were ready to rob and abuse the savage if they felt it to their advantage to do so, and once they had roused him to seek vengeance, the entire colony was forced to side with them for its own protection.

When the little armada reached St. Vincent, it found the enemy ready to receive it. The savages had built a sort of breastwork by placing their canoes end to end and filling them with sand; by lying prone behind this protection, they managed to withstand the gunfire of the French vessels as one after another discharged its broadside. Unable to dislodge the Indians by this mode of attack, the French headed their ships for the beach to make a landing; the Indians thinking they could now meet their foes man to man leaped from behind the canoes and rushed to the water's edge. This was just what the French hoped they would do. Loading their mortars with musket balls, they poured a volley into the Indian mob, killing quite a number and driving them back into the forest. For eight days the French ravaged the western part of the island, burning houses and plantations, slaying all who came in their way until they had driven the Caribs eastward into the Capesterre region. This done, they returned to Martinique.

The attack, thorough as it had been, did not put an end to the war. The savages had been defeated, not exterminated, and they now staged a comeback. At this time an incident occurred which roused the Indians of Martinique, who in turn rallied to them the natives of the nearby islands in a concerted movement against the French. A band of eight or ten Indians had been brought before Governor du Parquet accused of the murder of five Frenchmen. The accusation was no doubt a valid one, at least the council before which they were tried did not hesitate to pronounce them guilty. The Governor sentenced them to be clubbed to death with axes in the same manner as they had killed their victims, a sentence which was carried out after the Jesuit fathers had been given an opportunity to baptize them.

This execution, which may have been necessary, had the effect of infuriating the savages. Unable to attack the French successfully without assistance, they sent to the neighboring islands for reinforcements and soon a formidable army of two thousand men had surrounded the Governor's fortified residence. Realizing the seriousness of the situation, he sent his wife under a strong escort to Fort St. Pierre, where terrified by the showers of arrows she had been obliged to pass through, she gave premature birth to her child, the third she had borne her husband. Having thus placed his wife out of harm's way, he put his house in condition to sustain the assault. It came with terrific force, and soon the Governor realized that he lacked sufficient ammunition to hold out very long. When the Caribs saw the fire slacken, they would have charged the house had they not feared the huge dogs kept by the French to track down runaway slaves, dogs which they knew from past experience were more than a match for them. In fact, the savages were on the verge of retreating when they were joined by some fugitive blacks who had old scores to settle with their masters. Heartened by these allies, they at once started off to destroy the settlements. They burned houses, slaughtered the inhabitants, often with revolting cruelty, and bid fair to reduce the entire colony to ruin.

Matters now went from bad to worse.

The island of Martinique [says Du Tertre] was in a horrible state of confusion; the officers could no longer enforce obedience; they could not rally the inhabitants; each one took to flight, all forgot their duty to the public safety, thinking only of their own particular interests. Those who did not feel safe in their homes fled to the woods where the savages and blacks killed them with arrows and war-clubs.

At this moment, however, help came in the shape of four large Dutch vessels which sailed providentially into the harbor. From their decks the officers had noticed the fires rising in different parts of the island, and through their glasses had seen the inhabitants running wildly about. Suspecting a war with the Caribs or a slave revolt, they decided to land three hundred soldiers and lend a hand to the defeated French. Three times they charged the savages before the latter broke and fled to the jungle, leaving the French and Dutch masters of the field. Thankful for a breathing spell, the Governor purchased a supply of ammunition from the Dutch merchants and sent his men under the leadership of Guillaume d'Orange to pursue the fast retreating Caribs. D'Orange fought valiantly, and after nearly losing his own life in the attempt, succeeded in crushing the insurrection.

While these events were taking place in Du Parquet's domain, M. Houël was pursuing his plans to get rid of his brother-in-law as a partner and obtain the ownership of all their joint property for himself. Such a maneuver required delicate handling, and the Governor felt it would be better for him to go to France in person to see the business through. Wishing to keep the real purpose of his intended voyage a secret, he spread the rumor that he had been forced to return home because of urgent private affairs. On July 8, 1654, he appointed his brother the Chevalier Robert Houël and his nephew, Charles de Boisseret d'Herblay (whom we shall refer to as D'Herblay to distinguish him from his father), acting joint commanders to govern the island during his absence, warning them at the same time to keep a watchful eye on Mariegalante, which had been destroyed by the Caribs and rebuilt by the Chevalier the previous year.

Left to himself after the Governor's departure, the Chevalier discovered a rather sorry state of affairs. There were but twelve hundred men on the island capable of bearing arms, including three hundred Portuguese whom he did not consider reliable, while the stock of ammunition was low, and the prisons were filled with men condemned as lawbreakers. To quiet the persistent grumblings, Robert Houël, ably seconded by d'Herblay, ordered a general jail delivery, and conducted himself with such tact and moderation as to win the general approval of the colonists.

During February, 1655, word came to Guadeloupe of the arrival in the West Indies of a formidable English fleet under Admiral Penn, composed of no less than seventy ships carrying ten thousand men. It was the armada sent out by Oliver Cromwell to attack San Domingo which ended by capturing Jamaica instead. Though the expedition was aimed at Spain's West Indian empire, the French naturally felt alarmed when such a swarm of English Puritans entered the Caribbean. Rumors flew thick and fast telling of English schemes to drive the French from St. Christopher and from the other islands as well. Messengers scurried back and forth between the three governors with plans for coöperation and defense, until the fact was recognized that they could not break through this great fleet to help each other, and they decided that each one would have to act for himself. The Chevalier Houël for his part ordered all work to cease and everyone to join in fortifying the various places where the English might be expected to land. Trees were felled along the seashore closing up the roads leading into the interior; lookouts were posted at strategic points to discover the fleet and give the alarm to the inhabitants. When the English ships at last appeared, the entire colony sprang to arms and rushed to the shore. Admiral Penn headed for the roadstead at Basseterre with the intention of landing, but when he saw from his quarterdeck the settlers swarming towards the shore guns in hand, he wisely gave up the plan and coasting northward disappeared in the direction of St. Christopher.

The year 1656 brought considerable excitement to Guadeloupe and Martinique. A frightful hurricane, the worst in the memory of the oldest inhabitant struck Guadeloupe, and would have put an end to the colony had it not been for the help received from Martinique, which does not seem to have suffered so much from its violence. The storm, which was the third to visit the island in fifteen months, was ushered in by a strange rumbling in the forest which lasted for three hours; then came a series of whirlwinds of terrific violence that overturned groves of trees, wrecked houses, and swept away everything in their wake.

When these had passed, the sky turned a flaming color like redhot iron while blinding flashes of lightning followed by crashing peals of thunder struck terror into the hearts of the inhabitants. Suddenly the wind shifted to the west with a force that drove the ships anchored off Basseterre high up on the rocks, breaking them into pieces and drowning their crews. At four o'clock the next morning the real storm began, and in five or six hours it had uprooted all the trees in the vicinity, killed the birds, poultry, and animals, both wild and domestic, and destroyed the crops with such thoroughness that the colony stood face to face with starvation.

The storm [wrote Houël] did not leave us wherewith to feed a single man, the fierce burning winds have ruined our crops of peas and killed whatever vegetables the caterpillars did not eat; if the other settlements had been as badly damaged as ours it would have been necessary to abandon the island as we lacked enough to eat; it was necessary to see the extent of the damage to believe it.

Martinique, though it escaped the fury of the hurricane, experienced a convulsion of nature equally terrifying even if it did not do so much damage. Father Jean-Baptiste Feuillet has left us a vivid account of his experiences and of the terror it inspired among the inhabitants. An earthquake, lasting about two hours, overturned buildings and hurled terrified people to the ground. Even the sturdy stone residence of M. du Parquet was badly shaken and the unfortunate Governor obliged to seek shelter in a neighboring field followed by his family and household servants. Feuillet tells us that the village chapel after a violent shock remained standing for a quarter of an hour leaning like the Tower of Pisa, when a second quake knocked it back into position; a strange tale, but one that may well have been true. Even the ships in the harbor felt the effects of the seismic disturbance, and two that slipped their cables to gain the open sea were tossed about in the seething whirlpools formed by the settling of the ocean's bed.

Alarming as these visitations were, they were but minor misfortunes compared with the slave insurrection that took place toward the end of the year. Two Guadeloupe negroes named Pedre and Jean Le Blanc organized a conspiracy among the blacks of Angola, the slaves captured on the part of the African coast known by that name. These slaves lived for the most part in Capesterre and formed a different group from the Basseterre blacks who were natives of Cape Verde; but in order to make the uprising a success, Pedre and Le Blanc had enlisted the coöperation of the latter. The two leaders proposed to kill the whites, steal their women, and set themselves up as kings of Guadeloupe, one in Basseterre, the other in Capesterre. On the day set for the outbreak, the scheme was nearly wrecked by regional jealousy. Pedre and Le Blanc had gathered their men near a house in the Capesterre section where they were to await the coming of their allies. As the day wore on, however, the Cape Verde negroes failed to appear and at last the men from Capesterre realized they would have to carry out the plan by themselves or abandon it entirely. Rather than do the latter, they decided to attack. Bursting into the house they slaughtered the inmates, gathered what loot they could lay their hands on, seized whatever weapons they could find, and fled to the woods.

For twelve or fifteen days the negroes carried on a series of raids, attacking the outlying plantations, and killing all that fell into their hands. The colonists were terrified. No one seemed to know what to do to bring the slaves back to their duties; everyone feared the worst. Fortunately there was a Walloon gentleman named Despinay who stepped forward in this crisis and volunteered to march against the rebels with a detachment of twenty picked men, an offer which, needless to say, was gratefully accepted. He selected his men carefully, adding to them a number of Brazilian slaves to carry the provisions; and among the latter was one who, thanks to an abnormal sense of smell, could distinguish the tracks of a negro from those of a white man. The fugitives, knowing well that they would soon be followed, took to the mountains, hoping to reach Basseterre by unfrequented routes and compel the Cape Verde slaves to join them. The human bloodhound, however, quickly picked up their trail, and it was not long before Despinay and his men overtook the band and opened fire on them. Terrified at this sudden attack, the blacks fled helter-skelter each man for himself with the colonists hot on their heels, and in a short while the entire band was captured and brought in for punishment. The two would-be kings were drawn and quartered, some were torn asunder alive, others were hanged, while the young boys had their ears cut off and afterward were let off with a sound flogging. Governor Houël evidently considered these punishments a matter of state policy for on his return he generously reimbursed the owners for all the slaves he had executed.

A similar disturbance, though one not accompanied by such violence, took place simultaneously in Martinique. The slaves of this island appear to have been more anxious to obtain freedom by flight than by attacking their masters; they had no ambition to dominate the colony like Pedre and Le Blanc. They sought safety among the Caribs of Capesterre who received them well at first, but then bore them off to sell on the Spanish islands. To stop this general flight, some owners put their slaves in irons; but this proved to be no solution of the problem as it served only to irritate them, and the evil grew like a plague that attacked even the most faithful negroes. To meet the situation, Du Parquet sent reconnoitering parties into Capesterre to discover their hideout. Presently someone brought him word of a road by way of Mt. Pelee, and a detachment of soldiers was dispatched to explore it, but they returned without finding any trace of the slaves. Guillaume d'Orange was now sent by sea to make a tour of the island for the same purpose, but his expedition was also a failure.

Now that they were so well reinforced by the blacks, the Caribs decided to renew their attacks on the settlements using their newly found allies as shock troops to carry on their raids. The blacks were armed with bows and war-clubs, disguised as Indians, and placed in the van on these marauding expeditions.

With a torch in one hand and a club in the other, they bore down on their prey during the night, set fire to the houses, and beat down the inmates as they rushed forth into the open. In time these fellows grew bolder, making their attacks in broad daylight, on one occasion breaking into the home of a planter at Morne de Riflet despite the efforts of a detachment rushed there from the nearest fort. It is to M. d'Orange's credit that his slaves refused to desert him and fought valiantly against the Caribs and their fugitive allies. Perhaps harsh treatment of their slaves on the part of certain planters may have been at the root of the trouble, for D'Orange was known for his humane attitude toward those working under him.

For two years the problem of runaway slaves continued to beset the colonists of Martinique, until seeing they could never hold them as long as the Caribs were ready to shelter them or lend them canoes for making their escape, they gathered together and drove the Indians into Capesterre. The savages, tired of the continual warfare, then made overtures of peace and sent a delegation to M. du Parquet on October 18, 1657, under a safe conduct guaranteed by one of the missionaries. The Governor was confined to his house at this time through illness, but pleased at the opportunity to end the long-drawn-out struggle, he had himself carried to the fort on a stretcher where he received the emissaries with gifts of knives, axes, and cotton cloths. Peace was declared, hostages were exchanged, and the following day M. d'Orange visited the Caribs in Capesterre where he called on them in their homes and received pledges from them not to harbor any more runaway slaves.

While the treaty prevented the slaves from finding asylum in Capesterre, it did not cut off the possibility of their escape from the island, and Du Parquet soon found it necessary to take precautions to prevent their reaching the coast. For a time he detailed his own personal guards to do police duty about the island, but this soon proved too great a task for so small a body of men. He therefore conceived a plan to raise money by a special tax which would be devoted to employing men for this purpose. Strange to say the colonists refused to ratify this measure, though it was in reality a sort of insurance against the loss of slaves. This might have been the end of the matter if a ship belonging to the Governor had not been wrecked while patrolling the approaches to the island. Alarmed at the number of slaves which the Caribs from the neighboring islands were now able to spirit away, the planters themselves decided to raise a sufficient sum by taxation to maintain with the Governor's financial assistance a coastguard vessel and employ men to police the shores.

The time has now come for us to take leave of M. du Parquet and see his great property pass into the hands of others. For some time he had been suffering from gout, so Du Tertre tells us, a strange ailment for one who could not have indulged in high living to any extent, and recently his condition had been aggravated by the worries of the slave revolt. Toward the end of the year, however, he had recovered sufficiently to make a short journey to Case Pilote where he and Mme du Parquet had been invited to act as godparents to the child of M. de la Vallée, captain of the *quartier;* and here he suffered the shock which brought about his death. The day after the ceremony he chanced to be standing in the public square when a habitan named Bourlet approached him, and in an insolent manner boasted that there were many who would refuse to pay the tax recently voted and were ready to kill those responsible for its enactment. Under ordinary circumstances Du Parquet would have drawn his sword on the insolent fellow, but realizing his condition he prudently withdrew into the guardhouse. Two days later he learned that Bourlet had sent an agent to the Quartier du Prêcheur to rouse the planters. Springing into the saddle, Du Parquet set forth after him with his guards. By sheer force of personality he succeeded in nipping the uprising in the bud, not only here but at Fort St. Pierre and the Carbet as well, for he held his own with such energy that no one dared oppose him, and the tax was quickly collected.

It was, however, his last effort. The exertion and excitement of the past few days were too much for the ailing man, and feeling that his time had come, he retired to the residence of the Dominican fathers where he spent three hours preparing for death. From there he was carried to his home, and died a few days later on January 3, 1658, shortly after midnight, surrounded by his wife and children. Father Feuillet, who was present at his death, gives us an intimate description of the way he met his end. After bidding farewell to his family, he devoted himself with the help of Father Boulogne, his confessor, to his religious duties. Sending for Judge Fournier, he caused him to destroy in his presence the indictments he had brought against Bourlet, the instigator of the recent mutiny, whom his officers wished to put to death, and tendered him his forgiveness. He also withdrew his permission given a Dutch merchant to buy a plantation on the island, as he wanted the law forbidding heretics from owning property to continue in force after his demise. These matters attended to, he turned his attention to more spiritual affairs and continued his devotions with the help of the priests who had gathered about him until he passed away.

The following day his body was taken to his private chapel where Fathers Boulogne and Borde celebrated a mass for the repose of his soul. The funeral was conducted with all the pomp the colony could muster. At ten o'clock in the morning a procession left the chapel for the Church of St. Jacques headed by four companies of the militia numbering six hundred men, who marched with reversed arms to the sound of muffled drums. After them came the clergy reciting the office for the dead, followed by twelve guards in scarlet cloaks embroidered each with a white cross. Eight of the more prominent habitans bore the casket on their shoulders, marching ahead of three officers who carried respectively the Governor's helmet, his gloves, and his sword bound in crepe. From the Governor's residence to the church, the road was lined with women, children, and slaves who had come from nearby plantations and villages to show their respect for the deceased ruler. High Mass was celebrated, after which the body was interred in the churchyard amid salvos from the guns of the fort.

In this manner, amid the general mourning of his people, did the Governor of Martinique depart from this world. Of that great triumvirate which for nearly twenty years had governed and misgoverned the French West Indies, Jacques Dyel du Parquet was considered by his contemporaries as the most public spirited and the best fitted to rule. Under his able guidance Martinique had been raised from a small settlement to a prosperous colony, and the large islands of St. Lucia and Grenada had been added to the French domain. His piety and considerate treatment of the clergy, so different from the bullying attitude frequently adopted toward them by Houël and De Poincy, may account in some degree for the approval given him by all but one of the contemporary historians, for the writers of the early accounts were nearly all clergymen; but setting aside this natural bias, the records show that Martinique during his administration was comparatively free from the numerous dissensions that mar the history of St. Christopher and Guadeloupe.

~ XII ~

TRIALS AND TRIBULATIONS
OF OWNERSHIP

SHORTLY after the return of M. de Thoisy to France in 1647, Father du Tertre had elected to follow him and since that time had been living quietly at the Dominican convent in Paris working on his history of the French West Indies. While thus engaged he was suddenly surprised, early in the year 1655, to receive a visit from Jean Faudoas, Comte de Cérillac, a man who had certain plans of his own for colonizing in America for which he needed the advice and assistance of Father du Tertre. M. de Cérillac was a restless sort of man who had become imbued with the spirit of adventure and was burning with a desire to establish a colony in some hitherto uninhabited part of the New World where he could carve out a fortune for himself and add to his glory. Father du Tertre, who by this time had seen enough of pioneer work to realize its hardships, to say nothing of the expense involved, did everything in his power to dissuade the young man, painting in lurid colors the difficulties he would have to face; but at last, seeing his listener still determined on his adventure, suggested that he try to buy the island of Grenada where the preliminary work of colonization had already been done. Here he might with reasonable luck be able to make his venture pay at the end of the first year. Unlike most persons whose hearts are set on undertakings of this sort, Cérillac had the good sense to listen to the voice of experience; he even went so far as to persuade the priest to act as his agent in the matter, commissioning him to go with a gentleman of his retinue to Martinique and close the deal with Du Parquet.

Du Tertre set forth with his traveling companion for Nantes where he was to take ship for the West Indies. They set sail on the eleventh of July, but scarcely had they cleared the harbor when the ship was pounced upon by an English frigate and taken to Plymouth. Here the pilot, a Huguenot, made a false charge against the priest, accusing him of having distributed arms to the crew to promote an uprising against their captors. Fortunately Du Tertre was able to convince the authorities of the absurdity of such an accusation which, had it been true, would probably have led to his prompt hanging. Kept a prisoner for six weeks, he was at last able, through the influence of friends at home, to obtain his release; and thanks to the efforts of the French ambassador, he was not only set free, but his property consisting of books, sacred vessels, and 1,500 francs in cash was given back to him. On his return to France, M. de Cérillac induced him to make a second attempt. The following year saw him in Holland where he could get a vessel to take him safely through the waters patrolled by English ships, for England was then at peace with the Netherlands. He sailed from the Texel in July with M. de Maubray, Cérillac's agent, and Father Feuillet who was returning to the scene of his evangelical labors. After a long, tedious crossing they reached Martinique on the twenty-eighth of September.

On landing the travelers immediately sought audience with Du Parquet to tell him of their plans, and to secure a ship for a survey of such islands as might be for sale. We are not familiar with the details of this voyage, but Du Tertre later reported to his principal that he had visited most of the islands and made exhaustive inquiries about them from persons qualified to speak. In the end both he and Maubray agreed that Grenada was by far the most promising of those available for purchase, and they decided either to negotiate for its acquisition or return to France empty-handed. On sounding M. du Parquet, they found him willing to consider their proposition, so they went to Grenada and made a thorough examination of the place, as well as of the neighboring Grenadines, particularly Carriacou, which boasted of an excellent harbor. Grenada, they later reported to Cérillac, was half again as large as St. Christopher, and despite the broken condition of its terrain along the Basseterre coast, which was due to the hills and mountains skirting the shoreline, it had excellent ground farther inland where horses and wagons would be able to go as soon as it was opened up. Numerous rivers gave an ample supply of water, while a large number of sturdy trees proclaimed the fertility of the soil. There was plenty of game on land and swarms of fish in the surrounding waters. After taking soundings, they found that St. George's Harbor had enough depth and was sufficiently large to shelter a fleet of fifty sail. In addition to this, it would be possible to cut through the neck of land separating the harbor from the lagoon and open up additional anchoring space for smaller vessels. The fort, Du Tertre found, was an excellent one, stoutly built, though he could not wax equally enthusiastic over the church, which he described as a rather poor affair made of branches and reeds. The population of the island numbered three hundred souls who lived for the most part on plantations around St. George's Harbor, or the region to the north of it, and found protection from Carib assaults in little forts built at strategic points, one for every six plantations, to which they retired at night. The priest dilated particularly on the house constructed there for Du Parquet with a redoubt adjacent to it, which, of course, Cérillac would use as his residence.

Negotiations for the purchase of this island were long and protracted. Du Parquet said at first that he would sell for cash only and would take no notes or other arrangements for time payments, nor would he lease the property. As there was a deposit of pearl oysters on a sandbank near the island which would be included in the sale, he put his price at 100,000 francs.

OWNERSHIP

During the *pourparlers* held with Du Parquet to iron out differences, Maubray acted with consummate tact and diplomacy, and was the one who in the last analysis was responsible for the successful outcome of the affair. The principal clauses in the bill of sale provided that Du Parquet should cede to Cérillac the ownership and all rights to Grenada and the Grenadines, together with slaves, cannon, muskets, munitions of war, buildings, equipment; in short the Count should obtain everything pertaining to the operation of the colony. The Governor also yielded to Cérillac his political position as ruler of the island subject to the King's approval. As soon as the deal was closed, all workmen, indentured servants as well as slaves, would labor for the benefit of the new owner, while Du Parquet pledged himself to supply the island and defend it against all comers until the Count took charge of it, either in person or by deputy, which was to be not later than the coming St. John's Day (December 27), after which date the maintenance of the property would be at the purchaser's expense. There was little higgling as to the price, the 30,000 *écus* agreed upon, that is, ninety thousand francs, being nearly the same as the sum originally demanded. One-half of this was to be paid before taking possession of the property, the second half within a year. It was a big price, Father du Tertre admitted, but the island was well worth it, and in three or four years the Count should have been able to take out in profits ten times the amount put in. Indeed, the priest went on to say, with what was probably considerable exaggeration, something of a boom had started when the news got out that a new proprietor was to take possession, and many planters were making ready to move to Grenada.

De Tertre and Maubray returned to France immediately after the conclusion of the affair. M. de Cérillac was pleased with the work of his agents and at once began preparations to take up his residence in his newly acquired domain, anxious, no doubt, to please those who were so eagerly awaiting his arrival. For this purpose he made elaborate arrangements. Large sums were spent to collect a force of 400 men and charter a ship for their transportation. Then trouble began. The ship was to have been ready to sail by October 7, 1657; but when Cérillac appeared at Havre with his band of colonists, the vessel was not nearly ready, and he was obliged to place his people in two tenders where they were fed at the shipowner's expense for two months in the most economical manner possible. The Count with a small, select group stopped at the neighboring port of Honfleur, patiently waiting for the ship to start, and using up all his substance to purchase food.

At last, after much delay and considerable bickering, all was ready. Cérillac with his followers took their places on board and the anchor was weighed. Whether from spite or from a desire to save further expense, for the ship appears to have been a third-rate hulk, the owner had given orders to his pilot to run her aground before she cleared the harbor. This worthy seaman obeyed his orders only too well; he set the main course while still in the channel, a performance that astonished the critics lined up along the shore, and proceeded to run the ship squarely into the dyke at the entrance to the port. His duty done, he then jumped ashore and disappeared. Fortunately the damage was not excessive, and the vessel was brought back to the shipyard where it was repaired in about a month, seemingly at Cérillac's expense.

By the first Sunday of December the vessel was prepared to leave and the order was again given to weigh anchor. A severe storm was brewing outside, and scarcely was she under way when the skipper advised turning back. It would have been only common sense to have done so, but Cérillac, whose nerves were on edge from the continual delays he had experienced, was so obsessed by a fear that the owner might be preparing another coup that he gave strict orders to keep the ship on her course. When night came on the storm increased in violence, and the many weaknesses of the vessel began to show themselves. The

OWNERSHIP

tiller worked loose from the rudderstock, the seams opened up, letting in water with such rapidity that the pumps could not keep up with it, and the passengers, unable to keep a foothold on the deck in the terrible sea, were tossed about like corks, while the guns, breaking loose from their lashings, rolled about like so many battering-rams. For three days the storm lasted, taking the lives of twenty persons whose bodies were thrown overboard with little ceremony. Then, fearing his ship would founder, the pilot made for the English coast and succeeded in coming safely into Portsmouth. Here the Count, after some words with his captain, abandoned his plan of going to Grenada in person, and dispatched his lieutenant there to act as Governor and his personal representative. He himself did not go there until 1661.

This new governor, a man named Dubuc, arrived in Grenada some time during the year 1658. His character, from all we can learn, was far different from that of M. de Valmenière who ruled his people in a wise and humane fashion; and it was not long after his arrival that a large number of habitans, disgusted at the new incumbent's harsh ways, returned to Martinique. Instead of taking the hint from this desertion, Dubuc became worse than ever, venting his spleen on those who had remained by a hundred injustices and tyrannies. Matters finally came to a climax so that the remaining colonists rose against him and dragged him before a tribunal, presided over by the local blacksmith which sentenced the unfortunate official to be hanged. But here a point of etiquette arose. The Governor pleaded that he was a gentleman and as such was entitled to the more refined process of beheading. The executioner, however, demurred; his experience had been limited to more plebeian methods of killing, and he feared he could not do himself justice with an axe. The problem was finally settled by the simple process of running the victim through with a sword, which, no doubt, gave satisfaction to all concerned.

When news of this execution, which to legally trained minds

smacked too much of lynching, reached France, the government sent over a man-of-war with a commissioner to conduct an investigation. This official soon learned that the whole affair had been conducted by a group of irresponsible, lower-class people, most of whom had already fled the island, and he therefore decided to take no action in the matter.[1]

While the Comte de Cérillac was thus busy with his thankless task of making Grenada a profitable colony, important events were taking place in Martinique. The day after the death of Governor du Parquet his widow, putting aside her feelings for the moment, addressed herself to the task of securing the inheritance of her late husband's domain for her sons, Dyel d'Esnambuc, aged eight years, and Louis Dyel du Parquet, aged five. She called on her council, composed of Fathers Boulogne and Benin, superiors of the Dominican and Jesuit orders, respectively, and the leading officers and habitans of the island, to decide what measures to take to secure from the King the governance of Martinique (with a regent, of course) for young Dyel d'Esnambuc. After mature deliberation, the Council determined to entrust a clergyman with the affair, and Father Feuillet was chosen, the two superiors having excused themselves because of pressing business. He left the following day for St. Christopher to find a ship that would take him to France. At his departure the militia companies proclaimed Mme du Parquet Governor of the island and took the oath of fidelity to her.

When Father Feuillet reached St. Christopher, he went at once to M. de Poincy's chateau where he remained three weeks waiting for a vessel to sail. Toward the end of January, 1658, he managed to secure passage in the ship of Captain Béliard, and after a rather tedious voyage reached Flushing on the twenty-first of March and was in Paris six days later. Here he found plenty of opposition to the wishes of the Council of Martinique; for the powerful Knights of Malta were anxious to unite the governor-generalship of Du Parquet's domain to that of St.

[1] Best account of this event is found in Labat, *Nouveau voyage*, II, 142.

OWNERSHIP

Christopher under their own representative, De Poincy. On the other hand, MM. de Miromenil and des Hameaux, relatives of the Du Parquet family, sided with their kinswoman, and reminded the King and Cardinal Mazarin strongly of the services M. du Parquet had rendered his country. Eventually this pressure brought results—this and a sum of money surreptitiously paid a certain person whose name Du Tertre represents in his text by a series of dots—and on September 15, 1658, the King signed letters patent appointing the sons of Du Parquet Governors of Martinique, St. Lucia and their dependencies.

The King in making this appointment was evidently influenced by the commendable work done by the distinguished Belain d'Esnambuc and his no less distinguished nephew. As a matter of common justice, it seemed to him only proper to continue the rights of governorship to the third generation of a family which had founded the French West Indian empire, and done more than any one else to develop it. The right of ownership remained as a matter of course in the family, since Du Parquet had bought the property from the defunct company, and the King by his commission now confirmed the right of overlordship. Dyel d'Esnambuc was appointed Governor with his brother as successor in case of his death. To govern the island during their minority, that is until they were twenty years of age, Mme du Parquet was named the actual ruler, and to assist her the King selected her brother-in-law, Adrien Dyel de Vaudroques, thus placing the Du Parquet family in supreme command.

While Father Feuillet was thus bringing the business entrusted him to a successful conclusion, trouble was brewing in Martinique. A group of malcontents had managed to stir up opposition to Mme du Parquet's rule. Father du Tertre mentions the names of several men prominent in this disturbance, yet he felt them to be merely tools whose actions were inspired by those who kept behind the scenes. The trouble appears to have been caused principally by regional jealousy. Mme du Parquet, who was a native of Paris, had made a practice during the lifetime of her husband of using her influence with him to further the interests of the Parisians who had come to the island, and raise them to important positions. As a mark of gratitude these people were accustomed to hold celebrations in her honor on New Year's Day and on her birthday. The Norman citizens, who came from Du Parquet's own Normandy, felt somewhat piqued, to put it mildly, at the publicity enjoyed by the Parisians, and sought to go them one better. This led to competition; competition led to arguments; arguments, to brawls and fisticuffs. To prevent the island from becoming divided hopelessly into two irreconcilable factions, the Governor forbade all celebrations; but this did not alleviate the bitter feeling engendered by the Parisians' monopoly of lucrative positions. From that time on the Normans were the open enemies of Mme du Parquet.

The second cause of trouble was the return of M. de Maubray. This gentleman had become acquainted with du Parquet two years before when he came to Martinique to arrange for the purchase of Grenada for the Comte de Cérillac. On his return to France, he had had some disagreement with the Count, and was now back in Martinique to offer his services to the Governor. He landed shortly after Du Parquet's death and was at once welcomed by Madame who felt immensely relieved to see once again a man whose judgment and character had inspired her with the greatest confidence when she had met him on the occasion of his previous visit. From that time on no public meeting was held without his being invited to attend and give his advice. Such a state of affairs was, of course, quickly seized upon by the malcontents who regarded it as another reason for justifying their hatred of the late Governor's widow, and their feelings were heartily shared by the man whom Du Parquet had appointed as his lieutenant five years before, Médéric Rolle, Sieur de Gourselas. Unpleasant rumors, as might be expected under the circumstances, were soon spread about Mme du

Parquet and Maubray, rumors which solicitous friends quickly brought to her ears; but she refused to let them influence her conduct, and continued to retain Maubray as the power behind the throne.

The explosion came when an attempt was made to enforce an ordinance, passed during Du Parquet's regime, to limit the number of bales of tobacco exported from the island. Maubray was, of course, blamed for this unpopular measure; accusations were rife that he was planning to seize the government. An indignation meeting was held in the Quartier du Prêcheur where the complainants demanded that Maubray be driven from Martinique as a menace to the public peace; and the decision would have been carried out, had not Gourselas persuaded them to modify their demands so that Maubray should merely retire to Case-Pilote for two months, after which time he should leave the island. In consideration of this concession on the part of the insurgents, Mme du Parquet agreed to repeal the ordinance.

This arrangement, however, proved but a lull in the storm. From his new residence at Case-Pilote, Maubray continued to exert his influence by correspondence. The malcontents, who had spies everywhere, managed to intercept several of these letters; these gave them, so they claimed, evidence that the writer was plotting with the English of Barbados to have them send over a force to rescue Mme du Parquet—probably the last thing he would have thought of doing. Furthermore, a rumor, far more plausible than the former, soon got around to the effect that Maubray was scheming to seize the island for himself and hold it directly from the King. The rage of the colonists on hearing these tales, which they doubtless swallowed whole, can well be imagined. They proceeded in a body to Madame's residence and forced her to sign an order expelling M. de Maubray from the island; and once it was signed they quickly saw to it that it was carried out. Scarcely had the signature dried when Maubray was unceremoniously hustled on board a ship and sent to Antigua.

On July 22, 1658, a meeting of the Council was held under the presidency of Mme du Parquet at which representatives of the seven militia companies presented their grievances against the administration. They pointed out that the late governor had promised to reduce their dues from one hundred pounds of tobacco to fifty; they complained also that they were badgered by creditors who prevented them from taking back their property after they had paid their debts; that the judge administering local justice was incompetent; and that the habitans were not properly represented in the Council. There were many other causes of complaint, but these few will show the general drift. The Council saw the justice of the complaints and immediately took steps to remedy them. Gourselas was continued in his office of acting-governor; the dues were reduced to fifty pounds, though fifty more could be assessed for public works in time of necessity; a new judge was appointed; M. de Plainville, one of the leaders of the revolt, was named representative of the habitans with a permanent seat in the Council; and finally, Madame agreed not to punish any colonist for taking part in the recent disturbance.

With these concessions wrung from the head of the government, the matter might have ended had not the spies intercepted some further letters written to Madame by Maubray in the same vein as his previous correspondence. When the habitans learned their contents, they assembled under the leadership of Plainville and declared void the oath of fidelity they had taken to Mme du Parquet. The Council called a meeting on the sixth of August to discuss the situation, and Gourselas, who was to preside, was sent to bring the lady to the sitting. When she had taken her place, one of the deputies approached her and gave a signal at which several men rushed forward, seized Mme du Parquet, placed her in a carriage, and drove her to the Prêcheur where she was imprisoned in one of the storehouses.

In order to justify these rough and extralegal proceedings, the Council passed a resolution condemning Madame for her improper administration of the government and declaring her deposed and dispossessed of all her rights. In addition to this her officials were dismissed in favor of men appointed by the Council which was now to have complete charge of the political and economic affairs of the island. The annual dues were set at fifty pounds of tobacco with no additional assessment for emergencies; the inhabitants were forbidden to board ships anchored in the harbor; and all munitions were to be taken to Fort St. Pierre and placed in charge of Plainville who was to act under the authority of M. de Gourselas.

These decrees of the Council were in a sense a sort of democratic rebellion against the proprietors and in the interests of the people. For example, it had been customary for years for vessels entering port for purposes of trade to pay for the privilege of doing business by donating a certain amount of gunpowder which was kept on the Governor's premises subject to his control. The Council now decreed this was to be stored in the fort where the colonists could get at it. Similarly the regulation forbidding citizens from boarding the vessels was to protect the public by preventing speculators from cornering the merchandise and selling it later at ruinous prices. When the Council adjourned, the militia companies took the oath of fidelity to the newly appointed officers and promised to serve faithfully the King and the little Sieur d'Esnambuc, whom they hoped His Majesty would eventually appoint as their Governor.

Though the disturbances died down after the imprisonment of Mme du Parquet, there was yet considerable unrest due to the lack of a lawful ruler appointed by the King. Suspicion became rife; accusations of disloyalty flew right and left. As an example of this state of affairs, a rumor was started that something in the way of a rule of conduct could be found among Mme du Parquet's books which would give the clue to her highhanded actions. The new judge, Louis Duvivier, Sieur de la Giraudière, took it upon himself to investigate the matter. He went to the gubernatorial residence and after ferreting about in the library unearthed a copy of Machiavelli's *Prince* which he read with horror. It was enough; here was the source of all of Mme du Parquet's tyranny and her justification of it. He brought the offending volume before the Council, and that august body, concurring in the judge's findings, ordered it to be burned by the public hangman, a ceremony which was carried out amid the approving cries of all right-minded persons.

There were some, however, who felt uneasy at the cavalier-like treatment accorded to Mme du Parquet. After all she was the widow of the late Governor, the mother of the children who had inherited the island; it was one thing to depose her, quite another to throw her into prison. Hoping to find some excuse for releasing her, Gourselas went to see her and persuaded the unfortunate woman to sign a paper resigning her power until the King had declared his pleasure regarding Martinique, asking only to have her property restored to her. She also agreed to write to His Majesty requesting an amnesty for all who had taken part in the recent disturbances. Returning triumphantly to St. Pierre with this document, Gourselas read it to the public. The effect was immediate; arms were set aside and quiet was restored. But only for a moment. A servant of Mme du Parquet, one of those garrulous menials who knows it all, started the report that his mistress had signed only under pressure, not of her own free will. Trouble broke out again; crowds began to gather. In desperation Gourselas first allowed the irate insurgents to blow off steam by seizing a few relatives of the Du Parquet family and running them off the island, then he sent a messenger to Madame asking her to disavow the statement of her lackey and offer a guarantee that the paper signed by her was valid. This she did, and Gourselas read her statement to the Council which on the motion of M. de Plainville ordered Mme du Parquet deposed.

Now that her power was ended, there was no further need of treating her harshly, and the Council, perhaps somewhat ashamed of its conduct, brought her back to her home, even throwing a guard about the premises for her protection. M. de Gourselas as Acting-Governor took up the management of the island's affairs, while she, no longer responsible for its government, and perhaps somewhat chastened by her recent experience, set herself to win back the affections of her people, a worthy endeavor in which she succeeded so well as to bring about a decided reaction in her favor.

Scarcely had the question of government been settled, when trouble again broke out with the Caribs. It has been a tedious task to tell the story of these interminable wars which offer but little variety.of detail; but this one will be the last as it deals with the final expulsion of the Indians from Martinique.

Since the death of M. du Parquet, there had been peace with the Caribs; not the sort of peace which inspired much confidence, but at least it afforded a breathing spell to the war-weary colonists during the intermittent hostilities of the past few years. Lulled into a false sense of security, the French had recently been in the habit of going into the Capesterre section to hunt game. The savages noted one group in particular that made a practice of dividing itself into two bands: one to do the actual hunting, the other to remain behind and guard the camp. Seeing the white men defenseless, they burst into the camp one day and killed the three who had been left there. When the hunters returned and saw the carnage, they rushed off into the woods and made their way to Case-Pilote with all possible haste.

The following day the savages woke to the realization of what they had done and what the consequences might be. To ward off punishment, they sent a delegation to Fort St. Pierre to explain that this massacre was the work of Caribs from St. Vincent or Dominica who had landed without their knowing it. There being no one to contradict them the apology was accepted, and besides the French were then busy with their own internal disagreements. Feeling secure, the Indians now came to visit the settlements, mingling with the colonists as though nothing had happened. On one occasion a chief named Nicolas came with a few braves to Fort St. Pierre and sat down in a public place to drink with some French acquaintances. Here he was seen by a citizen called Beausoleil, a ruthless sort of man who was one of the leaders in the revolt against Mme du Parquet. Beausoleil was looking for an excuse to attack the Caribs, for like men of his stamp he had no use for members of a savage race and little scruple as to the means he used to rid himself of them. Seeing his opportunity, he gathered from nearby saloons a band of from sixty to eighty men all well armed, well primed with liquor, and ready for business. The Frenchmen opened fire on the Caribs as they were peacefully seated in the public square, killing five at the first volley and eight others as they fled to various places of safety; the rest were thrown into the guardhouse. Nicolas himself managed to escape in his canoe, closely pursued by Beausoleil and his men in their boats. When surrounded by the French, the Carib leapt overboard and swam underwater to escape the musketry fire, coming up unexpectedly with stones he had picked off the bottom which he used as missiles to throw at his pursuers. The struggle continued for some time until one of the Frenchmen shot him dead.

Greatly encouraged by his initial success, though the attack had been made without the knowledge of the officials, Beausoleil now on his own responsibility preached a crusade to drive the Indians from the island. When M. de Gourselas heard of this, he decided it was time for him to take a hand in the proceedings. The Council was immediately called and after due deliberation it was decided to declare a war of extermination that would settle the Indian problem once and for all. Calling together the militia companies, Gourselas selected six hundred men, most of them planters rather than indentured servants, of whom he placed two hundred in a fleet of five barks commanded by François Rolle de Loubière, while the rest were divided into two bands: one to go overland by way of Mt. Pelee, the other by way of Morne des Gommiers. Beausoleil was given command of one of the barks with orders to proceed to Capesterre and anchor at a certain place in the northern part chosen as a rendezvous. Father Benin acted as chaplain of the naval division, Father Boulogne, of the land forces.

The Caribs, warned of these preparations by their spies, proceeded to fortify their country against attack. Learning that the main army proposed to take the route by Mt. Pelee, they dug a number of deep holes across the path, filled them with poisoned arrows planted points upward, and covered these pits with grass and branches. Then they advanced to meet the French, checked them for a moment with a light skirmish, then broke and fled, hoping to draw them into the trap. But as night came on, an officer, wise in Indian methods, suspected some such trick and persuaded the leaders to make a detour and approach the settlements from another direction. The scheme worked better than he expected. The Indians seeing a body of men approaching from another quarter thought it was an additional force, and terrified at the huge numbers they felt must be pouring down into Capesterre fled to their village where they spread panic among those stationed there. Some chiefs, however, had sufficient nerve to rally the more courageous among them to put up a fight. Placing themselves in battle array, they marched toward the French army. The French were ready to receive them. Better equipped and more numerous than the savages, they had no difficulty in breaking their defenses. At the first onslaught the Carib host broke and ran for their canoes, while the French advanced to the villages where they burned the houses and slaughtered all on whom they could lay their hands. Those who escaped the sword, fled to Dominica and St. Vincent leaving the French at last in complete and undisputed mastery of Martinique.

M. de Loubière now arrived with his fleet bringing lumber for the construction of a fort for a settlement the French intended to plant in Capesterre as a protection against a possible return of the Caribs. Father Boulogne was appointed chaplain of the place, and a small chapel, called St. Jacques, was erected there for his use. The new village was established on the northern shore of the island. To encourage men to enlist in the garrison of this fort and settle in the new colony, various concessions were made. Each man was given a bonus of 120 pounds of tobacco, an exemption from taxes for ten years for himself, his servants, and his slaves; and in consideration of a fat capon paid yearly to Mme du Parquet, he was excused from all seigneurial dues.

A reaction in favor of Mme du Parquet now set in. The more orderly element, headed by Gourselas and Loubière, also felt it time to rid the island of the leaders of the recent revolt, especially as word had come announcing the King's intention of looking into the matter and punishing the mutineers. Beausoleil was the first to go. He had been sent on ahead in his ship, as we have said, to Capesterre, and when he failed to be at the rendezvous, Loubière had him arrested on a charge of insubordination and expelled from Martinique. Similar charges were preferred against Plainville and a few others who were now forced to follow him into exile. With the expulsion of the leading rebels, it became possible to restore Mme du Parquet to her lawful position. The former judge was reinstated in his office in place of La Giraudière, the officers exiled because of their loyalty to her came back, and on the twenty-first of October the Council again acknowledged her as its ruler.

At this time Mme du Parquet received word that the King had recognized her elder son as Governor of her husband's domain, and had appointed her brother-in-law as her legal adviser. The news pleased her immensely; it enabled her to return to France to seek the cure she could not obtain on the islands for a paralytic stroke she had recently suffered. For some time she delayed her departure, hoping M. de Vaudroques would arrive before she left; but as the days went by and he did not come, while her condition became rapidly worse, she at last decided to sail. Placing the government entirely in the hands of M. de Gourselas, and taking her two little daughters and a few gentlemen of her suite with her, she boarded a ship bound for St. Malo in August, 1659. During the crossing her sufferings grew worse, and a month after leaving Martinique she died in mid-ocean. The captain wished to preserve her body for burial beside that of her husband; but a storm arose and the superstitious crew ascribed its violence to the presence of a corpse on board the ship. To avert a threatened mutiny, he was obliged to yield, and the remains of Mme du Parquet were buried at sea.

As soon as he heard of his kinswoman's death, Vaudroques arranged to sail for Martinique to take up his duties as regent for his nephews. He arrived there in the latter part of November. His administration was brief and none too popular. The principal event during his rule was the treaty of peace signed by the French, English, and Caribs which will be discussed in the following chapter. A curious incident also occurred at this time that might have led to a complete change in the ownership of the island had not the principal figure in the undertaking suddenly fallen from the King's favor and been dismissed in disgrace. The famous Minister of Finance, Nicolas Fouquet, had for some reason or other planned to found a large estate in Martinique. For this purpose he sent over two agents to take charge of the business, and these men, after looking over the available ground, selected a vast plot at Trois Rivières, south of the Cul de Sac Royal, which their master purchased, and then drew up plans for laying out a handsome estate. Special workmen were imported from France to construct the elaborate residence planned by the distinguished minister. This might not have been so objectionable, had not the agents and workmen insinuated themselves with the inhabitants and attempted by means of subtle propaganda to wean them away from the lawful owners of the island, not a very difficult task considering the enormous influence of M. Fouquet. M. de Vaudroques presently became alarmed at the possibilities of this campaign and called a meeting of his Council; after he had explained the situation, it stood behind him to a man. An ordinance was passed limiting the number of artisans which the agents could bring to the island, and restricting their activities to the premises on which they were to work. All this might not have availed much, considering the power of the man they were trying to thwart, had not the King suddenly thrown him into prison for his peculations and turned over the management of his finances to Jean-Baptiste Colbert, an action which put an end forever to Fouquet's schemes in Martinique.

Shortly after this, on October 24, 1662, M. de Vaudroques died. To replace him, the leading inhabitants hit upon the idea of selecting the names of some of the prominent colonists and sending them to the King with the request that he appoint one of them as governor-regent for young D'Esnambuc. Gourselas, Loubière, La Forge, and Valmenière were those chosen; but the Du Parquet family in France thought differently about the matter, as they wished to have one of their number rule instead of an outsider. Their views prevailed with the King who appointed a kinsman of D'Esnambuc, M. de Clermont, who came to the island in June, 1663.

~ XIII ~

END OF THE PIONEER PERIOD

M. HOUËL, as we have said in a previous chapter, returned to France in the year 1654 to acquire, if possible, M. de Boisseret's interest in Guadeloupe. Evidently this was a matter that could not be rushed as he remained in France for two years, during which time he took advantage of his opportunity to look around by marrying a Mlle Hencelin. After the nuptial festivities were over, he again attacked the problem of Guadeloupe, and made Boisseret an offer for his share of the island. M. de Boisseret declined. He had invested a large sum of money in the enterprise from which he was receiving a comfortable income, and being well along in years, he expected it to support him to the end of his days. Unable to gain his point by persuasion, M. Houël flew into a rage in his brother-in-law's presence, creating such a scene that the aged man suffered a stroke and died the selfsame day. This brutal course of action on the part of the Governor defeated its own purpose, for it put an end to any possibility of his getting control of the property, at least until such a time as the heirs had taken it over and were in a position to negotiate for its sale. Such being the situation, M. Houël began his preparations to return to the West Indies; but before he left mutual friends managed to effect a reconciliation between him and his sister who, naturally enough, held him responsible for the death of her husband.

The Governor arrived in Guadeloupe in the latter part of

1656, and immediately set to work to rid himself of the persons in a position to dispute his absolute mastery of the island—his brother, to whom he had already promised a third of his holdings, and his nephew, who would now be in a position to claim a share of his father's property. He first tackled the Chevalier, telling him he no longer needed his services, since he now had a wife quite competent to look after his interests during his absence, and sent him back to France despite his protests. Next he called M. d'Herblay to his house and criticized him bitterly for his handling of the recent slave insurrection, emphasizing his failure to pursue the slaves himself instead of detailing the business to M. Despinay, and winding up his faultfinding with a blunt accusation of cowardice. Enraged at this insult, the young man denied the charge, and drawing his sword challenged his uncle to step outside and settle the matter man to man. The affair would have been serious if bystanders had not rushed in between the two. For this threat D'Herblay was thrown into jail until both he and his irascible uncle had cooled off, when he was released on promise of good behavior.

For a brief while a truce was observed between the two men, then trouble broke out afresh. The Governor took it upon himself to force a sale of his late brother-in-law's property, hoping in this manner to compel D'Herblay to accept the situation in exchange for a goodly sum of money. This measure met with violent opposition on the part of the nephew, especially as Houël saw to it that the sales were made to his own henchmen, and that a good share of the property was bought for his newborn daughter. Though these transactions netted 1,529,000 pounds of tobacco, M. d'Herblay, outraged at this arbitrary disposal of his father's property, lost his temper and threatened his uncle, an action for which he was promptly placed on board the first ship sailing for France and sent back home.

Having thus rid himself of his two troublesome relatives, M. Houël embarked on a course of action that led him from one difficulty to another. For some time past, guard duty had become so burdensome to the inhabitants that they had even been willing to pay a tax for hiring men to take their places. Under pretext of exempting them from this onerous duty and the tax they paid to avoid it, Houël abolished both, but in place of the tax he doubled the seigneurial dues to which he also added an assessment of sixty pounds of tobacco per habitan to help pay the judgment De Thoisy had secured against him. The uproar caused by this drastic raising of taxes was prodigious. The habitans seized their arms, vowing they would drive the tyrannical Governor from the island and put M. de Téméricourt (D'Herblay's younger brother) in his place. Unable to weather the storm, Houël at once bowed to popular clamor and signed an order abolishing all seigneurial dues, the *corvée*, and half the taxes used for military expenses; in addition to these concessions, he granted an amnesty to all who had taken part in the protest. This last promise was violated as soon as the disturbances had died down, for Houël promptly shipped Téméricourt back to France and expelled a hundred planters who had taken a prominent part in the trouble. M. Houël was going to be the undisputed master of Guadeloupe at all cost.

Having failed in his first attempt to increase his revenue, the Governor now decided to obtain by a ruse what he had failed to secure by an edict. For this purpose he suggested to the officers and habitans in his confidence a scheme whereby a tithe levied on all property would replace the poll tax. Having convinced them of the blessings of such a change, he drew up a petition for them to sign asking him to make the substitution. Those first approached were induced to put their names to the document by a verbal promise to exempt them from payment of the new tax, and these in turn undertook to persuade their friends. Thus the petition was circulated throughout the island, every man requested to affix his signature doing so for the reason usually given in such circumstances, namely, that everyone else was signing. Consequently when some complained after the passage of the new tax—and many did—Houël was able to point out blandly that he had made the change only at their written request. To make matters worse, he even went so far as to levy the tithe on those to whom he had promised exemption. Though he succeeded in raising considerable money by this means, the measure did him little good, for presently he was to need all the good will of his colonists to help him ward off the blow now being prepared against him in France.

When Téméricourt arrived in France and presented himself before his mother with an account of Houël's latest doings, she began at once to make plans for recapturing her children's inheritance. It was impossible now to misinterpret Houël's intentions with regard to the Boisseret family, and she decided to begin operations by sending D'Herblay back to Guadeloupe to force his uncle to yield him his father's share of the island. This, Mme de Boisseret believed, would not be too difficult, for she had heard of the strong anti-Houël sentiment among the colonists and of the friendly feeling they had toward her sons. Casting about for an older man to take the lead, her choice naturally fell on her brother, the Chevalier, who had earned the good will of the people by waiving all taxes during his brief administration. For this purpose she signed a contract with him on April 12, 1659, by which she ceded him half her property rights to all the slaves, cattle, and plantations, valued at about thirty thousand francs, with the understanding that he would pay half the expenses of the proposed expedition. The Chevalier Houël, thus bound to his sister's cause by financial interests as well as by personal inclination, made haste to prepare for the undertaking. Fearing Houël might hear what was going on, he avoided the ports of Havre, Dieppe, and other towns where ships bound for the West Indies were usually equipped, and chose instead a place on the Somme River in northeastern France where he could make his preparations in absolute secrecy. He arranged to take with him a number of prospective colonists, and also a hundred trained soldiers in case he met with resistance in Guadeloupe.

END OF THE PIONEER PERIOD

Meanwhile family conferences were being held by Mme de Boisseret for the purpose of arriving at some peaceful solution of the problem at which Houël was represented by his brother-in-law, M. Hencelin, and Madame by several relatives including the Chevalier. Numerous letters were exchanged, and finally the Governor indicated his willingness to settle on the basis of a division of Guadeloupe between himself and his nephews. He realized on reconsideration of the matter that his original offer to buy out his relatives involved the disbursement of too large a sum of money, and he therefore offered to cede to them instead a part of the island. This arrangement would leave him in complete control of the balance, namely, that region he had ruled and developed for so many years. If his nephews chose to form an alliance with him for mutual protection against a common enemy, that was one thing, but they would be in no position to interfere with the way he managed affairs in his own bailiwick. The idea appealed to Mme de Boisseret, her sons, the Chevalier, and all concerned.

With this understanding the Chevalier set sail with his two charges, fully determined to use force if necessary to bring Houël to terms. They arrived at Mariegalante in July, 1659, where they prepared to put into practice a piece of sculduddery they had planned before leaving home. Témericourt was induced to write a letter to the local commander saying he had just arrived from France in an ailing condition and requesting food supplies. The commander naturally hastened on board at once with a canoe-load of provisions, only to find Houël and D'Herblay also there to receive him. The ailing man proved healthy enough and was able to join his fellow-plotters in seizing the commander —which was done in the most courteous manner possible—and taking him ashore. Here the trio entered the fort and ordered the garrison to lay down their arms while they read a manifesto, previously concocted by them in their leisure moments, by which they proclaimed themselves the lawful rulers of the island and demanded an oath of fidelity from the assembled soldiers.

They evidently made a good impression on their audience for about twenty men offered to follow them on the next stage of the adventure.

That night they sailed to Guadeloupe and anchored the next morning at Grande Anse. The Chevalier landed at once with his two nephews and proceeded to a house he owned in the vicinity, whence he sent Téméricourt to Fort Ste. Marie with strict orders not to disclose their plans for forcing Houël's hand until he had made himself master of the district. To gain the loyalty of the habitans proved to be an easy task, for they had always liked the Chevalier and the Boisseret brothers as much as they disliked the Governor, whose recent action in imposing the tithe was regarded as the last straw. The Chevalier now reëmbarked and steered his vessel around the cape to Basseterre, sailing under the guns of the fort, where Houël from a point of vantage gazed at it suspiciously. Rounding a point of land on which the Dominican convent was located, he came to anchor out of sight of those in the fort. Immediately a flock of canoes, led by the superior of the Dominicans, Father Beaumont, put off from shore to visit the stranger. The father was amazed at seeing his own friends back again, this time ready to assert their claims to the island. He gladly took charge of a packet of letters to Governor Houël, promising to deliver it without delay, in which the new arrivals advised him of their plans. After he had departed the Chevalier landed his little army and drew it up in battle array; then with drums beating and flags flying, he marched to the banks of the Rivière des Pères where he took up a position he could easily hold in case of attack.

Among the letters sent Governor Houël was one written by his brother which set forth his own personal demands in the scheme for partitioning the island. It was a long-winded epistle, though perhaps not more long-winded or verbose than the average correspondence in those days, in which the writer explained the sacrifices he had made for many years past in looking after the Governor's interests in Guadeloupe, and with amazing

END OF THE PIONEER PERIOD

nerve he calmly stated that he had made the voyage principally in the hope of being of use to his dear brother in the pending negotiations. Then, coming down to the business at hand, he calmly demanded that Houël cede him half of his remaining share of the island after he had yielded half of the entire property to his nephews in accordance with the plan they had agreed upon before leaving France. This would have given the Chevalier half the island, leaving Houël one-quarter and his nephews one-quarter. He based his preposterous demand on certain promises he said Houël had made him in times past to share the government with him in recognition of his services. Knowing Houël's character as we do, we can readily understand just how he must have felt on receiving this proposal. Wild with rage, he summoned his Council which issued an edict on the twenty-ninth of July declaring the Chevalier and D'Herblay disturbers of the peace and guilty of lese majesty. But to his astonishment he soon learned that most of the colonists sided with the intruders, for when he ordered them to march against the Chevalier, they suddenly found they had no ammunition for such a purpose.

Now the wisdom of the Chevalier's preparations in bringing a company of soldiers with him became apparent. He sent word to his brother of his intention of obtaining his rights by force if necessary. Suiting action to words, the invaders crossed the Rivière de Pères and advanced to the Rivière des Galions where they took up a position within range of the Governor's residence. Seeing his enemies ready to attack, Houël decided to compromise, for he knew only too well by this time how the colonists felt toward him, and saw very clearly that he could not rely on them in a struggle against his brother. It was therefore agreed by both sides to submit the question to a board of arbitrators consisting of four representatives of each party who should choose a ninth to act as umpire. The man selected for this important post was the Chevalier de Sales, nephew of the great St. Francis de Sales, who was then residing at St. Christopher. The meetings, which lasted some seven weeks, took place in the Dominican convent—most of the board were clergymen—and were marked by heated arguments that on some occasions nearly led to blows. At the first meeting, held on the third of August, the board drew up a resolution intended as a sop to the Governor's feelings, by which the Chevalier and D'Herblay were to have the same authority in judicial matters in their portions of the island as the Governor enjoyed in his, subject, nevertheless, to his retaining the title of governor of the entire island, without prejudice to their rights, and commander-in-chief of all the troops when they were assembled together as one army. This done, the board proceeded to work out the following plan of partition.

To M. d'Herblay was assigned the district bounded on the north by the Rivière aux Gouyaves, which is located in the northern part of the isthmus connecting the two main parts of the island; on the east by a line running north and south along the crest of the mountain range separating Basseterre from Capesterre; and on the south by the Rivière du Bailly, emptying into the sea near Fort Madeleine. D'Herblay also received the shores and islands of the Grand Cul de Sac, the huge bight into which the Rivière aux Gouyaves empties, with the exception of the Case aux Lamentins just east of that river. He also obtained the district around Fort Ste. Marie, subject to certain restrictions, Mariegalante, which he later erected into a marquisate for himself, the little island of Desirade, and the still smaller island of Petite Terre. Governor Houël received all the rest, consisting of what was roughly known as Capesterre and that large eastern section of Guadeloupe known as Grande Terre.

All this was a bitter pill for Governor Houël to swallow, and he made at least one effort to disgorge it. His henchmen received orders to annoy the Chevalier and his nephews on all possible occasions; and many among them did, even going so far as to try to prevent them from using the public thoroughfares. From annoyances they progressed to insults, until matters reached such point that De Poincy thought it wise to intervene in his capacity as Governor-General before it was too late. A duel between the Chevalier and M. Hencelin was the signal for his dispatching a representative with an order commanding them to bury their differences and try, at any rate, to live in peace. Their mutual friends in France, hearing of the quarrel, besought the King to use his influence to compel the Governor of Guadeloupe to assume a more friendly attitude toward his nephews. His Majesty accordingly sent an order to De Poincy giving him authority to restrain Houël from interfering with the rights of Mme de Boisseret and her family.

Nevertheless the wrangling continued until the colonists themselves took sides, and matters came to such a pass that bloodshed seemed imminent. To make a last stand against his kinsmen, M. Houël went to France, where he hoped to convince the authorities of the validity of his claims. He was closely followed, however, by his brother. The matter of the partition was put before a board of arbitration headed by the Duc de Bournonville, Governor of Paris, which rendered a decision on October 18, 1660, confirming the original deal with certain modifications that appeared to suit the interests of both the contesting parties. M. Houël effected a reconciliation with his sister and presently returned to Guadeloupe giving all the impression that everything had been settled amicably. But if any believed the millenium had come, they did not know their man. There was still fight in the old lion, and he soon gave evidence that he would not take the board's decision lying down. Within two months after his return to Guadeloupe, he accused his nephews of entering into a plot to assassinate him and ordered all habitans who found them wandering about the island with weapons of any sort in their hands to sound the alarm and rush them to the nearest prison. In other words he practically declared them outlaws. To ensure the enactment of his orders, he caused a decree to this effect to be posted in the public places throughout the island. As was to be expected, disorders took place, the people siding for or against the Governor. Brawls, fights, murders now became the order of the day, until at last it was evident that some drastic measures had to be taken to prevent the total ruin of the colony. For this purpose the King dispatched Alexandre de Prouville, Marquis de Tracy to take charge of the situation; but as he does not appear on the scene till later on, we shall postpone discussion of his work until we have described the events that meanwhile occurred.

At this time a league of nations was formed between the English and French colonists of the archipelago for mutual protection against the Caribs. Governor Houël had the knack of handling the savages and keeping peace with them within his domain, but the other colonies, both French and English, had not been so successful and had suffered greatly from their depredations. In February, 1660, meetings were held at M. de Poincy's residence to consider the matter. There were present Governor James Russell of Nevis, Christopher Kaynall of Antigua, Roger Osborne of Montserrat, Governor Houël for Guadeloupe, and his brother representing the Boisseret interests. As a result of these conferences, an agreement was drawn up, to which all subscribed, pledging mutual aid against the savages. The contracting parties were to furnish the necessary forts, men, munitions, and share equally the burdens of a defensive campaign. It was decided, however, to leave Dominica and St. Vincent to the Caribs as places where they could live without molestation, with the understanding that any missionaries dwelling there for the purpose of evangelizing the natives should be protected. To meet the expenses of the league, both French and English agreed to pay within six months forty thousand pounds of sugar each to agents at Basseterre, St. Christopher, who were to hold it subject to the orders of Governors Houël and Osborne to whom the conference entrusted the management of the league.[1] To Houël was also entrusted the business of signing a treaty of peace with the Caribs in behalf of the members.

[1] Copy of treaty is found in Oliver, *History of Antigua*, I, xxvii.

END OF THE PIONEER PERIOD

Scarcely had the delegates dispersed when two men, M. de Loubière and Christophe Renaudot, arrived from Martinique. While the conference was still in session, M. de Vaudroques had heard of it and had hastily called a meeting of his Council to discuss the advantages of joining the league. The decision was favorable, and these two gentlemen were selected as emissaries to arrange for the admission of Martinique. They had gone first to Guadeloupe to see Houël, as it was he who had advised Vaudroques of the plan, and had urged him to fall in with it. M. Houël, however, out of respect for the Governor-General sent them to him, and the latter, not to be outdone in courtesy, pointed out that the Governor of Guadeloupe had been charged with the business of making peace with the Caribs, and it was to him they should apply. Back again in Guadeloupe, they were informed by Houël that in view of the recent war waged in Martinique against the savages, it would be necessary for its inhabitants to make a definite peace with them before entering the league. He also offered to arrange a meeting between the white men and the chiefs to facilitate negotiations. Back in Martinique, Loubière and Renaudot reported the conditions imposed upon them to M. de Vaudroques. He at once called an emergency meeting of the Council at which it was decided to ask the two emissaries to journey again to Guadeloupe to arrange a peace with the Caribs according to the Governor's suggestions. They were to point out to him, however, that the Caribs had been the first to break the truce in Martinique, where they had massacred the colonists seemingly without cause, carried off five hundred slaves belonging to them, and committed so many acts of hostility as to make it highly inadvisable for the inhabitants ever to receive them again on the island or give them land before they had made restitution for the slaves they had stolen. It was also darkly hinted that the Council would reimburse its agents for any expenses they might incur in persuading certain influential chiefs.

Armed with these powers, MM. de Loubière and Renaudot

returned to Guadeloupe where they found awaiting them some fifteen chiefs from Dominica and St. Vincent, hastily summoned by Houël. The meeting was held at the Governor's residence of Houëlmont, and on March 31, 1660, an agreement was finally reached by which both parties promised to live at peace with each other, forget the past, and restore prisoners. The Caribs also agreed to restrain their people from attacking the French and English provided they were left undisturbed in Dominica and St. Vincent. It was indeed a notable victory for the white men; they had driven the Indians from their principal possessions and were now left to enjoy them in peace.

This victory was the last event in which De Poincy took part. The veteran governor had now reached his seventy-seventh year and was beginning to suffer from the infirmities of age. He fell ill—Du Tertre does not tell us the nature of the illness—and though he felt his end approaching, did not relax in his supervision of the colony, but even took measures to increase the proprietor's revenue. He published an edict changing, and increasing, the seigneurial dues from one hundred pounds of tobacco to one hundred and ten pounds of sugar, a change which the colonists accepted philosophically, as they figured the Governor would probably die before the time came to collect them; and in this they were right, for M. de Poincy passed away in April, 1660.

Unlike the death of his great contemporary, M. du Parquet, De Poincy's demise did not excite universal mourning. His administration, despite the many things it accomplished, was marked with outbursts of harshness that frequently drove colonists from the island.

A man of spirit [Du Tertre describes him] a great politician, generous on occasions, affecting the grand manner in his festivities and building projects, well disposed toward his friends and servants whose fortunes he sometimes made, subject to bias and severe to excess toward those who did not have his interests at heart.

M. de Poincy had ruled St. Christopher and his dependencies

END OF THE PIONEER PERIOD

for over twenty years, and it must be admitted that generally speaking the colony grew and prospered under his supervision. It is easy enough to criticize his severity, which in some cases amounted to downright cruelty, and he certainly was not so admirable a character as Du Parquet; but he dealt with a pioneer community composed principally of persons who could not by any stretch of the imagination be called the best element in France. He also ruled over a vast horde of blacks, not the civilized negroes of modern times, but savages fresh from the African jungle; and he had ever to be on the alert against the Indians of the neighboring islands and possible attacks by unfriendly Spaniards. Taken as a whole, it was a job demanding fearlessness and determination, and with these virtues De Poincy was well supplied. De Poincy was buried at Basseterre with the pomp and circumstance to which his position entitled him. He was succeeded in his office by M. de Sales.

Scarcely were the funeral services over when the new Governor was given a chance to show his mettle. A number of colonists had urged him to signalize the beginning of his administration by a general reduction of taxes. De Sales was not unwilling to comply with this request, though he felt obliged to put off the decision until more pressing matters had received his attention, and with this answer the majority of the inhabitants was satisfied. But there was a certain man named Brisson, captain of one of the militia companies, a notorious drunkard and brawler, who gathered together a following of thirty or forty kindred spirits to foment a rebellion for the purpose of overthrowing the proprietors and holding the colony in allegiance directly from the King. De Sales was equal to the occasion. De Poincy might be dead but the new ruler was quite able to handle the situation, and show the rebelliously disposed that there would be no trifling with his government. He called the militia to arms and at once dispatched a messenger to summon Brisson to him; then deciding to take no chances, he set out with a small group of followers for Brisson's plantation to attend to the matter himself. On reaching the rebel's home, he asked for an explanation; but the fellow answered in such an insolent manner that the Governor had no choice but to order him placed under arrest. Brisson, as soon as he heard the command, rushed into his house, seized a pistol, and fired it point blank at De Sales, wounding him severely; then as he reached for another weapon, one of the Governor's men returned the fire and brought him down. Thrown promptly into prison he was as promptly tried, convicted, and sentenced to be hanged, drawn, and quartered, a sentence immediately carried out in all its gruesome details, the head being placed on a pole in the public square as a warning to rebels. M. de Sales had shown himself capable of meeting any situation.

The cause of this revolt had been taxes. For fifteen years heavy taxes had been levied at St. Christopher to obtain, so it was said, the ninety thousand francs due M. de Thoisy; but though twenty times that amount had been raised, the ex-Governor-General does not seem to have been paid in full. The same was also true in Guadeloupe where, despite the enormous sums raised by various methods, the debt due De Thoisy still remained unpaid. De Sales, once he had asserted his authority, set himself to undoing much of the harm done by his predecessor. He recalled many of De Thoisy's sympathizers, the "Patrocles" who had been expelled by De Poincy. He gave them back their homes, their cattle, their furniture; he paid their debts, and even in some cases reimbursed them for their losses from the property belonging to the Order of Malta. On the whole, so Du Tertre says, he ruled more as a father than as a governor.

With the death of De Poincy there passed from the scene the second of the three great governors of the French West Indies who, after the days of Belain d'Esnambuc, ruled their island possessions contemporaneously for so many years. In truth, it was shortly after their demise that the era, which might be called the pioneer period, came to an end—the period of initial settlement and expansion during which the French spread out from St. Christopher over those islands that were to become theirs. Furthermore, the break between the old and new periods was now marked by the appearance of a new factor: the French West India Company, a corporation founded by the government to supplant the owners, take over their possessions, and bring the islands under centralized control. From now on new faces appear, and the work of organization falls into different hands.

The reason for this change in policy was due to a realization by the authorities that the valuable trade of the West Indies was slipping away from the French merchants. From the earliest days when D'Esnambuc first planted his colony on the shores of St. Christopher, the Dutch had been encroaching on the island trade, and in spite of all that could be done, their activities had increased. With the elimination of the Company of the Isles and the giving of greater authority to the new governors, this trade had tended to grow, especially as the French sea captains and merchants were obliged by law to pay a heavy duty to the King for the privilege of trading in the islands, and it grew until the Dutch were sending from 100 to 120 ships every year to take advantage of this profitable business. To rectify the situation, a prominent Parisian banker suggested forming a French company with the assistance of the government to take over this trade, and closing the islands to foreign vessels gradually, as the amount of business was too great for the French to handle all at once by themselves. There were others who shared the same opinions; France was slowly awakening to the immense losses she had been incurring by her failure to keep this lucrative trade in her own hands.

Fortunately, King Louis XIV had at his elbow the great financier, Jean-Baptiste Colbert, who at this time was beginning to turn his attention to the West Indian situation. During the year 1662 a report was placed in his hands giving an account of the troubles in Martinique. The island, so the report said, was in a state of anarchy due to the maladministration of M. de

Vaudroques, who for the past four years had been running the place for his own personal interests. Such a situation deserved immediate attention, for Colbert considered Martinique the principal island of the group, and he determined to send out a representative who would take steps to restore order. On November 19, 1663, he gave the Marquis de Tracy a commission appointing him the King's Lieutenant-General of all his lands and islands in the Western Hemisphere, Canada as well as the West Indies. Armed with this authority, the Marquis set sail in February of the following year and reached Martinique in June, after stopping a while at the French colony in Guiana. M. de Clermont, who now commanded at Martinique, was somewhat alarmed at the arrival of this prominent nobleman armed with plenipotential powers, for rumors had been brought him by the Dutch traders of the plan to form a huge company to take over the West Indies. Nevertheless, it was necessary to give the new arrival a decent reception; and he would have done so at once had not the habitans attended to it on their account, for scarcely had the ship dropped anchor off Fort St. Pierre when a delegation swarmed over the side to lay before the Marquis their complaints against Governor de Clermont, complaints which had been accumulating for some time and which they now hoped would receive proper attention. M. de Tracy greeted them with such affability that they left his presence firmly convinced he was the man to set matters right.

M. de Tracy then sent an officer ashore to present his orders to the Governor and see what sort of a reception awaited him. Anxious to gain the good will of the King's representative, Clermont received the messenger in so gracious a manner that he returned to his superior with an enthusiastic report of the Governor's hospitality. In this the officer was not mistaken, for on stepping into his gig the Marquis was welcomed with salvos of artillery that boomed continuously across the water during his progress toward the shore.

The Governor [says our authority] was waiting for him at the landing-place with the principal citizens of the island. He received him there, and after having tendered his submission led him to the public square where the habitans were awaiting him drawn up in battle array. They saluted him with a burst of musketry. He entered the church where the *Te Deum* was sung, and again the guns were fired to show the joy with which they received him.

M. de Clermont offered his guest Du Parquet's house as a residence, but he declined it, preferring to take lodgings in town where he could attend to business more readily. He spent the first week learning the ropes, registering his commission, receiving the oath of fidelity from the Governor, the clergy, the Council, and the people. By the seventh of June he was ready to begin his investigations. He found the island as a whole greatly in debt to the Dutch traders, and the colonists in debt to each other, so that the courts were clogged with suits and countersuits. The administration of justice was in a chaotic condition because of this, while Jews and heretics had got out of hand and were insolently practicing their religions under the very noses of the faithful. The Marquis, in view of this state of affairs, decided to dispense with the courts and try the cases himself. Before his tribunal nobles and commoners, rich and poor, citizens and strangers appeared, and were judged according to the merits of their respective cases; and thus in a short while he was able to do more than the judges had done in years. Two things made him feared and loved by the people: his inflexible attitude toward anything that touched the King's authority, and his refusal to be reached by appeals to his private interests. He refused to accept even the most insignificant gifts, such as presents of food made him by the Governor, and lived very simply on what provisions he could buy. Before leaving the island, he drew up a code of regulations governing the religious, mercantile, and social activities of the colonists that was to form the basis for future conduct.

After finishing his work at Martinique, De Tracy proceeded to Guadeloupe where another job of similar character awaited him. Prior to leaving, however, he received a visit from M. du

Coudray, a gentleman sent by Houël with certain suggestions which the Governor hoped would make a favorable impression on the Marquis. Du Coudray told him of a handsome present prepared for him, a collection of horses, cattle, and slaves, worth seven or eight thousand francs, awaiting him when he reached Guadeloupe. Having stressed this point, the emissary proceeded to offer several arguments justifying the Governor's treatment of his nephews. But M. de Tracy, indignant at what was palpably a bribe, cut him short and spurned the gifts, bluntly informing the astonished messenger that anything he might say in favor of his master would be useless, for he (Tracy) was bound to call him to account for the many complaints lodged against him. Furthermore, he said he could see no way to protect the Governor of Guadeloupe from the consequences of an investigation unless the Governor went at once to France to lay his case at the feet of the King. As a mark of favor he would, however, withhold a letter he had with him ordering Houël to return to France so that the unfortunate man might give his people the impression that he had gone back voluntarily. A few days after M. du Coudray's departure, an emissary arrived from M. d'Herblay who was even more bluntly handled, for De Tracy did not mince matters and told him plainly that both the nephews must carry their case to the King ten days after he landed in Guadeloupe.

De Tracy arrived at Guadeloupe on the twenty-third of June, and no sooner had he anchored off Basseterre than Houël and D'Herblay both came on board to welcome him. For once the aggressive Houël was silent. In the presence of this distinguished nobleman armed with the King's authority, a man incorruptible, susceptible to none of the usual forms of pressure, and who, moreover, far outranked anyone who had ever been sent to the West Indies, Houël was tongue-tied and remained for some time without uttering a word until the Marquis put him at his ease with a few civil remarks. On shore M. Houël recovered his poise, and set about to receive the King's representative in the

END OF THE PIONEER PERIOD 267

grand manner. As in Martinique, the Marquis landed amid salvos, and as in Martinique he was offered a handsome residence which he likewise declined.

Several conferences were now held between MM. de Tracy, Houël, and d'Herblay at which the Marquis explained that as soon as they left for France, he would remove the local garrisons from their forts and replace them with the King's troops. De Tracy evidently persuaded Houël that he meant business for three or four days later the Governor was seen to embark on a Flemish vessel bound for France. The following day the Marquis repealed the two heaviest taxes Houël had imposed, an action which naturally caused universal satisfaction. Eight days after their uncle's departure, MM. d'Herblay and Téméricourt also sailed for France, leaving the island under the complete control of M. de Tracy.

While the Marquis de Tracy was thus engaged in bringing order out of chaos, Colbert was perfecting his plans for placing the islands in the hands of a strong company capable of managing them in a profitable manner. On April 17, 1664, the King issued an order commanding all members of the defunct Company of the Isles to bring before a specially appointed commission all papers in their possession pertaining to the sale of the islands by the company to the present proprietors. In May, Louis XIV signed the charter of the West India Company, a document granting the newly formed corporation all French colonies in South America, the West Indies, Canada, Acadia, and Newfoundland, with broad powers of government and management. The owners of the West Indian possessions, for their part, had no intention of surrendering their rights without a struggle. The wives of Houël and Cérillac, and the mother of D'Herblay filed protests to Parlement beseeching that august body not to register the charter; but in the end they were forced to yield. The Boisseret interests presently signed a contract with the company surrendering Mariegalante, Desirade, and their share of Guadeloupe. The following year the Knights of

Malta sold their property for five hundred thousand francs, and M. de Cérillac the island of Grenada for one hundred thousand, while Martinique changed hands for a hundred and twenty thousand francs. As might be expected, valiant old Houël balked, and probably with some justice, at the niggardly twenty-five thousand offered him for his share of Guadeloupe; in fact he refused to ratify the deal, retaining nominal possession of his property until the dissolution of the company in 1674 when his island, like all the others, was taken over by the Crown.

With the acquisition of these islands by the West India Company, we may fittingly bring our story of the French Pioneers in the West Indies to a close, for the pioneer work is done. Save for Dominica and St. Vincent, whose story belongs to a later period, the principal islands of the Caribbee group were now safely in the hands of the new company and destined to become in a brief decade the property of the Crown. From a tiny settlement on little St. Christopher, planted in haphazard fashion by a privateersman in search of fortune and adventure, French colonial enterprise had expanded until it had gathered to itself the fairest islands of the Lesser Antilles. In the face of tremendous odds, the pioneers had set themselves to the grim task of making their possessions fit places of habitation for Europeans. The Indians had been expelled, slave insurrections suppressed, Spanish attacks repulsed, starvation and disease overcome. Even neglect by those at home who had sponsored the undertaking could not dampen the determination of these hardy settlers. Despite all obstacles, they had cleared the land and in place of a wilderness had planted fields of tobacco and sugar cane. Towns had been built, forts erected at strategic places, and roads cut through the jungle. The New World was being compelled to yield its produce to feed the Old. Fortunately for the first fifteen years of colonial expansion, the adventurers had the benefit of the administrative abilities of the leading statesman of the age. Thanks to the skill of Cardinal Richelieu, money

END OF THE PIONEER PERIOD

was found to finance the embryo colony; and after the enthusiasm of the backers had cooled off, he reorganized the first company and supplied fresh capital for the work. Yet even his authority could not always cope with the situation. The colonies had been launched for the purpose of making money, but those sent out as representatives of the company naturally had no intention of letting any opportunity slip through their fingers to enrich themselves personally. Furthermore, the colonists had their own battles to fight, their own affairs to look after, and could not be expected to show too keen an interest in making a profit for the owners at home. Such being the case, they did business wherever they found it most profitable, and it chanced that the Dutch were able, because of their enormous and efficient merchant marine, to give the best service. The several governors, fully aware of the long distance separating them from France, ran things pretty much their own way. Thus it was that the company failed, and the governors after purchasing their islands from the defunct organization became owners as well as rulers.

Free now from all restraint, these men proceeded to build up a profitable commerce with the Dutch merchants; so that at the end of a dozen years, the West Indian colonies presented the curious anomaly of a venture founded by French capital, owned and ruled by Frenchmen, but yielding nothing to the mother country. Such a situation was contrary to the economic theories of the day. The idea of free trade—and we mean free trade in the eighteenth-century sense, that is the right of a colony to trade where it pleased—was not understood. It was a universally accepted theory that colonies existed for the mother country; that is why rulers granted them charters. Acting on this principle, Colbert soon turned his attention to the problem of the West Indies. He saw that the Dutch traders were enriching themselves at the expense of France, and at once proceeded to rectify the situation. The huge West India Company was organized to take over the islands from the owner-governors, French vessels were built to take care of the new business, and the entire system changed to direct trade into the proper channels.

In this manner the first phase of French West Indian history came to an end. The history of Europe now also underwent a change, and very soon there began that long struggle between France and England that did not end until the fall of Napoleon. France now became the great nation of Europe, and to keep her within bounds England attacked her on every front, in the New as well as the Old World, in the West Indies as well as in Canada. The French West Indian empire, after many vicissitudes, during which the islands changed hands repeatedly, was finally dismembered, until France, once mistress of the Caribbee Islands, now retains but Martinique, Guadeloupe, and a few dependencies.

APPENDIX

ISLANDS OF THE FRENCH WEST INDIES

Islands	Area in Square Miles	Date of First Permanent Settlement
Antigua	108	1632
Barbardos	166	1627
Dominica	290	1635
Grenada	133	1649
Guadeloupe	619	1635
Mariegalante	55	1648
Martinique	380	1635
Montserrat	32	1632
Nevis	50	1628
St. Christopher	63	1624
St. Lucia	240	1650
St. Vincent	140	1719

BIBLIOGRAPHY

Ballet, Jules, La Guadeloupe. Basse-Terre: 1894. 3 vols.
   This is far more than a mere historical treatise; it is a compilation of information on all conceivable subjects that might add to the knowledge of Guadeloupe. It deals not only with history, but with fauna, flora, geology, mineralogy, agriculture, commerce, industry, and administration. Volume I, covering the period between 1625 and 1715, is divided into three parts, each a large volume in itself. Volumes II and III cover the greater part of the eighteenth century. The author lived many years in Guadeloupe, holding several important business and government positions which gave him access to rare documents and a wealth of material unavailable elsewhere. The first installment of the work appeared in 1890, the last in 1902.

Biet, Antoine, Voyage de la France équinoxiale en l'isle de Cayenne entrepris par les françois en l'année MDCLII. Paris, 1664.
   Antoine Biet was a French priest who made a voyage to some of the Caribbee Islands in the year 1652. His work is divided into three main sections: (1) an account of his journey across the Atlantic to Guiana; (2) an account of the events in that colony for the next fifteen months; (3) a description of the country and the customs of the Indians. Most of this work deals with Guiana, but in the second section there is the account of a short journey made by the author to Barbados, Martinique, and Guadeloupe that yields some useful information concerning these places. He appears to have had difficulties with the Jesuit fathers in Martinique for he criticizes their missions severely.

Bouton, Jacques, Relation de l'establissement des françois depuis l'an 1635. Paris, 1640.
   This book deals exclusively with Martinique as its author, a Jesuit priest, spent a few months there and did not concern himself with the

other islands. It is the first French West Indian chronicle. Bouton treats briefly the historical events—there were only five years of history for him to tell about—and devotes most of his space to a description of the island, its produce, possible exports, geographical situation, the character of its inhabitants—whites, blacks, and Indians. The book is dedicated to the directors of the company. It was written probably for the purpose of presenting the colony in its most favorable light, at a time when the company was in bad repute, due to the disorders that were then taking place on the islands. Under the circumstances it is not improbable that the company may have inspired the book, or, at any rate, have aided in its publication.

Boyer-Peyreleau, Eugène-Édouard, Les Antilles françaises, particulièrement la Guadeloupe. Paris, 1823.

Like Jules Ballet's Guadeloupe, this book contains a general survey of the geography, fauna, and flora of the Antilles, a feature it shares with most West Indian histories. The narrative is carried down to 1823. Colonel Boyer-Peyreleau made several trips to the West Indies and was at one time (1802-9) aide-de-camp of the Governor of Martinique. In 1814 he was second-in-command of Guadeloupe. His work is the result of personal observations and research; but so far as our purpose is concerned, it gives little that cannot be found elsewhere as Du Tertre is practically his only source for the early period. It has an index, something unusual in a French book.

Coppier, Guillaume, Histoire et voyage des Indes occidentales. Lyon, 1645.

Coppier was one of the early colonists of St. Christopher, poor in purse but of fair education. He came as an indentured servant and served his allotted time of three years, taking part in the skirmishes against Don Fadrique. Eventually, after many vicissitudes, he returned to France to live in a fairly prosperous manner. His book, thrown together in haphazard style, contains, nevertheless, some interesting details of the events which occurred during his time.

Dampierre, Jacques de, Essai sur les sources de l'histoire des Antilles françaises (1492–1664). Paris, 1904.

This work is invaluable for anyone writing on the early history of the French West Indies. It is a critical bibliography of French literature dealing with the period from the first settlements to 1664, particularly with the books and pamphlets written by travelers who visited the islands during the first part of the seventeenth century. Great pains have been taken to give the reader all the biographical information possible concerning these early authors with helpful comments as to their qualifications for making observations.

Daney, M. Sidney, Histoire de la Martinique depuis la colonisation jusqu'en 1815. Fort Royal, 1846.

A comprehensive history which covers the subject from the first colonization of the island to the year 1815, written by a member of the Colonial Council of Martinique. The work is well done and written in an interesting narrative style. The author is obviously familiar with the important documents, but unfortunately he wrote in the West Indies where he did not have access to the archives of the home government.

Dessalles, M. Adrien, Histoire générale des Antilles. Paris, 1847. 5 vols.

A large comprehensive history of the French West Indies from the beginning of colonization to the French Revolution. The author, who came from a prominent family of Martinique, had at his finger tips the documents collected by his grandfather, Pierre Regis Dessalles which he embodied in the third volume of his work. In order to edit these papers, he was granted access to the Archives de la Marine in Paris where, of course, he found ample material for his history. For the period which concerns us, however, he relies chiefly as he himself tells us, on Father du Tertre. He gives an enormous amount of detail.

Dessalles, Pierre Regis, Histoire Legislative des Antilles; ou, Annales du Conseil Souverain de la Martinique. Edited with notes by M. Adrien Dessalles and forming the third volume of his Histoire générale.

Dessalles was born in Martinique and at an early age was appointed an assessor to the Sovereign Council. Here he undertook to write a history of the island and for this purpose collected valuable documents, but for various reasons was never able to complete the work. Instead, he satisfied himself with publishing certain select documents or résumés of them, and these were afterwards republished in the history written by his grandson, Adrien. There are but a few documents that fall within our period.

Du Motey, Henri Renault, Guillaume d'Orange. Paris, 1908.

A biography of a prominent pioneer in the early history of Martinique, St. Christopher, and Guadeloupe. It throws considerable light on contemporary events.

Du Puis, Mathias, Relation de l'etablissement d'une colonie françoise dans la Guadeloupe. Caen, 1652.

This is the work of a Dominican father. It is entirely historical, being devoid of those digressions on zoology and botany that are so frequently found in contemporary books. It is particularly useful to those who wish to study the events of Governor Houël's stormy administration; in fact, nearly half the book is devoted to his activities. The author does not depict Houël in a favorable light; on the contrary, he does full justice to the Governor's animosity toward the Dominicans. In addition to this, the book gives a history of the island from the founding of the first colony and contains in Part II a valuable dissertation on Indian customs.

Du Tertre, Jean-Baptiste, Histoire générale des Antilles. Paris, 1667–1671. 4 vols.

This work is the backbone of all accounts dealing with the first forty years of French colonization in the French West Indies. Enough has been said in the text to give the reader an idea of Father du Tertre's career and his opportunities for compiling such a history. Volume I starts with the foundation of the colony at St. Christopher and ends with the death of Governor de Poincy; Volume II deals with natural history, customs, agriculture, and trade; Volumes III & IV published four years later, take up the narrative where Volume I left off and bring it down to 1668. No one was better qualified to write a history of the Caribbees than Father du Tertre. He made several voyages to the islands and lived there long enough to become acquainted with local conditions and to know personally the principal actors in the drama. From these men he obtained an enormous amount of information that could never be unearthed today by even the most conscientious historians. In addition to this he had access to all the important documents in France, many of which he quotes *in extenso*, so that parts of his work read more like a collection of state papers than a historical narrative. While at Paris he also made several trips to seaports such as Havre, Honfleur, and Dieppe, where he interviewed sea captains and adventurers who had made the voyage to the West Indies, men who could throw light on certain ambiguous points. All this material Father du Tertre wove together into an interesting, homogeneous story, extremely readable besides being authoritative. There are slight mistakes, of course—he himself admits them—but they are trifling compared to the vast amount of accurate information he has given us.

Great Britain. Privy Council, Acts of the Privy Council of England. Colonial Series. London, 1613-1680.

Great Britain. Public Record Office, Calendar of State Papers, Colonial Series. London, 1574-1660.

Haring, Clarence Henry, The Buccaneers in the West Indies in the XVII Century. New York, Dutton, 1910.

A scholarly work on the subject based on careful research among the early records and state papers. It is interestingly written and is one of the best books on the subject produced in recent times. For our purpose it gives a summary of the early history of Tortuga.

Harlow, Vincent Todd, ed., Colonising Expeditions to the West Indies and Guiana, 1623-1667. London, 1925.

This edition, compiled for the Hakluyt Society, contains several early narratives dealing with the West Indies and Guiana. The account of John Hilton, chief gunner of Nevis, tells of the settlement and early history of that island as well as of St. Christopher by the English. The voyage of Sir Henry Colt also throws some light on the subject. Mr. Harlow has prefaced these stories with an introduction giving an interesting account of the first colonies on these islands.

Histoire de l'Isle de Grenade.

This work covers the history of Grenada for a period of ten years (1649-59) and is written in the form of annals. It gives a detailed account of the events that took place in the island during this period, evidently having been written by one who witnessed them. The author does not mince matters in his narrative. He describes the life of the colonists in all the stark brutality that was often found in these early settlements. It is not the sort of book that would be used by promoters as a prospectus for attracting colonists or investors, and for this reason is valuable to those who wish to know what actually did take place. It is unfortunately marred by the tendency of the author to disgress from his topic and to moralize on the events he describes. Dampierre believes it was written by a priest about the year 1660.

Jeaffreson, Christopher, A Young Squire of the Seventeenth Century. London, 1878.

An interesting picture of life at St. Christopher in the latter part of the seventeenth century, told in the letters of a colonist, one Christopher Jeaffreson. This falls outside the period of our narrative; but the introduction by John C. Jeaffreson gives much valuable information about the settlement and early history of the island.

Labat, Jean-Baptiste, Nouveau voyage aux isles de l'Amérique. La Haye, 1724.

Father Labat shares with Father du Tertre the distinction of being one of the two most valuable chroniclers of the early French West Indies. He spent eleven years on the islands (1694-1705) principally in Martinique and Guadeloupe, and being an unusually keen observer, his account of what he saw and learned is of immense value. He gives considerable history, but his descriptions of the various industries, the fauna and flora, the customs of the people, and his own experiences enlivened by clever anecdotes, are probably better even than those of Du Tertre.

La Roncière, Charles de, Histoire de la marine française. Paris, 1899-1932. 6 vols.

A monumental work on the French navy in all its ramifications from the earliest times to the Treaty of Utrecht in 1713. It is the result of years of research in the French archives, and may be considered *the* outstanding authority on the subject. The account in Volume IV of the founding of the French colonies in the Caribbees is brief but accurate, and full of valuable information, reinforced by copious footnotes.

Margry Pierre, Origines transatlantiques. Belain d'Esnambuc et les Normands aux Antilles. Paris, 1863.

This brochure is the result of painstaking research on the part of a great scholar who unearthed an enormous mass of material on French colonial history. It gives information concerning D'Esnambuc unknown up to that time, and traces his life from the very beginning to his death in 1636. Valuable and interesting genealogical data about the Belain family are also included.

———— "Origines françaises des pays d'outre-mer," published in Revue Maritime et Coloniale. Paris, 1878.

This is a study appearing in serial form and dealing with the history of the Dyel du Parquet family which for many years ruled, and at one time owned, the island of Martinique. It was into this family that D'Esnambuc's sister married. These articles like all the writings of Pierre Margry are based on careful research and give much that would be difficult to find elsewhere.

Mercure François, XXIII. 325-33.

Mims, Stewart L., Colbert's West India Policy. New Haven, 1912.

A scholarly work fortified with abundant footnotes and citations from the sources. It is purely an economic history, and gives an excellent account of the economic forces at work in the founding of the French West Indian colonies.

Moreau de Saint-Méry, Médéric Louis E., ed., Loix et constitutions des colonies françoises de l'Amérique sous le vent. Paris, 1784-90.

This is a collection of laws and decrees gathered by an enterprising French lawyer of San Domingo who wished to codify the laws of that island. As San Domingo had obtained much of its early legislation from Martinique, Saint-Méry included in his work many legal documents dealing with the history of the Caribbee Islands.

Newton, Arthur Percival, European Nations in the West Indies 1493-1688. London, 1933.

This is one of "The Pioneer Histories" series brought out under the editorship of V. T. Harlow and J. A. Williamson, authorities on West Indian history. It is written by a competent scholar, and though, because of the scope of the work, the portion dealing with the Caribbee Islands is necessarily abridged, it is useful to us as it shows the relation of our subject to West Indian history as a whole.

Oliver, Vere L., The History of the Island of Antigua, London, 1894-1899.

Pelleprat, Pierre, Relation des missions des P. P. de la Compagnie de Jesus. Paris, 1655.

This is a book dealing principally with the activities of the missionaries written by a Jesuit father who had been to the Caribbees in person and had visited St. Christopher, Mariegalante, St. Vincent, Martinique, and Grenada. He made two journeys to the West Indies in 1651–53 and 1654–55. What interested him most in his sojourn was the religious situation he had to face, and it is to him one turns for much information on this subject which is not disclosed even by Father du Tertre. He tells at length of the missionary activities of the priests in various islands, the conversion of many Huguenot colonists, the difficulties which Irish Catholics experienced with their Protestant masters, and the work done among negro and Indian slaves. The book contains little concerning secular history.

Provins, Pacifique de, Relation du voyage des isles de l'Amérique. 1646.
Father Pacifique was a Capuchin at St. Christopher and was among the first missionaries to come there in 1635. As he spent almost his entire time on this island, his narrative deals chiefly with the events there in the missionary field.

Purchas, Samuel, His Pilgrimes. Hakluyt Society Edition. Glasgow, 1905.

Rochefort, Charles-César de, Histoire naturelle des Antilles de l'Amérique. Lyon, 1667. 2 vols.
Little is known of the author, though it is generally believed that he was a Protestant minister who had traveled extensively in the Lesser Antilles. He was a friend of Governor de Poincy who supplied him with considerable information and numerous documents. There is little historical narrative in the book; it is, as its title indicates, a natural history, and thus contains much on subjects falling under the broadest meaning of the term. There are several chapters dealing with the Carib Indians. Du Tertre in his book frequently attacks Rochefort's accuracy; in fact, he appears to have had a grudge against the man as he accuses him of plagiarizing his own work, even to the extent of copying the mistakes.

Saint-Michel, Maurile de, Voyages des isles Camercanes en l'Amérique qui font partie des Indes Occidentales. 1652.
A book by a Dominican father in which he tells of his observations on his journey to the Caribbees. It deals principally with conditions as he found them, chiefly in St. Christopher, Guadeloupe, and Martinique, but does not tell much about historical events.

BIBLIOGRAPHY

Smith, John, Works. Edited by Edward Arber. Birmingham, 1884.

Southey, Thomas, Chronological History of the West Indies. London, 1827. 3 vols.

> A year by year account of the events in the West Indies from the earliest times to 1815. For his French sources during the period we are studying, the author relies almost entirely on Du Tertre. Southey's book is an old one, and much has come to light about the pioneer period since he wrote it, especially about the British colonies.

Williamson, James A., The Caribbee Islands under the Proprietary Patents, London, 1926.

> An excellent treatise telling of the early settlements on Barbados and St. Christopher. It deals principally with the English, but there is a good summary of D'Esnambuc and his work. It has also a good account of the important Carlisle Patent.

INDEX

Adriensen, Abraham, 186
Anguilla, French colony on, 33
Angola, negroes of, 224
Annatto tree, dye from, 4
Anne of Austria, queen of France, 118, 145, 206
Annunciation, Fort, 195, 197 f.
Anse à Louve, 73
Antigua, 2, 4, 25, 32, 191, 239; naming of, 7; raided by Caribs, 104; unsuitable for colonization, 33
Arawaks, 4
Armada of Don Fadrique, 26, 29
Arms (bearing of), discouraged by Du Parquet, 179
Assumption, 8
Aubert, Mlle, women from Hospital Saint-Joseph housed by, 119
Aubert, Sieur Jean, 99 f., 102, 108 f., 136, 194; captaincy, 124; escape to St. Christopher, 121; governor of Guadeloupe, 109 ff.; Houël persecutes, 121 ff.; plantation purchased by Houël, 121; Poincy supported by, 131 f.; subordination of, 117
Aubigny, Prince d', 208 f.
Auger, Sieur (founder of a settlement on St. Croix), 190
Augramert (Indian chief), 200, 202

Banyan tree, 41 f.
Barbados, 28, 239; naming of, 8
Barbuda: Houël's expedition against, 169; Littleton acquires, 24; traffic privileges granted by Charles I, 16 and note.
Baron, Captain (Indian chief), 53, 111
Basseterre (Guadeloupe), 52, 53, 57, 103, 121, 135, 222 f., 254, 266; Thoisy's fortifications at, 151; Thoisy's commission read at, 152
Basseterre (St. Christopher), 21 and note, 69, 74, 90, 102, 115, 120, 127, 136, 138; Spanish armada attacks, 30 ff.; evacuation by the French, 32; capital of the French West Indies, 39
Basseterre, Fort (St. Christopher), 73
Beaufort (general), 154 ff.
Beaumont, Father, 254
Beausejour, 215
Beausoleil (a leader in the revolt against Mme DuParquet), 244 ff.
Beculat, René de, Sieur de la Grange Fromenteau, *see* La Grange Fromenteau, René de Beculat, Sieur de
Bedel, Noël, 95
Belain, Catherine, 10
Belain, Nicolas, Sieur d'Ensambuc et de Canouville, 10
Béliard (captain), 165 f., 169, 236
Bell, Philip, 203
Bellestre, daughter of, 70 f.
Benin, Father, 236, 245
Benin (coast of), 40
Bermuda, 202
Biet, Antoine, 178
Boisfaye, Jean François Parisot de, 134, 136 f., 149 ff., 171
Boisseret d'Herblay, Jean de, 207 f., 213, 249
Boisseret family, Mariegalante, Desirade, and Guadeloupe surrendered by, 267
Boisseret, Mme de, 252 f., 257, 267
Bonnard, Marie, *see* Dyel du Parquet, Mme Marie (Bonnard)

INDEX

Bontemps (captain), 134, 141, 147 f., 149 f.
Borde, Father, 228
Boulogne, Father, 228, 236, 245
Bourlet, (leader of revolt against Du Parquet), 227 f.
Bournonville, duc de (governor of Paris), 257
Boutain (commander of a vessel from La Rochelle), case of, 149 f., 154
Bouton, Jacques, 108
Bréchet, Nicolas, 45, 57
Breda (captain), 144
Breton, Raymond, 45, 49, 57, 105, 168; L'Olive berated by, 53 f.
Brezé, Armand de Maillé, marquis de, 118
Brissac, Charles de Cossé de, 10
Brisson, 261
Buccaneers, 2, 80 f., 86
Bugaud, Clement, 116

Cahuzac (commander of fleet to expel the English from St. Christopher), 25 ff.
Camot, Antoine, 139 f., 143 ff., 180; Mariegalante charter lapsed, 190
Canada, Champlain's colonies in, 18; French colonies in, 3
Cannibalism, 7
Canouville, François Belain de, 10
Capesterre (Guadeloupe), 119, 256; habitans petition for remission of dues, 150 f.; Thoisy's commission read at, 152
Capesterre (Martinique), 244 f.
Capesterre (St. Christopher), 21 and note, 102; churches of, 75; slave insurrection, 100
Capitalists, French, *see* French capitalists
Capuchins, 39, 75, 108, 140; Des Marets befriended by, 114; expelled from St. Christopher, 131, 142 f.; La Grange befriended by, 72 f,; La Grange favored by, 69
Carbet, Rivière du, *see* Du Carbet, Rivière
"Cardinale, La," (ship), 19, 22, 28, 37

Carénage, 64 f.
Caribbee Islands, 1 ff.; discovery of, 6; fertility of, 3; French dominant in, 1; location, 1; prosperity, 2; Spaniards fail to colonize, 8; volcanic origin, 3
Caribs, 4 ff., 193 f., 196 ff., 200 ff., 260; attacked by the French, 50 ff., 218; Aubert friendly with, 109; conversion of, 39; defeated by French at Guadeloupe, 103; execution at Martinique, 219; expulsion from Martinique, 244 f.; expulsion from St. Christopher, 20; Guadeloupe a headquarters for, 6; Martinique attacked by, 60 f.; massacre on St. Bartholomew, 187; massacre on Grenada, 198; massacre on Mariegalante, 191; massacre on Martinique, 243; mission of St. Vincent destroyed by, 214; peace with French at Martinique, 61, 108, 226; raids of, 54 f.; raids on Dutch Protestants, 212; raids on Grenada, 213 ff., 216; raids on Guadeloupe, 79; raids on Martinique, 107, 225 f.; raids on St. Christopher, 17; raids on St. Lucia, 203; slaves sheltered by, 225 f.; treaty with Aubert, 111; treaty with French and English, 258
Carlisle, Charles Howard, 1st earl of, 24, 28
Carmelites, 75
Carpenters, shortage of, 106
Carré, Father, 45, 56
Cartagena, 26, 32; Fontenay raids, 93
Case du Borgne, 119
Case-Pilote, 65, 227, 239, 243
Castries, 4, 204
"Catholique, La" (ship), 19
Cattle hunting on Tortuga, 84
Cayenne, ship from, 215
Cayman islands, 97
Cayonne (St. Christopher), 78, 210; church at, 75
Cayonne (Tortuga), 87, 92 f., 97
Cérillac, Jean Faudoas, comte de, 230 ff.; governor of Grenada, 233;

INDEX

Grenada sold by, 268; voyage to Grenada attempted, 233 ff.
Cérillac, Mme (wife of Jean Faudoas, comte de Cérillac), 267
Champlain, Samuel de, 18
Chantail (captain), 16
Charles I, king of England, colonization of St. Christopher favored by, 15
Charles, Fort, 73, 141
"Chateau, The," 73 f.
"Citadel, The," 73
Clergy, persecuted by Houël, 168; residence for at Guadeloupe, 56 f.
Clermont, Jean Dyel de, 248, 264 f.
Colbert, Jean-Baptiste, 2, 248, 263 f., 267
Colonists, English, *see* English colonists
Colonists, French, *see* French colonists
Colonization, economic reasons for, 3
Columbus, Christopher, 6
Commissioners of Foreign Plantations, 203
Company of St. Christopher, 18, 36 f., 269 (line 2); dissolution of, 38, 44
Company of the Hundred Associates, 18
Company of the Isles of America, 38, 44, 116, 263; bankruptcy of, 205 f.; charter amended, 147 f.; dues protested by habitans 150 f.; failure explained, 269
Conception, 8
Cotton, Martinique colonists compelled to grow, 77
Council, chosen by Houël, 149
Council of war, appointed by Thoisy, 151
Coutis, Sieur (leader of colony on St. Lucia), 218
Coutume de la côte, 80
Cromwell, Oliver, 222
Cul de Sac Royal, 59, 64, 135, 212

"David of Lubeck" (ship), 32
De Boisfaye, Jean François Parisot, *see* Boisfaye, Jean François Parisot de
De Guinant, *see* Guinant, de
De Poincy, Philippe de Lonvilliers, *see* Poincy, Philippe de Lonvilliers de
De Sabouilly, Jean Soulon, Sieur, *see* Sabouilly, Jean Soulon, Sieur de
De Sales, Charles, *see* Sales, Charles de
Des Galions, Rivière, 57, 110, 255
Desirade, 256; sold to Houël, 207 f.; sold to West Indies Company, 267
Des Marets, Sieur (ex-captain of St. Christopher), 113, 115, 129
Des Martinaux (messenger from Thoisy to Houël), 159
Des Pères, Rivière, 254 f.
Despinay (a Walloon gentleman), 224, 250
De Thoisy, Noël, Sieur de Patrocles, *see* Thoisy, Noël, Sieur de Patrocles de
De Tracy, Alexandre de Prouville, Marquis, *see* Tracy Alexandre de Prouville, Marquis de
D'Herblay, Charles de Boisseret, *see* Herblay, Charles de Boisseret d'
D'Herblay, Jean de Boisseret, *see* Boisseret d'Herblay, Jean
Diablotin, Mount, 3, 6
Dieppe, merchants, 50, 78 f.; traffic in indentured servants, 23
Dominica, 1, 3 f., 6, 44, 47, 199, 268; Aubert visits, 109; Caribs, 191 f.; Caribs establish headquarters in, 54; Caribs to be unmolested on, 258; Esnambuc takes possession of, 59 f.; Roman Catholic mission on, 60; Survey of, 43
Dominicans, 49, 65, 228; convent on Guadeloupe, 256
D'Orange, Guillaume, *see* Orange, Guillaume d'
Dragon's Mouth, 8
Dubuc (governor of Grenada), 235
Du Carbet, Rivière, 46, 227
Du Carenage, Rivière, 204
Du Coudray (messenger from Houël to Tracy) 266
Du Fort, Rivière, 59
Du Halde (lieutenant-governor of St. Christopher), 66
Dulcina, *see* Barbuda

Du Mé, Captain Le Roy, leader of pro-Houël party, 160 ff.; 190, 192
Du Motey, Henry Renault, *Guillaume d'Orange*, 169n
Du Parquet, Jacques, see Dyel du Parquet, Jacques
Du Parquet, Mme Marie (Bonnard) see Dyel du Parquet, Mme Marie (Bonnard)
Duplessis, Jean, Sieur d'Ossonville, 43 ff.; death of, 51; son of, 112; widow of, 100, 109
Du Pont, Jean, 59 ff.; Caribs pacified by, 61; prisoner at San Domingo, 61
Du Puis, Mathias, *Relation de l'etablissement d'une colonie française dans la Guadeloupe*, 169n
Du Puy, Father, 190
Duquesne (Indian chief) daughter of, 197 f.
Du Rivage, François, 122 ff.; sentenced to galleys, 124
Du Roissey, Urbain, Sieur de Chardonville, 11 ff.; Richelieu commissions, 19; Basseterre defended by, 30 ff.; desertion of colony, 33; d'Esnambuc confers with, 26; expedition to Ireland, 22; lands at St. Christopher, 16; return to France, 17 ff.; return to St. Christopher, 1628, 22; St. Christopher (southern part) acquired by, 21
DuSarrat, Jerome, Sieur de la Pierrière, 139, 150, 170; Beaufort murdered by, 156; governor of Martinique, 157; plot against Beaufort, 154 ff.
Dutch, Martinique rescued by, 220 f.; Spanish fleet annihilated by, 102
Dutch merchantmen, 21 f.
Dutch merchants: Martinique in debt to, 265; trade increased, 263; trade monopolized by, 269
Dutch Protestants, 211 ff.; on Guadaloupe, 211 f.; on Martinique, 212
Du Tertre, Jean-Baptiste, 31 f., 47, 52, 54, 59n, 65 f., 86n, 105, 121, 127, 155, 171 f., 176, 181, 190, 194n, 213, 227, 237, 262; captured by the English, 231; Cérillac's agent, 230 ff.; Houël unfriendly to, 178; mutineers dispersed by, 163; quoted, 220, 260; Thoisy's partisan, 159 ff.
Dyel d'Esnambuc, Jean-Jacques, 241, 248; governor of Martinique & St. Lucia, 236 f.
Dyel de Vaudroques, Adrien, 62, 237, 246, 259, 264
Dyel de Vaudroques, Adrienne, 10, 30, 61
Dyel de Vaudroques, Pierre, 10, 61
Dyel du Parquet, Jacques, 138 f., 154, 169, 191, 265; agriculture restored by, 178; arms (bearing of) discouraged, 179; Aubert advised by, 109; authority threatened by judge, 106; Caribs besiege, 220; Caribs of St. Vincent attacked by, 218; Caribs pacified by, 226; clergy well-treated by, 229; death of, 228 f.; defeated by Poincy, 140; deposition of, 241 f.; discipline restored by, 178; Dutch Protestants accepted by 212; Dutch Protestants rejected by, 211; exchange proposed, 164; governor-general, 209; governor of Martinique, 62, 105 ff.; Grenada, aided by, 215; Grenada and Grenadines sold by, 232 f.; Grenada annexed by, 193 ff.; hospitality of, 64; imprisoned by Poincy, 141; islands purchased by, 209; lieutenant-governor of Martinique, 63; receives Thoisy, 135; residence damaged by earthquake, 223; restored to Martinique, 170, 172; return to France, 221; St. Lucia annexed by, 193, 199 f.; St. Lucia colonized by, 204; St. Lucia massacre attributed to, 203; uprising quelled by, 227; Warner betrays, 140 f.
Dyel du Parquet, Louis, 236 f.
Dyel du Parquet, Mme Marie (Bonnard), 154, 173, 220, 227; death of, 247; governor of Martinique, 236 f.; imprisonment, 240 ff.; opposition to, 237 f.; reinstatement of, 246
Dyel du Parquet, Simon, 30 f., 61
Dye wood, 82, 84

INDEX

Earthquake, 223
Edict requiring permission of Company of St. Christopher for trading, 37
English armada, 221 f.
English colonists, 1 f.
English colonists on Nevis, 24
English colonists on St. Christopher; Cahuzac attacks, 27; establishment, 12 ff.; French territory encroached on, 25; Don Fadrique's armada attacks, 32; success of, 22
English colonists on St. Lucia, 199 ff.
Epidemic, 105
Esnambuc, Pierre Belain d', 10 ff., 237; Basseterre (St. Christopher), defended by, 30; boundary settled by, 41 f.; commissioned by Richelieu, 19; death of, 63; despair of, 35; domain of, 10; Du Roissey confers with, 26; Du Roissey deserts, 33; estate of bought by Poincy, 69, 73; governor-general, 45; landing at St. Christopher, 16; leads colonists to Montserrat, 33; leave refused, 62; opposed to attacking Caribs, 50; plea for reinforcements, 25; residence in Basseterre, 39; return to France, 17 f.; return to St. Christopher, 34; St. Christopher (northern part) acquired by, 21; statue in Fort de France, 63; vigor renewed, 36
Esnambuc, Fort d', 215 f.

Factors, 116; depredation of, 120
Fer-de-lance, 46, 64, 107
Fernandez de Fuermayor, Rui, see Fuermayor, Rui Fernandez de
Feuillet, Jean-Baptiste, 223, 228, 231, 236
Fichot (leader of settlement on St. Martin), 185 f.
Figueroa, Gabriel de Valle, see Valle Figueroa, Gabriel de
Flemish soldiers, 213
Fontenay, Timoléon Hotman de, 90; attempt to recapture Tortuga, 97; conquers French at Tortuga, 92; surrenders Tortuga to Spaniards, 96
Fort, Rivière du, see Du Fort, Rivière

Fort de France, 59, 63, 65
Fouquet, François, 44, 108
Fouquet, Nicolas, 247 f.; letter to Houël, 132 f.
Fournier (judge), 228
Francis de Sales, Saint, 255
Freedom, old French law of, 40
French capitalists, complaints of, 36 f.
French colonists, 1 f.
French colonists on St. Christopher; alliance with English against Indians, 17; alliance with English against the Spaniards, 26; economic problems, 36; English encroach upon, 25, 27, 41; recruits for, 39; Spanish armada attacks, 29; Dutch trade with, 36
French colonists on St. Lucia, 204
French Guinea Company, 40
French merchants: duty paid by, 263; trade lost by, 263
French sea captains, duty paid by, 263
French West India Company, 263
French West Indian empire, dismembered, 270
Fromenteau, René de Beculat, Sieur de la Grange, see La Grange Fromenteau, René de Beculat Sièur de
Fuermayor, Rui Fernandez de, 83

Galions, Rivière des, see Des Galions, Rivière
Gardien, Father, 140
Genip-tree sap, 4
Giraud (captain), 131
Giron (captain), also known as Couarlay, 28, 33 ff.
Gourselas, Médéric Rolle, Sieur de, 238 ff., 248
Grand Cul de Sac, 256
Grande Anse, 133, 216, 254
Grande Terre, 256
Greater Antilles, 1
Grégoire (captain), 165 f.
Grenada, 1, 8, 193 ff., 214, 229 f., Caribs attack, 197; Caribs invade, 214 ff.; sold to Cérillac, 231 ff.; sold to Du Parquet, 209; sold to West India Company, 268

INDEX

Grenadines, 209; sold to Cérillac, 232 f.

Gryphon, Pierre, 45, 56

Guadeloupe, 1, 46 ff., 99, 102; Caribs depart from, 54; charter for, 44; clergy arrive at, 105; De Tracy reforms, 265 f.; discovery of, 6; Dutch Protestants on, 211 f.; epidemic at, 105; food shortage and unwholesome living conditions, 48; France still possesses, 270; French colonization of, 47 ff.; hurricane, 222 f.; peace and prosperity of, 112; St. Christopher overshadowed by, 63; slave insurrection, 224 f.; sold to Houël, 207 f.; sold to West India Company, 267; sugar cane industry, 213; survey of, 43; taxation on, 251

Guébriant, Mme Renée de Bec de, 208 f.

Guiana (French), 12, 102, 116, 199, 264

Guinant, de (protégé of Sabouilly), 139, 146, 164; Thoisy represented by, 137 f.; governorship of St. Christopher promised to, 136; report to Louis XIV, 172

Habitans, 48 ff.; complaints against de Vaudroques, 264

Hameaux, Jean Dyel des, 237

Haquet (governor of St. Lucia), 217

Harbors, 4

Havana, 32

Havre: Cérillac at, 234; traffic in indentured servants, 23

Hawley, Henry, 28

Hedouin, Mathurin, 127 ff.; threat to kill Marivet, 133

Hein, Peter, 26

Hempteau, Father, 108

Hencelin (Houël's brother-in-law), 253, 257

Hencelin, Mlle, see Houël, Mme (Hencelin)

Herblay, Charles de Boisseret d', 221 f.; deported to France, 250, 267; Houël's persecution of, 257; plot against Houël, 253 ff.; property assigned to, 256; Tracy greeted by, 266

Herblay, Jean de Boisseret, see Boisseret d'Herblay, Jean d'

Heretics, on Martinique, 265

Hides, tax on, 89

Hilton, Anthony, 24 ff., 28; governor of Tortuga, 81 f.; Nevis colony founded by, 25; St. Christopher colony destroyed, 24; death of, 82

Hilton, John, 29

Hispaniola, 6 f.

Honfleur, 234

"Hopewell" (ship), 15

Hospital, at St. Christopher, 73

Hospital Saint-Joseph, Paris, 119

Hotman (brother of Timoléon Hotman de Fontenay), 93 ff.

Houël, Charles, Sieur de Petit-Pré, 78, 116 ff., 138, 141, 193, 213, 221, 258; Aubert unfairly treated by, 121 ff.; chief justice, 148; clergy persecuted by, 168; clergy reconciled with, 168 ff., and note; company's interests disregarded by, 205; council appointed by, 149; deported to France, 267; Dutch Protestants welcomed by, 212; expense account challenged, 206; good works, 178; governor of Guadeloupe, 117; Guadeloupe offer refused by, 268; Herblay's plot against, 253 ff.; incites colonists to march on Basseterre, 159; islands purchased by, 207 f.; Le Fort agreement, 171; letters received by, 254; marriage of, 249; plague stricken, 168; Poincy feud, 125; Poincy visited by, 120 f.; Poincy's cobelligerent, 153; Poincy's order of restraint to, 257; position in regard to Boisfaye, 152; property assigned to, 256; refuses to go to Fort Royal, 164; sister reconciled with, 257; reign of terror, 166; reimbursements for executed slaves, 225; return to Guadeloupe, 132; return to Guadeloupe (1656) 249 f.; Sabouilly threatened by, 177; Saints (islands) annexed by, 190; ship furnished for Thoisy, 139; taxes raised by, 251; Thoisy defied by, 150 f., 165 ff.;

INDEX 289

Thoisy opposed by, 145 ff.; Thoisy presents, 134; Thoisy's assassination plotted by, 158; Tracy received by, 266 ff.; verdict against, 174
Houël, Mme (Hencelin), 249, 267
Houël, Robert (The Chevalier), 191, 221 f., 250, 252 f., 257 f.
"Houëlmont," 121
Howard, Charles, 1st earl of Carlisle, *see* Carlisle
Huguenots, 84 ff.; persecutions, 89
Hunt, right to, 76
Hurricane, 3, 14, 222 f.
Hyacinthe, Father, 143

Imbaut, Sieur (colonist of Grenada) 214
Indentured servants, 22 f., 27, 32, 37, 40, 49; desertion of English by, 29; term of service, 36
Indians, *see* Arawaks; Caribs
Indigo, 77
Island of Association, 82

Jamaica, 2, 222
James (captain), 84, 86 and note
Jeaffreson, John, 13, 15 f., 34, 76
Jerome, Father, 39
Jesuits, 75, 108, 171, 212, 219; Thoisy resides with, 165; Dutch Protestants rejected because of, 211 f.; dwelling on Martinique, 65
Jews, 179, 211, 265
Jubilee, 133
Judge, expulsion from Martinique, 107
Judicial system, 147 f.
Judlee (captain), 202
Justice, administration of at Martinique, 265

Kairouane (Indian chief) 196
Kaynall, Christopher, 258
Knights of Malta, 181, 210, 236, 262; West Indian property sold by, 268

Labat, Jean-Baptiste, 5, 40
La Bazilière (captain), 151, 162, 166
La Fayolle, Mlle de, 119, 127 ff.
La Fontaine (an officer of Guadeloupe), 51, 173, 176

La Fontaine, Haussier de, 139 f., 143 ff., 179 f., 190
La Forge, Charles de, 160, 248
La Giraudière, Louis Duvivier, Sieur de, 241, 246
La Grange Fromenteau, Mme, 70 ff.
La Grange Fromenteau, René de Beculat, Sieur de, 66, 112, 129; insubordination, 75
La Mare, Nicolas de, 105, 214
L'Anse-Noire, Rivière de, 215
La Paix, Father, 122, 168
La Pierrière, Sieur de, *see* Du Sarrat, Jerome
La Ramée, de (colonist of Guadeloupe), 110 f., 166, 173
La Rivière (captain), 194 ff., 216 f.
La Rivière, Joachim Monnier de, 110
La Roche, Fort de, 87, 93
La Rochelle, 132; Huguenot refugees from siege of, 84
La Soufrière, Mount, 47
La Tour, Savinien de Courpon, Sieur de, 186 f.
La Vallée, Philippe Levayer de, 60, 66, 227
La Vernade, Roi de Courpon, Sieur de, 88, 103 f.; expedition against Thoisy, 170 ff.; Poincy's ambassador to Warner, 137
La Violette, 183
League of Nations, 258
Le Blanc, Jean (slave), 224
Le Breton, Sieur (governor of St. Lucia), 217
Le Cercueil, Yves, *see* Le Fort, Sieur, pseud.
Le Comte, Jean, 138, 141, 215; Du Parquet joined by, 198; governor of Grenada, 195
Leeward Islands, 1; Columbus sails through, 6
Le Fort, Sieur, pseud. of Yves Le Cercueil, 154 ff., 170, 191, 199
Le Gendre, Jacques, 187
Le Hazier, du Buisson, 190
Leigh, Charles, 199
Leigh, Sir Olive, 199
Le Marquis, Sieur, 215

INDEX

Le Normand (Judge), 158
Le Pas, Captain, *see* Lepelletier, Jean, known as Captain Le Pas
Lepelletier, Jean, known as Captain Le Pas, 195
Lesperance, Auvray de, 107, 150; house fired, 155
Lesser Antilles, *see* Caribbee Islands
Letters of ennoblement, 117
Leumont, Claude Clerselier de, 120, 126 ff., 132, 138, 141, 147, 149; emissary to Houël, 153; expelled from St. Christopher, 131; Houël's troublemaker, 150; Thoisy supported by, 135
Le Vasseur (governor of Tortuga), 85 ff.; assassination of, 92; character changed, 88;
Le Verrier (leader of expedition to Virgin Islands), 181
Liénard, Charles, Sieur de l'Olive, *see* L'Olive, Charles Liénard, Sieur de
Littleton, Thomas, 24, 81
L'Olive, Charles Liénard, Sieur de, 42 ff., 78 f.; Aubert opposed by, 110; Poincy received by, 68
L'Olive, Mlle (widow of Charles Liénard, Sieur de L'Olive), 207
Lonvilliers, Robert de, 88, 131 *et passim*, 136 ff.; governor of St. Christopher, 125; governor of St. Martin, 187; prosecution of, 149; return to St. Christopher, 171
Lorimer (captain), 195
Loubière, François Rolle de, 244 f., 248, 259
Louis XIII, king of France, 38 f., 40, 66, 67; company's requests granted by, 117; death of, 118
Louis XIV, king of France, 263, 267; decree of 1645 to amend charter of Company of the Isles of America, 147 f.; *lettres de cachet*, 172; sovereignty over St. Christopher, 211

Machiavelli, Niccolò di Bernardo, *Prince*, 242
Madame, 119*n*

Madeira, 135
Mademoiselle, 119*n*
Madonna, statue of, 89
"Magazin de Monsieur," 74
Maldonado, Francisco, 184 f.
Malta, Knights of, *see* Knights of Malta
Manatees, cargo of, 110
Manchineel tree, juice of, 5
Mansel (captain), 173
Marc, Father, 39, 89
Margry, Pierre, 194; *Origines françaises des pays d'Outremer*, 209*n*
Mariage, Sieur Charles, 216
Mariegalante, 6, 169, 180, 190 f., 206, 214, 221, 253, 256; sold to Houël, 207 f.; sold to West India company, 267
Marivet, Antoine: acting governor of Guadeloupe, 126 ff., 132 *et passim;* jailed, 128; judge, 146
Martin (nephew of Le Vasseur), 91 f., 97
Martinique, 1, 4, 44, 225, 229, 237, 259; agriculture on, 178; arms (bearing of) discouraged at, 179; Boutain's trial, 150; Carib insurrection at, 220 f.; code of regulations, 265; Du Sarrat governs, 139; Dutch Protestants forbidden, 211 f.; earthquake on, 223; English armada at, 222; Esnambuc colonizes, 58 f.; France the present possessor, 270; French colony prospers, 61; Guadeloupe aided by, 222 f.; guard established on, 179; habitans revolt, 240 ff.; league of nations joined by, 259; L'Olive and Duplessis take possession of, 46; naming of, 8; Orange takes refuge in, 169; report sent to Colbert, 263 f.; revolt at, 154 ff.; St. Christopher overshadowed by, 63; sold to Houël, 209; supplies needed, 105; survey of, 43; Tracy reforms, 264 f.
Maubray, de (Cérillac's agent), 231, 233, 238 f.
Merchants, Dutch, *see* Dutch merchants

INDEX

Merchants, French, *see* French merchants
Merifield, Ralph, 13, 15 f.
Miromenil, Jacques Dyel de, 237
Misery, Mount, 39, 41 f., 100 f., 140
Montmagny, Chevalier de (governor of St. Christopher), 210
Montserrat, 2, 4, 25; French at, 33; naming of, 7; patent to traffic in granted by Charles I, 16 and note
Morne des Sauteurs, 198, 215
Murphy, John, 82

Negroes (African), 82; conversion of, 41; insurrection on Guadeloupe, 224; insurrection on St. Christopher, 100; Poincy seizes, 70; sold to French on St. Christopher, 39
Nevis, 2, 28, 32, 139, 141; English colony on, 23; naming of, 7; patent to traffic in granted by Charles I, 16 and note.
Nichols, John, 201
Nicolas (Indian chief), 243
Noailly, Philbert de, 194
Normans, on Martinique, 238
North, Roger, 12
Notre Dame, Church of, 74

Ogeron, Bertrand d', 98
Ojeda, Alonzo de, 7
Old Road Bay, 14, 24
Old Road Town, 73
"Olive Branch" (ship), 199
Orange, Guillaume d', 169*n*, 221, 225; estate of, 65; expedition against Barbuda, 169; gathering at house of, 161; Houël's action against, 169; Houël persecutes, 166 ff.; priests befriend, 167; slaves loyal to, 226; survey of Guadeloupe, Dominica and Martinique, 43 ff.
Orange, Rivière d', 161
Order of Malta, *see* Knights of Malta
Orphans, Poincy cares for, 73
Osborne, Roger, 258
Ossonville, Jean Duplessis, Sieur d', *see* Duplessis, Jean
Pacifique de Provins, Father, 39, 180

Painton, Thomas, 12
Paria, Gulf of, 8
Parisians, on Martinique, 238
"Patrocles," 262; persecution of, 175
Patrocles de Thoisy, Mme (de Thoisy's mother) 145, 180
Patrocles de Thoisy, Noël, Sieur de, *see* De Thoisy, Noël
Pedre (slave), 224
Pelee, Mount, 225, 244
Pelican, Pierre, 45, 56
Pelican Point, 29
Pelleprat, Father Pierre, 84
Penn, Admiral William, 222
Pernambuco, 211
Peronne, Demoiselle Louise, 10
Petit Fort River, 47
Petit-Pré, Charles Houël, Sieur de, *see* Houël, Charles
Petite Terre, 256
Philip IV, king of Spain, claims to West Indies, 26
Pinart, Jean, 181 f.
Pioneer period, end of, 262 f.
Pitrecotté (privateersman), 39
Plainville, de (leader of revolt on Martinique), 240 f., 242, 246
Plantations, interest of English in, 2
Plantation workers, method of securing, 22 f.
Planters, complaints against Poincy, 129
Plymouth, 32
Poincy, Philippe de Lonvilliers de, 67 ff., 193, 258; Aubert fairly treated by, 122; Capuchin fathers expelled by, 142; company's interests disregarded by, 205; complaints against, 112, 129; criminal action lapsed, 205; death of, 260; deportations of, 181 ff.; Du Parquet defeated by, 140; Father Feuillet entertained by, 236; governor of St. Christopher, 67; governorship confirmed, 210; Houël's feud with, 125; Houël's letter, 169; Houël's visit to, 120 f.; Le Vasseur and, 88 f.; miscarriage of justice, 133; nephews of, 164; plans to sell St. Christopher,

Poincy, Philippe de, (*Continued*) 99 f.; promotes uprising against Thoisy, 149 ff.; reappointed governor general, 113; reign of terror, 143 ff.; St. Croix captured by, 188 f.; St. Martin acquired by, 185 ff.; Thoisy resisted by, 131; verdict against, 174

Poincy, Sieur Robert de Lonvilliers, *see* Lonvilliers, Robert de

Pointe à Pitre, 4, 47

Pointe de Sable, 25, 27, 31, 41, 75, 116, 137, 138 f., 141, 143, 173

Pointe du Fort, 192

Port à l'Écu, 91

Port à Margot, 86, 97 f.

Portuguese, 211, 221

Priests, 39

Priests, shortage of, 106

Privateers, 11

Prosopopée de la nymphe Christophorine, 71

Providence Company, 81 ff.

Puerto Rico, 183 f.

Quartier de la Case Pilote, 65

Quartier du Carbet, 65

Quartier du Fort St. Pierre, 65

Quartier du Prêcheur, 65, 239 f.; mutiny of, 154 ff.

Quartiers (Martinque), 178

Quérolon (relative of Mme de la Grange), 70 f.

Razilly, Isaac de, 22

Renaudot, Christophe, 259

Renou (judge), 71 f.

Rich, Roland, 188

Richelieu, Armand Jean du Plessis, Duke and Cardinal de, 2, 25 f., 67, 117, 179, 268 f.; colonial expansion policy, 17; Company of St. Christopher dissolved by, 38; Company of St. Christopher formed by, 18; death of, 118; Du Roissey imprisoned by, 33; L'Olive reappointed by, 57; royal authority in the West Indies strengthened by, 44

Riflet, Morne de, 226

Rivière aux Herbes hospital, 178

Robert, Jeanne Petit, 128

Rochefort, Charles César de, 89

Roissey, Urbain du, Sieur de Chardonville, *see* Du Roissey, Urbain, Sieur de Chardonville

Roman Catholics, 38, 84; return to Tortuga, 92; persecutions on Tortuga, 88

Rosée (merchant of Lyons), 208

Rosselan, Louis de Kerengoan, Sieur de, 204

Roucou, 77

Royal, Fort, 64, 106, 118

Russell, James, 258

Saba, 60

Sabouïlly, Jean Soulon, Sieur de, 75, 99, 102 f., 108 f., 116, 138, 141, 147, 149; flight to Martinique, 132; Guinant supported by, 136; Houël defied by, 177; mutineers dispersed by, 163; Poincy defied by, 131; Thoisy supported by, 135 f.

Saint-André, Mlle Marie (Bonnard), *see* Dyel du Parquet, Mme Marie (Bonnard)

Saint-Aubin, Jacques de, 138, 141, 164

St. Bartholomew (St. Barts), 187, 210

St. Barts, *see* St. Bartholomew (St. Barts)

St. Christopher, 1, 4, 268; convents on, 39; English possession of, 63; boundary, dispute between French and English colonists, 41; eminent domain ceded to Knights of Malta, 210 f.; English colonists on (*see* English colonists on St. Christopher); French colonists on (*see* French colonists on St. Christopher); French evacuate, 32; French reoccupy, 34; hospital at, 73; invasion threatened by English and Spanish, 102; L'Olive's plantation in, 55; naming of, 7; patent to traffic in granted by Charles I, 16 and note; sale considered, 207; sold to Order of Malta, 210; taxes unpaid, 205; treaty of partition, 20

St. Croix, 187 ff., 210

Ste. Marie, 121, 126, 213

Ste. Marie, Fort, 158, 254, 256

INDEX

Ste. Marie, Rivière, 119
Ste. Rose, 46 f.
St. Eustatius, 28, 143, 186; Dutch at, 188; complaints against Houël, 123
St. George's (harbor), 194 f., 214, 216, 232
St. Jacques (chapel), 245
St. Jacques, Church of, 228
St. John, Alexander, 200
St. John, Nicholas, 199
St. John (island), 181
St. John, Fort, 199
St. Kitts, *see* St. Christopher
St. Louis, Fort, 73
St. Lucia, 1, 4, 193 ff., 199 f., 214, 229, 237; desertion of, 217; discovery of, 8; governors of, 216; massacre at, 216; sold to Houël, 209
St. Malo, traffic in indentured servants, 23
St. Martin, 28, 34, 143; French at, 33 f.; Poincy acquires part ownership, 185 ff.; sold to Order of Malta, 210; treaty of amity, 187
Saint-Martin, Sieur de (founder of the island of St. Martin), 186
Saint-Paul, Jean de, 105
St. Peter and St. Paul, Church of, 65
St. Pierre (Martinique), 242
St. Pierre, Fort (Guadeloupe) 47, 53, 57
St. Pierre, Fort (Martinique), 59, 65, 156, 227, 241, 243 f., 264
St. Pierre, Fort (St. Christopher), 68; demolition of, 73
Saints (islands), 190, 207 f.
St. Thomas (island), 183
St. Vincent, 6, 196, 268; French attack, 218; Caribs to be unmolested on, 258; naming of, 8
Sales, Charles de, 255; governor of St. Christopher, 261
Salt ponds, 13; dispute between French and English concerning, 75
San Domingo, 2, 222; buccaneers on, 80 f.; raided by Fontenay, 93
San Juan, 184 f.
Sea captains, French, *see* French sea captains
Second Hundred Years' War, 63

Seigneurial dues at St. Christopher, 260
Senegal Company, 40
Servants, indentured, *see* Indentured servants
Slavery on St. Christopher, 39 f.
Slaves, Brazilian, 224; flight from Martinique, 225 ff.; insurrection on Guadeloupe, 224 f.; *see also* Negroes (African)
Slave traders, 2
Society of Jesus, *see* Jesuits
Souches, Jean du Bouchet, marquis de, 134
Soulon, Jean, Sieur de Sabouïlly, *see* Sabouïlly, Jean Soulon, Sieur de
Sourdis, Henri d'Escoubleau de, bishop of Bordeaux, 67
Souvré de (messenger to the king), 210
Spanish claims to West Indies, 26
Spanish Main, 1 f.
Spanish possessions, 2
Sugar cane, cultivation in Martinique, 77 f.

Taxation: Guadeloupe, 251; St. Christopher, 261 f.
Techenel, Father, 173
Tegreman (Indian chief), 13 f., 20
Téméricourt, de (D'Herblay's brother), 251 ff.; Houël's persecution of, 257; deportation to France, 267
Texel, 231
Thoisy, Noël, Sieur de Patrocles de, 89, 138; action against Mansel, 174; assassination plotted, 158; assassination rumored, 165; authority repudiated, 154; commission presented by Houël, 134; council of war appointed by, 151; deportation to France, 173; Du Parquet receives, 135; embarkation at Havre, 134; failure to secure release of Du Parquet, 141 f.; Guadeloupe left by, 165; Houël opposes, 145 ff.; Houël outwits, 148; Houël receives, 135; Houël summoned by, 164; imprisonment at St. Christopher, 171; La Bazilière besieges, 162; La Pierrière

INDEX

Thoisy, Noël, (*Continued*)
pardoned by, 157; La Vernade captures, 170 f.; overtures to Houël, 153; Poincy repulses, 136; Poincy resists, 131 ff.; suit against Poincy and Houël, 174; supporters deported by Poincy, 181 ff.; unpaid, 262; Warner repulses, 137
Thomas (Indian), 197 f.
Thomas, Martin, 186 f.
Tibaut (nephew of Le Vasseur), 91 f., 97
Tobacco, 35 f.; cultivation forbidden in England, 76; Du Roissey's cargo of, 22; edict against raising of, 77 f.; exports decline, 77; growing of on Martinique, 64; growing of on St. Christopher, 13 ff., 16; Hilton's cargo of, 24; production limited, 76; shipment to Holland and England, 37
Tobago, 8
Toledo, Fadrique de, 26, 28 ff.
Tortuga, 80 ff.; buccaneers on, 80 f.; charter, 85 f.; Fontenay conquers, 91 f.; government of, 81; Huguenots on, 85; recolonizing of, 83; religious liberty on, 85; Spaniards attack, 87; Spaniards conquer, 82 f., 93 ff.
Tostain, Nicolas, 123
Tracy, Alexandre de Prouville, Marquis de, 258; Guadaloupe reformed by, 266 f.; Martinique reformed by, 264
Trade, settlers rights restricted, 115
Traitor, report concerning, 128
Treval, de (Poincy's nephew), 90, 138 f., 165; hostage, 171; prosecution of, 149
Trezel (Dutch merchant), 77 f., 176 f.
Trezel, Mlle, 176
Trinidad, naming of, 8
Trois Rivières, 247
"Trois Rois" (ship), 27

Turtles: cargo of, 110; gathering of, 55

Valle Figueroa, Gabriel de, 93
Valmenière, Louis Caqueray de, 216, 235, 248
Varon, François, *see* Du Rivage, François
Vaudroques, Adrien Dyel de, *see* Dyel de Vaudroques, Adrien
Vaugalan, Sieur de (leader of expedition to St. Croix), 189
Venables, Robert, 23
Vervins, Treaty of, 11
"Victoire, La" (ship), 19
Vieux Fort River, 47
Virgin Gorda, 183
Virgin Islands, 181; naming of, 7
Virginia, 203
Voléry (factor), 102
Volléry (captain), 127, 141

Walloon soldiers, 213
War canoes, Carib, 5
Warehouse at St. Christopher, 115
Warner, Edward, 14, 27, 30, 104
Warner, Sir Thomas, 12, 14 ff., 22, 34; complaint against Houël, 123; Esnambuc's rendezvous with, 42; Poincy aided by, 132, 140; Poincy welcomed by, 69; Queen's letter to, 135, 137; Querolon's mistake permitted by, 71; St. Lucia colonized by, 202
West India Company, 267 ff.
West Indies: French colonial empire, founded by Esnambuc, 63; French colonies in, 3
William III, King of England, 3
Windward Islands, 1
Women: Guadeloupe, 119; St. Christopher, 70 f.
Wood, right to gather, 76
Wormeley, Christopher, 81 ff.; governor of Tortuga, 82 f.

Yance (captain Indian chief), 52 f.